Praise for

Driving Honda

"Great investors profit by running counter to the crowd, and in this respect Rothfeder's superb and readable book is the story of a great corporate contrarian. It explains how Honda's idiosyncratic and often counterintuitive approaches to leadership, innovation, and growth have enabled it to prosper in a hypercompetitive industry dominated by giants."

—John A. Casesa, senior managing director, Guggenheim Partners

"*Driving Honda* is a fascinating look at one of the world's great iconoclastic corporations. Through extensive access to high-level Honda executives, Rothfeder dives deep into a corporate culture that sidesteps traditional hierarchy and remains devoted to individualism, accountability, and collaboration, proving that no organization is too large or established to stop thinking like a lean, flexible start-up."

—Keith Ferrazzi, author of the #1 *New York Times* bestseller *Who's Got Your Back* and *Never Eat Alone*

"In this highly readable and entertaining book, Rothfeder details how Honda has successfully navigated globalization through a unique strategy. This strategy should be a model for other multinationals to follow."

—Ray Kwong, senior advisor, USC U.S.-China Institute, and *Forbes* contributor

"This highly readable book reveals the key to Honda's success: a culture of openness, innovation, and relentless commitment to quality. It's a must-read for anyone interested in the future of manufacturing in America."

—Subir Chowdhury, author of *The Power of LEO* and *Power of Six Sigma*

ABOUT THE AUTHOR

Jeffrey Rothfeder is a veteran award-winning journalist and former editor in chief at *International Business Times.* He has written numerous critically acclaimed books, including *McIlhenny's Gold*, *Every Drop for Sale*, and *Privacy for Sale.* He previously was national news editor at Bloomberg News, editor in chief at *PC Magazine*, executive editor at Time Inc., and an editor at *Businessweek*. He lives in Cortlandt Manor, New York.

DRIVING HONDA

INSIDE THE WORLD'S MOST INNOVATIVE CAR COMPANY

JEFFREY ROTHFEDER

PORTFOLIO / PENGUIN

To all the men and women in the auto industry who believe that their jobs are to make individuals more mobile, economies stronger, machines more innovative, societies more equal, and manufacturing more beneficial—while protecting the environment.

PORTFOLIO / PENGUIN
An imprint of Penguin Random House LLC
375 Hudson Street
New York, New York 10014
penguin.com

First published in the United States of America by Portfolio / Penguin 2014
This paperback edition with a new afterword published 2015

Photographs provided courtesy of American Honda Motor Co., Inc.

ISBN 978-1-59184-473-0 (hc.)
ISBN 978-1-59184-797-7 (pbk.)

Printed in the United States of America
10 9 8 7 6 5 4 3 2 1

Set in Sabon LT Std
Designed by Jaime Putorti

CONTENTS

1

THE HONDA DIFFERENCE

Some of the people in attendance observed offhandedly that Soichiro Honda must have been spinning in his grave—or at least letting loose with one of his well-crafted profane tirades.

It was April 2000 when a ground breaking was held for a factory on a 1,300-acre site in Lincoln, an eastern Alabama town of fewer than 4,500 people at the time. A year earlier, Honda Motor Company had announced that it would construct its inaugural southern U.S. plant in this tiny hamlet. Because Honda had already made history in 1982 as the first Japanese carmaker in the United States by opening a manufacturing facility in Marysville, Ohio, the news that it was expanding into Alabama captured headlines around the world.

And raised its share of questions. For one thing, what and where was Lincoln? Other automakers that had already set up shop in southern cities—among them Mercedes, Toyota, Nissan, and Hyundai—chose large towns like Smyrna, Tennessee; and in Alabama, Huntsville, Montgomery, and Tuscaloosa. The companies wanted to be in cosmopolitan areas where the pool of potential workers who had experience with new manufacturing technologies and skill sets was sufficiently large. Moreover, they liked being able to offer visiting executives access to high-quality restaurants and hotels.

Honda, on the other hand, picked Lincoln precisely because it offered what the company wanted most: anonymity and no big-city spotlights or distractions. Indeed, during the search process for a property in Alabama, Honda executives rejected Birmingham, the first option presented to them, saying it was too big and crowded and, well, messy. And they told the state's industrial development officials that they wanted a site at which they could work unobserved and inconspicuously.

By those criteria, Lincoln was perfect. Before Honda arrived it was a sleepy flatland, left behind years earlier by farmers and defense factories, barely a pit stop on east–west I-20 between Birmingham and Atlanta. Even now, with a world-class automobile factory in its midst, Lincoln is easy to pass by without noticing; it has a few fast-food places to get a bite—Waffle House, Taco Bell, and Burger King—and a couple of franchise motels, like Days Inn and Econo Lodge. But no signs trumpet the Honda factory on the highway or anywhere in town.

Considering the depth of Honda's reticence—a single-minded self-preoccupation that manifests in the automaker's almost religious regard for internal innovation and individualism and a concomitant ineptness about promoting its accomplishments—the public ground breaking at Lincoln for Honda's new 1.7-million-square-foot plant was bound to be perilous. At least the weather cooperated; temperatures reached near eighty that day and the sky was a milky blue. A crowd of a few hundred town residents and invited guests were on hand to watch.

They heard short speeches welcoming Honda from Governor Don Siegelman, three-decade Lincoln mayor Carroll "Lew" Watson, and local congressman Bob Riley, as well as convocations given by the ministers of the area's primary black and white churches and gospel songs sung by a choir that combined the best talent from the two. The speakers mainly touted the jobs, tax receipts, influx of supplier factories, and population growth—all of it adding up to millions and ultimately billions of dollars in economic gains that would be drawn into the area by what would be built on this one unlikely spot of land. As Mayor Watson said later, with an impish grin and a syrupy drawl, "It was as if we won the lottery; in our wildest dreams, no one ever expected Lincoln to be in newspapers as far away as California or Tokyo." (That was the same conversation in which he pointedly took pains to erase any misconceptions I had about the origin of his town's name: virtually all southern cities named Lincoln, he said, are honoring Benjamin, the aide-de-camp to George Washington who accepted British general Charles Cornwallis's surrender at Yorktown, and not Abraham.)

Honda was represented by its leading global executive, CEO Hiroyuki Yoshino, and lesser officials from Honda of America and the Lincoln plant brain trust. Like every CEO in Honda's history, Yoshino rose through the ranks of engineering and research and development—an unspoken but unchallenged prerequisite for those following in the footsteps of Soichiro Honda, who was among Japan's most creative engineers when he founded the company. Other automakers, like other outfits in any industry, tend to fill top jobs with MBAs whose expertise lies in marketing, sales, or finance.

Having engineers in charge of the business fits Honda's personality perfectly—particularly, the company's bias toward an indispensable aspect of the engineer's craft. Namely, the necessity to tear apart design, development, strategic, or manufacturing decisions by trying out alternate solutions arrived at with the same analytical probing and intellectual fervor that produced the original option. Criticizing and rejecting ideas and knowledge deemed to be true—inverting conventional wisdom—is more valuable at Honda than repeated success using the same concepts. "No one will blame you for making a mistake if you tried something new; in fact you may be promoted for that," said Chuck Ernst, who conceived and oversaw the building of the Honda factory in Lincoln, an unconventional facility that resembled and performed like no other auto plant in the world when it was constructed. Before that assignment, Ernst had never built a factory from scratch. "However, you could fall out of favor if you're afraid to stray from what worked before—no matter how well it worked."

Or, as Satoshi Okubo, one of Yoshino's predecessors in the CEO's office, put it: "At Honda, it's sink or swim. They don't teach you step-by-step; they just throw you into the pool and let you figure it out on your own. If you don't know how to swim at first, you need to be aggressive to survive. We are to try out whatever we think is necessary to take ourselves to the next level."

The tradition of engineers at the helm has also suffused Honda's culture with the concept of *sangen shugi,* which some people translate as the three realities. In Honda's interpretation, *sangen shugi* means see it with your own eyes, go to the spot before making a decision. In other words, find out, say, what the customer wants or how a part should be designed so it can be assembled efficiently on the factory floor by asking the people who can show you—not just tell you—the answers face-to-face.

There's almost nothing about Honda's unorthodox DNA that hasn't been informed by the skepticism and curiosity—by the unpacking and then reassembling of knowledge and information—that characterizes the best of the engineering discipline. However, there is a downside to this: engineer CEOs are not, generally, inspiring or motivating public speakers. That's where having a more traditional sales or marketing background, in which communication skills are necessarily honed to try to persuade people to buy your product, is a distinct advantage.

And in this respect, in Lincoln, Honda CEO Yoshino did not deviate from the norm. Although gregarious and animated in small groups, at the ground breaking he appeared shy and halting; the speech itself was somewhat ham-fisted.

Some in the crowd couldn't hear him over the sound of the wind blowing across the open field in which they stood. But those who did pick up what he said heard a repeated theme: Honda has been successful because it is, above all, a company that focuses on doing one thing well—making engines that last a long time for cars, motorcycles, and so-called power products like lawn mowers, generators, snowblowers, and weed or garden trimmers. And Honda continually works to perfect this core skill to improve as a company. Yoshino pointed out that the Lincoln plant would be uncommon because Honda would build both cars and engines there; most other automakers don't even manufacture many of their engines and virtually none of them interweaves engine development and manufacturing processes as closely as Honda does to ensure that automobile design decisions are explored holistically.

And he added: "We earn more than ten million customers for these [engine] products every year. That makes us the largest engine maker in the world. The V6 engines we build here in Lincoln will give yet another meaning to the words 'Powered by Honda.' In this way, a phrase so important to our past will have even more power in the future."

With that and a few more words, the breaking of the ground was about to begin. A Honda public relations person took to the microphone to tell the luminaries on the stage to step down and pick up a shovel.

"Now, you may have noticed that everyone isn't using a shovel," he continued. "Well, Mr. Yoshino spoke earlier about the concept of 'Powered by Honda.' The tiller that he and Mayor Watson are using to break ground is one of those 'Powered by Honda' products. I want you to count down with me to the ground breaking. . . . Count down to this start-up of construction for Honda's new facility in Alabama.

"Five-four-three-two-one. Gentlemen—start your engine . . . and shovels."

The shovels were not the problem. The tiller, however, was. It wouldn't kick over. Yoshino first pulled the starter string smoothly and confidently, no response. Again, with a smile, dead. Then he yanked on it hard—there was sweat appearing on his brow and upper lip—just a cough from the machine. Now getting more nervous, Yoshino jerked on the rope with force, so hard that someone said it looked like he was going to strain a muscle. It didn't help. People in the audience were growing more and more embarrassed for the CEO and by the obvious irony of a dead Honda engine dedicating the company's crown jewel greenfield factory; they wanted to look away or whispered to their neighbor about how they wished they were anyplace else but here.

Then, something unexpected happened. Rather than give up or call for help from the Honda maintenance crew in the crowd, Yoshino tackled the balky tiller himself. More comfortable with technical complications than audiences anyway, he bent down and peered into the engine, casually playing with the spark plugs, the carburetor, the gas line. He flipped the choke. It took less than two minutes; then he stood up and pulled the cord. The engine came alive.

■

Those who believed that Soichiro Honda would have disapproved of what unfolded that spring afternoon on a nameless plot of land in the Deep South couldn't have been more wrong. Quite to the contrary, Honda-san would have been proud for this reason: though unfortunate, the mishap with the tiller revealed yet again that Honda Motor, the company Soichiro founded some fifty years earlier, is an awkward outfit built on paradox and contradiction, full of enthusiasm and warts, yet wholly original, influential, creative, enterprising, resourceful, and successful—just as he was. More than anything, that public faux pas in central Alabama reflected how well his company echoes his uniqueness as an engineer and a businessman and how his unconventional management style and improvised, even intuitive, organizational genius has permanently infected the corporation that bears his name.

Any number of Honda aphorisms would appropriately frame that Alabama misstep, sayings embedded deeply in the company's culture, but one maxim oft repeated by Soichiro Honda, who was fond of mistakes like these, fits best of all.

"Success," Honda said, "can be achieved only through repeated failure and introspection. In fact, success represents one percent of your work, which results only from the ninety-nine percent that is called failure."

To Soichiro, slip-ups were a sign of progress to come, a motivator to improve.

Soichiro Honda's business partner, Takeo Fujisawa, the management consulting genius whose personal style and temperament stood in sharp contrast to the founder's but who nonetheless forged a common bond with Soichiro that united the pair for more than two decades, had a more nuanced way of looking at mistakes. To him, it was the fear of failure that drove people to achieve the most, rather than failure itself.

Fujisawa was adept at *shogi*, a Japanese version of chess with at least one substantial variation: when you captured an opposing player's piece, it could be redeployed on your side. To Fujisawa that was an apt metaphor for business strategy. As he saw it, by outsmarting the competition, you not only vanquish a rival, you are enhanced by his losses. And the only way to avoid being beaten yourself is by constantly being on alert and ready to respond to the errors in judgment and in practice that could give your competitors an opening.

To make this point, Fujisawa quoted Kozo Masuda, a champion *shogi* player in the 1950s whom he idolized. Paraphrasing Masuda, Fujisawa would say, "I'm at my best in a match when I'm on the edge of victory or defeat. I've made many careless mistakes in my day and every one of them happened when I had some slack. . . . It's better for me to feel like my opponent's closing in on me."

But beyond the positive effects of failure, Honda CEO Yoshino's embarrassing moment and the way he recovered from it in Lincoln is still remembered today—still mentioned in the auto industry more than a decade later—because it exemplifies in miniature the odd traits, the slightly askew culture, that have made Honda one of the most successful multinational companies in the world, profitable every year of its existence.

As an auto company consultant who helped implement many of Toyota Motor's operational strategies described it: "When I first heard about what happened in Lincoln—everyone in the industry talked about it—I laughed and said, 'There goes that motorcycle company again trying to play in the big leagues of the auto industry.' And then a couple of days later I was driving to work and it hit me: Crap, Honda can make a mistake and rebound quickly, turn a negative into a positive; a few days after Lincoln and now everyone is asking, 'Could my CEO get the engine going?' Probably not—and he wouldn't even try. They're nimble and smart. To use a basketball term, they can go small or go big with equal skill."

That dexterity, he added, explains why Honda's product development, production, and management methods have been quietly studied by most of the other auto companies as well as other industrial firms, seeking to emulate its personality and manufacturing prowess.

What they've found is that the Honda Way is unorthodox and in most cases the opposite of the approach chosen by large manufacturers, including all of Honda's chief rivals in the auto industry, which generally are top-down, command-and-control businesses. You don't have to scratch the surface too deeply to see that Honda, instead, is driven by a series of grassroots, Eastern-derived principles that emphasize:

- individual responsibility over corporate mandates;
- simplicity over complexity;
- decision making based on observed and verifiable facts, not theories or assumptions;
- minimalism over waste;
- a flat organization over an exploding flow chart;
- autonomous and ad hoc design, development, and manufacturing teams that are nonetheless continuously accountable to one another;
- perpetual change;
- unyielding cynicism about what is believed to be the truth;
- unambiguous goals for employees and suppliers, and the company's active participation in helping them reach those metrics; and
- freely borrowing from the past as a bridge to what Honda calls *innovative discontinuity* in the present.

By following these strategic tenets that are the backbone of Honda's distinctive culture, many of them originally adopted or at least adapted by Soichiro Honda, the automaker has maintained the flexibility of a start-up even as it has grown to be the number-two Japanese car company producing some of the most celebrated and bestselling cars in the United States and across the globe. Richard Pascale, coauthor of the classic book *The Art of Japanese Management*, called Honda's decidedly eccentric approach the "Honda Effect," in which strategy is not a long-term concrete business plan but rather "the things necessary for the successful functioning of an organization as an adaptive mechanism." While Honda understands the importance of structure and systems, it is equally drawn to a singular slate of business precepts that foster continuous reinvention of products, people, and processes. Honda, Pascale wrote, exists "in a sort of restless, uneasy state, which enables it to get a great deal out of its people and itself."

The company's achievements and proprietary strategies and tactics are not as well known as those of its chief competitor, Toyota, about which much has been written. But quietly Honda has amassed a record of accomplishments that often surpass Toyota's. Honda has done this by drawing on fundamental business values that are virtually unchanged since the founding of the company, yet are far more inventive and suited to navigating the trials of the postglobalization environment than any other manufacturer's.

Among Honda's striking achievements:

- Founded in 1949, Honda is the youngest and most versatile automotive manufacturer in the world. The company designed and built its first car in 1963, the S500 roadster, some sixty years after Henry Ford's Model A debuted. Now,

Honda employs 140,000 people globally to make a panoply of products: cars, trucks, vans, SUVs, motorcycles, lawn mowers, snowblowers, and other power equipment.

- By a large margin, Honda is the preeminent engine maker in the world with an output of more than 20 million internal combustion motors annually.

- Honda has never posted a loss in its history. Its automobile operating profit ratios of about 5 percent consistently top the industry.

- Honda's stock price has nearly doubled since September 2008, when the global economy collapsed, and at the beginning of January 2014 stood at record territory of about 40. In that five-year period, Ford and GM (which had its post-bankruptcy IPO in 2010) have been relatively flat. A dollar invested in Honda U.S. ADRs (American depositary receipts) when initially issued in 1987 would be worth $800 at the beginning of 2014; the same amount invested in Ford would have returned only about $100. Since Toyota's U.S. ADR was issued in the 1990s, its shares are up 300 percent, while Honda's are up nearly 600 percent. Moreover, Honda's market capitalization of about $73 billion is well above Ford's and GM's.

- Honda automobiles rank high in sales in virtually every international market. In the United States, for example, the Accord, Civic, CR-V, and Odyssey are the number-one models (excluding fleet sales to rental companies, corporations, and government agencies) in the midsize, compact, compact SUV, and minivan sectors, respectively.

■ Honda vehicles are the most durable and longest lasting of any automaker, with 75 percent of its cars and trucks sold in the last twenty-five years still on the road, according to registration data from industry analysts Polk.

■ Within ten years of Honda's founding in a country whose economy was drained by war, political upheaval, and dozens of failures of major companies and banks, it had become the number-one motorcycle outfit in the world, besting more than two hundred competitors. Honda sells about 15 million motorcycles a year; the second-place company, Yamaha, produces only about 5 million motorcycles annually while Harley-Davidson struggles to reach 500,000.

■ In 1974, about three years after entering the U.S. car market, Honda stunned the American auto industry by introducing a four-door Civic that met stringent Clean Air Act emissions standards, which called for a 90 percent decrease in carbon monoxide, hydrocarbon, and nitrogen oxide levels by 1975 compared with 1970 vehicles. This was the first car in the world to qualify under the new rules and it hit the streets just as the large U.S. automakers and Toyota were lobbying Washington to soften these requirements, claiming it was impossible to economically produce an engine that accomplished the act's goals.

■ After trumping its rivals by becoming the first Japanese company to manufacture cars in the United States in 1982, Honda again outpaced its domestic competitors by introducing a luxury brand, the Acura, in 1986. Toyota's Lexus would not emerge for another three years. In addition, Honda built the first electric/gas hybrid, the Insight, in 1999, and the first fuel cell–powered vehicle, the FCX Clarity, in 2002. Indeed, Honda's research and development arm, whose mission is broadly to study human mobility, has designed a robot, named ASIMO (Advanced Step in Innovative Mobility), that can climb stairs, run, and follow oral directions; a computerized leg harness that assists people who have difficulty walking by supporting their strides in response to information obtained from hip sensors; and a new lightweight private jet, made entirely of composite materials with unique design elements, including laminar flow body, an exaggerated, tapered nose, and engines mounted over the wing, that reduce drag substantially. As a percentage of revenue, Honda earmarks more money for R&D than any other automaker.

- In terms of industrial performance, Honda surpasses the rest of the auto sector in almost every meaningful benchmark: factory utilization is routinely above 90 percent; production hours per car is in the teens; no automaker can make as many different vehicles on the same assembly line with virtually no turnaround time between models as Honda (this is known as Honda's flexible manufacturing system); and compared with its rivals, Honda plants produce more cars per square foot and are typically the least expensive to build.

When the Japanese automakers—principally Toyota, Honda, Nissan, and Mazda—began selling cars in volume in the United States in the 1970s, they brought with them an operating philosophy that American companies found to be odd and of questionable value: lean manufacturing. In the auto industry, mass production had worked well since the days of Henry Ford, producing iconic vehicles in large batches with unskilled workers manning discrete stations on the assembly line. There was plenty of waste—too much inventory, supplies, workers, and space—but GM, Ford, and Chrysler were making big profits so there was no need to disrupt the system.

And the Detroit 3's dominance—and confidence in their operating model—probably would have endured a while longer had events not conspired to make the timing of the arrival of the Japanese companies so fortuitous. The rise of OPEC and the subsequent oil embargos of 1973 and then 1979 sent gasoline prices soaring and engendered dread among Western drivers that the availability of oil could not be taken for granted anymore. Suddenly, the ideal car had a new set of criteria: instead of fancy, engorged designs, big chassis, and powerful engines, people sought high gas mileage and motors that ran efficiently and inexpensively for much longer than those of the typical American cars of that period did.

The Japanese automakers delivered the desired gas mileage and sales ballooned, although initially drivers were skeptical about the quality of Japanese-built products. For much of the post–World War II era "Made in Japan" meant cheap knockoffs or plastic knickknacks. It didn't take long, however, for people to realize that Toyota and Honda built very good cars; they were reliable, budget-conscious, and easy to repair, and spent much less time in mechanics' bays than American automobiles. And as these cars caught on—and seemingly impregnable American companies began to lose market share rapidly—the lean manufacturing techniques that the Japanese used gained legitimacy. Perhaps, business theorists if not the U.S. auto companies posited, mass production had run its course.

Toyota, the least shy among the Japanese automakers, took full advantage of the budding interest in Japanese manufacturing methods, opening its kimono to numerous Western academics and think tanks—and subsequently enjoying the acclaim (and increased sales) from being the subject of a bestselling book that introduced the intimate details of lean manufacturing to the West, *The Machine That Changed the World*, by MIT professors James Womack, Daniel Jones, and Daniel Roos. The Toyota Production System, or TPS, and Toyota itself had become the new high bars for manufacturing in the post-Ford age. Indeed, by the late 1990s, even the Big 3 U.S. automakers had overcome their resistance to "lean" and actively, if unsuccessfully, tried to implement it in their factories.

Stated simply, lean manufacturing is concerned with eliminating waste in production. It is an ongoing process that seeks factory floor "continuous improvement," as the lean proponents call it, by reducing work flow; throughput time, or how long each specific manufacturing activity takes; the number of employees needed to do a job; the amount of supplies required; raw materials; parts and finished products on hand; and on and on as the production process narrows to its most stripped-down and efficient components.

But as the authors of *The Machine That Changed the World* put it, the greatest distinction between lean manufacturing and mass production can be found in their objectives: "Mass producers set a limited goal—'good enough,' which translates into an acceptable number of defects, a maximum acceptable level of inventories, a narrow range of standardized products. . . . Lean producers, on the other hand, set their sights explicitly on perfection: continually declining costs, zero defects, zero inventories and endless product variety."

Presented that way, what company could afford not to adopt lean production? Indeed, hundreds of American manufacturers felt compelled to spend hundreds of millions of dollars to emulate

Toyota since the MIT professors published their book and dozens of magazine articles piggybacked on the topic. Most of these companies—as many as 75 percent, lean consultants concede—shelved the effort within a year or two.

These failures are not an indictment of the goals or even the techniques that exemplify lean manufacturing, but rather they are evidence that lean, as a factory production concept, was misunderstood from the start. Because Toyota appeared to be radically different from every manufacturer that Westerners had known before, and outwardly at least one of Toyota's most distinctive characteristics was its production system, lean manufacturing was confused with Toyota's corporate culture. It was assumed to be the reason for Toyota's success, the genetic code of the organization, rather than the tool Toyota used to be successful. To a great extent, even Toyota was fooled by this. Viewed through this blinkered lens, lean manufacturing became known as an operational strategy when in actuality it is a set of tactics.

Which raises the question: what type of corporate DNA—which set of operational attributes—best suits a lean manufacturing company? For better and worse, Toyota offers some clues. At its best, Toyota is a disciplined company with a rigid command-and-control hierarchy that enabled it to maintain unwavering supervision over a global production system built on improvement and minimalism. Rules, systems, processes, and training modules were developed in Toyota City, the company's headquarters in Japan, and distributed throughout Toyota's network by people taught at the home office. That's not the only way or even the most desirable way to implement lean systems. But as Toyota has proven, if a company is sufficiently diligent about sustaining centralized control, it can effectively train and manage workers throughout the organization to rigorously apply lean methods to their day-to-day activities.

However, recently at Toyota, we had the opportunity to observe how ineffective even the most intelligently orchestrated lean methods could be when a company's operational culture abandoned them. As Toyota's growth exploded through the 1990s and into the 2000s, instead of an obsessive focus on preserving and enhancing lean techniques at all of the company's factories and on training the next generation of lean gurus who would teach others out in the field, management's attention had shifted to other priorities: for one, to overtake General Motors as the top-selling auto company in the world, and for another, to expand globally at an increasingly rapid pace. That meant producing more cars, new designs, and customized models than at any other time in the company's history.

With its altered agenda, Toyota had become much more ordinary, closer to being just another automaker. Its production system was still lean, but its culture and strategic direction were tilted toward escalating sales growth, a hyperactive set of goals that were not aligned anymore with its manufacturing approach. On the factory floor, critical lean concepts, such as a strong emphasis on quality control throughout the assembly process, were still practiced, but Toyota's management in Japan gave lean outcomes short shrift. And before long, this neglect from headquarters served to attenuate lean efforts at Toyota operations around the world.

The disconnect within Toyota finally became public in 2009–10 when Toyota recalled more than 15 million vehicles globally, the largest extended recall ever. Although these repairs covered everything from faulty spare tire carriers to oil hose leaks to fuel pump problems in all types of models, the most prominent malfunction involved unintended acceleration—the car takes off, or feels like it is about to, even when braking.

In early 2010, the National Highway Traffic Safety Administration (NHTSA) received dozens upon dozens of complaints about sudden acceleration in Toyota vehicles, and the automaker recalled well over 6 million cars in the United States alone and another 2 million in other countries. NHTSA ultimately linked five deaths to this issue, which the agency determined was the result of gas pedals that were stuck partially depressed or trapped under the floor mat. In addition, Toyota faces hundreds of wrongful death and personal injury lawsuits related to these flaws in its cars. In October 2013, Toyota lost a wrongful death civil case in Oklahoma and immediately settled for an undisclosed amount before the jury could award punitive damages. Now, Toyota is in negotiations to resolve the outstanding litigation, published reports say.

Toyota management conceded that internal dysfunction led directly to these quality problems. "Toyota has, for the past few years, been expanding its business rapidly," Akio Toyoda, the company's CEO, said. "Quite frankly, I fear the pace at which we have grown may have been too quick." He added that the company's priorities "became confused, and we were not able to stop, think, and make improvements as much as we were able to before."

Toyoda's apology was no doubt sincere, but he wasn't fully forthcoming about how pronounced and dangerous the misalignment between company management's goals and the lean concepts that essentially define Toyota's operations had become. A group of Toyota workers in the United States told me that the real failure in the unintended acceleration episode was not that Toyota quality control workers did not know about it soon enough but rather that their attempts to notify higher-ups about the problem were thwarted. Indeed they had heard complaints from U.S. drivers in the months leading up to the recall, but no one would listen. In theory, this shouldn't happen in a lean environment where workers are expected to go as far as stopping the assembly line when something is amiss and offer possible solutions to issues that threaten the quality of the product, to take control of their jobs and responsibility for the items that they build. "When we mentioned that something was wrong with the gas pedals—and as people started complaining about them—one supervisor told us, 'Let's just ride this out; Japan doesn't want to hear this. Let's not raise too much of a fuss right now,'" one of the workers said.

The supervisor's stance might not have been the result of a direct order from Toyota City; however, many Toyota employees in the United States got the message about management's preferences in a company memo that circulated a few years earlier. Under the heading "Wins for Toyota Safety Group," Toyota executives boasted of $100 million in savings gained not by, for example, quality improvements, but by persuading U.S. regulators to agree to a more limited recall of Camry and Lexus models with defective floor mats than they had initially requested. The memo also includes millions of dollars in additional savings achieved through lobbying for delays to safety and other regulations.

Those savings and more have been frittered away by Toyota's foot-dragging on the balky gas pedal issue. Because Toyota failed to report internal knowledge about acceleration problems in its vehicles in a timely fashion, the automaker has paid upward of $70 million in fines to the U.S. government. And in March 2014, Toyota settled a Justice Department criminal investigation into its activities for $1.2 billion, the largest penalty of its kind ever imposed on an auto company.

This incident highlights how seductive it is for a large company to mistakenly believe that lean production techniques could be a proxy for corporate culture—that a successful lean strategy by default produces high levels of product quality and safety, customer service and organizational candor, and transparency. That temptation is what drove many Western multinationals to embrace lean in the past few decades, hoping that it would magically transform bloated and inefficient organizations into streamlined businesses that could deftly navigate rapid changes in global market conditions; however, they scuttled these efforts in disappointment after finding out that their organizational character was ill suited for the type of company they aspired to be. In Toyota's case, that erroneous notion about lean methods was finally shattered when the automaker's management ideology no longer viewed continuous improvement and quality control as priorities. As Toyota's new, more aggressive strategic thrust took hold, the company's executives learned to their dismay that implementing lean tactics without a sympathetic organizational culture to nurture them was an exercise in futility.

Although Honda never made the miscalculation that culture could be subordinate to the tools and techniques used by the organization, the company is nonetheless often misguidedly characterized as being similar to Toyota in its operating principles. In large part that is because like Toyota, Honda is fanatical about lean precepts such as reduction of waste, efficient and ergonomically sound factory floors, just-in-time parts logistics, and minimization of product defects. However, those facets of plant excellence are assumed by Honda to be the price to participate at the superior level the Japanese companies have chosen for making cars; they are the obvious prerequisites of being a first-class manufacturer—but they are not Honda's identity.

Indeed, I've spent nearly five years researching Honda and can count on five fingers the times that anyone who works for the company mentioned lean manufacturing. The opposite is true as well: I've never had a serious discussion with a Toyota insider that didn't begin and end with hand-wringing over lean techniques.

In its broadest expression, Honda and Toyota differ the most in the relationships between corporate headquarters and the companies' many factories and offices around the world. When it is functioning smoothly, Toyota encourages global employees to think on their feet and recommend solutions to roadblocks, but inevitably ultimate power at Toyota resides in Japan. Local decisions must climb the chain of command and gain approval from the executive suite in Toyota City. By contrast, Honda is a decentralized organization that gets its strength from independent decision making at each of its facilities.

Or as James Womack, one of the authors of *The Machine That Changed the World*, explains it: "I wouldn't call Toyota a top down organization but rather it's sort of bottom up, top down, bottom up, top down. They have rules that must be followed and upper management wants to be involved in critical changes. Honda is more relaxed about that; it comes closest to being a bottom up organization."

A tangible illustration of this distinction between the two companies comes from a former Toyota plant engineer who now works for Honda in Lincoln: "When I was at Toyota, I was asked to create a new assembly line at an existing factory. It was easy; my supervisors in Japan gave me the blueprint and said, 'Here's how we do it, follow the plan.'

"At Honda a few years later I had to oversee the setting up of the line at the Lincoln engine plant. The experience was so different. The only instruction I got was, 'Go to the Anna engine plant in Ohio, study how they do it, talk to the workers and the managers about what they like and don't like, what they would fix and what they would leave unchanged, and then make a better one in Lincoln.' I took this to mean, understand what they've done, and then advance it."

While Toyota is permanently coupled with lean, Honda clearly sees itself in another light—as a big manufacturer embodying the spirit of an entrepreneurial small business exemplified by these traits:

questioning common beliefs, innovation springing from risk taking and examining mistakes, open lines of communication, local control, and accumulated knowledge linking the global company like a bridge. Moreover, Honda views the factory as an elegant web of interchangeable tools and activities, rather than a series of discrete operations that can be leaned, streamlined, and automated to meet certain predetermined benchmarks that, in turn, squash the enthusiasm for creativity and contributing to improvements in the plant out of the local workers. It's worth noting in this regard that Honda's factories are the least automated among carmakers, yet Honda enjoys the highest profit margins. These characteristics and the way Honda employs them are striking because they have largely gone unexamined and yet provide a valuable cultural framework for multinationals struggling with the challenges of maintaining excellence, corporate values, localization, and continuous advances in design, development, engineering, and products throughout a far-flung network of factories and R&D centers.

Certainly Honda has had slip-ups. For example, the road into China, which Honda pioneered among Japanese companies, has been thorny (as it has been for most multinationals), although Honda appears to be on the verge of succeeding, and the devastating Japanese tsunami in 2011 caught the company unawares and vulnerable to the shortage of a single but critical part. But because of its uniquely downsized corporate culture, Honda has adroitly used those failures as vehicles for continuous improvement.

The value of Honda's unparalleled and extremely creative industrial model has taken on increased importance recently as the world's manufacturing landscape is becoming increasingly more chaotic. After a period of unprecedented manufacturing retrenchment in the West, when one factory after another was shuttered and tens of thousands of jobs were lost each month to new plants in low-cost nations like China, Thailand, Romania, and India, the concept behind this sweeping job migration—globalization—is losing its luster. It's not just wage inflation in these and other countries precipitating this change of heart. Instead, multinational manufacturers—most of whom, including majors like General Electric, John Deere, and Xerox, are unprofitable in emerging economies, a fact that they prefer to not break out in their earnings reports—are learning that placing a factory in a distant country to serve other parts of the world creates a new set of problems they didn't foresee.

For example, by establishing factories thousands of miles away from research and development centers, which are generally considered skilled facilities that should be close to headquarters, manufacturers found that the quality of their products and factory productivity suffered, as did their ability to respond quickly to a sudden shift in customer preferences. Equally troubling, multinationals discovered that products made in an Asian country could be literally lost at sea for weeks during shipments to the West, leaving the company uncertain about when and in what shape the items would arrive. If the wrong goods were shipped, which happens all too frequently, the company could face millions of dollars in mislaid inventory.

These issues and others, including the influence of state-owned companies and the strength of nationalism in many emerging nations, have put a quick end to globalization, at least as it has been defined up until now. Multinationals are hastily rethinking their factory footprints, turning away from low-cost nations to be closer to their customers and skilled workers in the West. Virtually every leading manufacturer has retrenched in this way, rejecting offshoring in favor of what is popularly known as reshoring.

The CEO of Siemens USA, the electronics giant, describes it thus. "The labor components—the need to choose where to set up manufacturing facilities based primarily on where the wages are cheapest—is not the major driver anymore," says Eric Spiegel. "Instead other factors—access to skilled labor, modern infrastructure, the ability to drive innovation with world-class R&D, where the customers are, and capabilities like new manufacturing technologies—propel decisions about new factories."

But like globalization, this strategy, too, is full of potential obstacles. This new manufacturing era, which can be called localization, requires that companies set up full-scale operations—factories, engineering sites, research facilities, suppliers, and logistics channels—in key areas around the world to profitably and efficiently provide individualized products customized for each particular region. The centralized command-and-control structure that characterizes many multinationals is precisely the wrong culture for this type of global strategy, which essentially calls for separate businesses in each locale, connected to a larger corporation but relatively independent of it.

Indeed, Honda is one of the few companies prepared for localization. For evidence, consider that over the past few years Honda has quietly remade itself from a Japanese multinational with smaller operations around the world into an automaker whose largest subsidiary is an autonomous U.S.-based producer of cars for the Americas, followed by similar operations in China, Japan, Thailand, Brazil, and numerous other places as well as separate businesses making motorcycles, power products, and new technologies like robots and alternative energy equipment. Honda's ability to morph to a large degree seamlessly into a localized company of many different self-operating units around the globe is a testimony to the strength of its self-consciously decentralized structure and its embrace of local autonomy and independent workers. All of which springs directly from the entrepreneurial, do-it-yourself roots planted firmly by Soichiro Honda.

Which is, after all, why the dead tiller engine in Lincoln, Alabama, and CEO Yoshino's casual kick-start were so telling.

2

THE SMELL OF OIL

"There's something wrong with that man—and his company, too."

At least three auto industry experts said they heard Eiji Toyoda, one of the founders of Toyota Motor, utter those words about Soichiro Honda. They all hastened to add that by the time Toyoda said this in their presence he was elderly and retired. His tone was playful, not bilious as it probably had been decades earlier when he had to dodge Honda's unpredictability in a weary postwar Japan.

For his part, Soichiro Honda surely relished the compliment. He was the least likely Japanese industrial giant of his generation. In a country where conventionalism, reticence, and humility are among the most admired traits, Honda rejected all three; he believed genius arose from idiosyncrasy.

"Nonconformity is essential to an artist or an inventor," he told his workers on more than one occasion.

Indeed, Honda was in the thrall of the unconventional. Well before anyone thought of calling it a syndrome, he was infatuated with shiny new objects—more because they were different than new.

Born in 1906 in a tiny hamlet outside of Hamamatsu, in Shizuoka Prefecture, about two hours south of Tokyo on the Pacific coast, Soichiro Honda's first real brush with mechanical novelty came in the 1910s when a Ford Model T drove down the dirt roads of his village. Honda's father, Gihei, was a blacksmith who also fixed bicycles. Intrigued by his father's dexterity and the tools he had to work with, Soichiro repaired bikes as well but didn't find them particularly challenging. He was fascinated by the mechanics of mobility, but the way bicycles worked was too pedestrian.

However, seeing the Model T was a revelation, especially in his sleepy community, where bicycles were just catching on. "I could not understand how it could move under its own power," Honda was to say many years later. "And when it had driven past me, without even thinking why, I found myself chasing it down the road as far as I could run.

"I was enchanted by the smell of that oil. I leaned over a spot of oil on the ground and put my nose right up to it, and rubbed my hands in the residue. From that moment on, I only had one fixed idea, and that was to invent machines and to get greasy with machine oil and lubricant."

For the days and weeks and months after that, Soichiro couldn't take his mind off the magnificence of motor-driven engines. Whenever he could, he traveled with his grandfather to examine the inner workings of a nearby rice-polishing mill, which had one of the few mechanical engines in his remote area.

"The sound of the machine was my first music," Honda recalled. "From the veranda of our wooden house, I could see the blue smoke it emitted. Going to the mill became a habit. I loved the noise of the combustion motors, the smoke . . . and I stayed there for hours, watching the machine while my grandfather tried to talk me into going back."

And at fifteen, in 1922, the allure of motors had become too overwhelming to merely view from a distance. Soichiro dropped out of school and left home to seek a job working on internal combustion engines in Tokyo. He was hired as an apprentice at Art Shokai, an automobile and motorcycle repair shop.

Art Shokai's owner was impressed by Honda's innate technical expertise, but at that time well-traveled craftsmen still held sway over the tiny global auto industry; as the old-timers saw it then, it should take years of watching and training before an individual was given his own set of tools to work on a car. This expectation was obviously anathema to Soichiro's peripatetic personality. And it's impossible to say what he would have done next if he had been forced to apprentice for a decade or so. But an unforeseen tragedy rendered this possibility moot.

What became known as the Great Kanto earthquake struck the Japanese mainland in September 1923. The deadliest quake in the nation's history, the episode lasted as long as ten minutes and leveled Tokyo as well as the port city of Yokohama. More than 140,000 people died. Among the more dramatic anecdotes still told to impress visitors with the strength of the quake, a ninety-three-ton, fourteen-foot statue of the Buddha was lifted up and moved two feet by the undulating movements of the earth.

Art Shokai was spared by the event, but most of the shop's surviving mechanics had to leave their jobs and return home to deal with their families' losses and rebuild their houses. Soichiro's town was too far away to be affected by the quake. So he filled in for the missing workers and became a full-fledged mechanic, repairing automobiles well before anyone his age was usually allowed to.

Five years later, when he was twenty-one, Honda had mastered servicing cars so well that he moved back to Hamamatsu and opened a branch of Art Shokai in his hometown. It was a small business, a two-person shop that plodded along, making just enough money to keep the doors open. The shop's fortunes changed, though, in the late 1920s when Honda produced his first automobile-related invention: a wheel with cast-iron spokes. Until then, wooden spokes were ubiquitous, but on the demanding unpaved or pockmarked roads that existed at the time, these wheels cracked with troubling regularity, routinely propelling cars into ditches or each other, and stranding motorists. Consequently, Honda's new cast-iron supported wheel was a significant breakthrough, an idea he first thought of when still working on bicycles, which greatly improved automobile comfort and reduced accidents.

Licensing money poured in from automakers around the world, and despite the global depression, Honda became a very rich man. Never one to be stingy with newfound wealth, he took up motorcycle racing on the back of his new Harley-Davidson; he spent a great deal of time carousing with geishas on motorboats he built himself; he had an auto accident or two, going overboard on rickety bridges above streamlets; he drank a lot. And he planned his next auto industry triumph. This time, piston rings.

Still among the most elaborate parts of an engine, piston rings failed often in the early days of internal combustion motors. Their main task is to close the gap between the piston and the cylinder during the compression cycle, sealing gases and oil in the combustion chamber. Piston ring gap tolerances are minuscule—as little as a thousandth of an inch—and must be machined perfectly or the engine could seize up.

Soichiro Honda was convinced that he could make piston rings better than anyone else. He told one of his associates at the time: "I just need to look at something once to know how to build it." He would come to regret saying that. From a man who decades hence would be called the Henry Ford of Japan, this statement displayed perhaps youthful but striking naïveté about the complexity of high-quality manufacturing.

To back up his boast, in 1936 Honda founded the Art Piston Ring Research Institute. His designs were, not surprisingly, stellar and even inventive. But the pistons themselves were far less than satisfactory. He had overlooked quality control on the assembly line and in the raw materials he used; he had no benchmarks for ensuring that tolerances on the actual part met blueprint specifications and that each piston was a replica, relatively at least, of the one before it. Out of Honda's first fifty piston rings, forty-seven were rejected by Toyota, Art Piston Ring's most important account.

He learned from failure, though—a lesson that he embraced with enthusiasm and would frequently tell others to heed, so frequently that it became one of the bedrock principles of Honda Motor. Soichiro realized that he didn't know enough about metallurgy to be able to determine how specific metals would react in the manufacturing process, and thus, he didn't have enough basic information to control the quality of his products. To fill this hole in his knowledge, at age thirty, he enrolled at the Hamamatsu School of Technology and took on a full schedule of courses involving steel-making, machining techniques, stamping, tool-making dies, and manufacturing parts from designs. He went to classes diligently, but was expelled at the end of his second year for ignoring his exams. Nonetheless, Soichiro continued to go to school at Hamamatsu, sitting in on classes. He also visited dozens of factories to observe how they worked with metal.

Finally, satisfied that he knew enough about piston rings to produce them in volume to any customer specifications, Honda quit school in 1939, three years after enrolling. He never received a diploma, which he described as "worth less than a movie ticket. With the ticket, you can at least enter the movie house and spend an enjoyable evening; but a diploma is by no means a sure ticket to life. I don't give a damn for the diploma. What I want is the knowledge."

That he obtained. Enough so that before long he held twenty-eight patents related to piston rings and piston ring manufacturing. And with that expanding portfolio, Honda founded a new company, Tokai Seiki Heavy Industry, to make the part. In short order, Honda's firm would employ two thousand people and become the sole supplier to Toyota and Nakajima Aircraft Company, two of Japan's largest businesses.

A success for the second time in his relatively short life, Soichiro's self-confidence, never in limited supply, bubbled over. As he later described the first bumpy decades of his career: "I would have to put in the necessary time, but nothing could stop me from succeeding. I just wouldn't give in, no way . . . There are qualities that lead to success. Courage, perseverance—profound belief in something allows every individual to find an immense inner force and to overcome his or her failings. I let no one disturb my concentration . . . Even hunger could not disturb me."

Perhaps more germane for what was yet to come in his life, Honda would never again take manufacturing for granted or underestimate the intelligence, skills, and level of attention, even the inventiveness, needed to make superior products.

However, Honda's restlessness—or, more to the point, his impatience to bestride an industry, not just to be a bit player in it—soon got the better of him. Repairing machines and manufacturing small parts for big products was not enough; he was convinced that there was something else, something that would be much more celebrated, in store for him. So in 1945, one month after World War II came to a close, Honda sold his shares in Tokai Seiki to Toyota Industries for about $5,000.

By that time, Soichiro had already adopted some of the

eccentricities that he would continue to display for the rest of his life; his small frame was lit up by colorful, often loud, suits and, inevitably, stark red shirts; his balding head was frequently topped by a dashingly tilted fedora. And thus decked out, he told Toyota's managers that he was taking a "human holiday" for the next twelve months.

"To tell you the truth, the execs at Toyota, the serious, sober company that it was, thought that they had seen the last of this strange, erratic little man," said a Toyota historian.

Soichiro lived his vacation to the hilt. Most people in Japan were in desperate straits and much of the country was razed by the war—its economy dependent primarily on the largesse of the United States—but Honda had lots of money to burn. He took up moonshining, converting medicinal alcohol into sake, and gave bottles of his formula to friends as gifts. He partied nearly every night, usually with a coterie of associates at a liquor store where they would drink from a drum of alcohol that the owner had secretly sold Honda. He learned to play the Japanese bamboo flute, drew designs for fantastical products, tinkered with engines in his shed, and built machines for making salt and Popsicles.

He was married and had children by then but that didn't make him more productive or temper his revelry during his hiatus. On many days he could be found perched in his family's garden, staring off into space. As one neighbor recalled: "He didn't even pull a single weed. He just sat there on a rock from morning till night." He had the reputation, another neighbor said, for being "a wizard at hardly working."

But in a moment of frustration, his wife, Sachi, lashed out at him—and unwittingly launched the most important phase of Honda's business career. Sachi had just returned home after riding her bicycle for hours through Hamamatsu and adjoining villages in a futile attempt to buy rice on the black market. Exhausted and angry—and finding Soichiro blithely toying with his tools and machines in the backyard—she reproached him. "For once, you try going out and buying the rice," she said.

"No way did I want to do that," Honda would recall later. So he told Sachi that he'd build her a motorized bike. (Motorcycles were virtually impossible to find, and gasoline wasn't readily available either in the rubble of postwar Japan.) Remarkably, Sachi was placated, although it would take Soichiro months to complete this ambitious effort. If Sachi's initial inclination was to punish Soichiro for being idle and insensitive while she struggled to keep food on the table, agreeing to have him take on the challenge of designing an engine-driven bicycle certainly did not accomplish her aim.

Indeed, Soichiro undertook the task with a degree of enthusiasm and industriousness that had been missing for almost a year. Cleverly, he realized that the hundreds of tiny abandoned engines that generated energy for the Mark 6 wireless radios in Japan during the war—and that littered the burned-out streets of every Japanese city—could be retrofitted to power a bicycle. He combed through every town in the area and collected all the government-surplus motors that he could find, subsequently spending hours to modify each one so that they could be used for transportation.

Making a fuel tank was an even bigger obstacle. Ideally, tin-plated sheets of steel would be formed to create the reservoir because the rust from ordinary steel could degrade the oil and weaken the performance of the fuel. But tin-plated steel was almost impossible to obtain because of controls on the economy. Instead Honda used old metal hot-water bottles, the circular containers that doubled as bed warmers, which he found in a swap shop.

It was not one of Soichiro's proudest or most sophisticated designs, but given the parts limitations and the adjustments he had to make to the engines he was pleased that the bicycle's motor even started up. In fact, it almost didn't. Because gasoline was at a premium, Honda was forced to use raw pine resin as fuel; it didn't burn well under any conditions, but certainly not at first and the engine could take a half hour to kick over.

Those problems notwithstanding, Sachi was pleased; she hadn't fully realized how needlessly arduous her shopping trips were until the motorized bike made them so much more convenient. And seeing her excitement—later Honda would call her reaction the "Joy of Buying," which occurs when a product exceeds a customer's expectations, and seeking that response would become one of his company's most fundamental motivating principles—Soichiro recognized that there probably was a market among Japanese housewives for the motor-powered bicycle. Although unwieldy and balky, the bike was clearly an improvement over pedaling and would satisfy a dire need among his neighbors, who daily had to travel long distances to buy food and avoid starvation.

It would take Honda at least a day to build each motorized bicycle. They sold instantly. But after producing a few hundred, he ran out of free government-surplus engines—and had to shut down the operation.

This experience, though, drew Honda out of his human holiday. He was invigorated again, buoyed by the prospects of starting his third business; this time, making motorcycles—frames and engines—from scratch. No other manufacturer in the world made both. Rather, they farmed out one or the other job. (In fact, most automobile companies at the time—and even now—outsource engine production, keeping for themselves frame manufacturing and vehicle design and assembly.) Honda had experience in stamping and metallurgy, engine design and production, and overseeing assembly lines. With that combination of skills, Soichiro believed that he was unusually qualified to produce an entire bike.

That goal, however, would have to wait a few years. At first, in September 1948, Honda opened up a small factory in Hamamatsu that primarily manufactured engines. This was a twenty-person shop, backed by his father, who had sold his life's savings, about ten thousand square meters of timberland, to be the first investor in Honda Giken Kogyo (Honda Motor Company). The plant produced remarkably sturdy and reliable two-stroke motors that bicycle shops and black-market dealers attached to any frames they could get their hands on. These strange-looking bikes could reach speeds of about 12 miles per hour and were extraordinarily successful in the domestic market. They were perfect for Japan, where money was scarce, but they were far too crude for the rest of the world.

In the early days of Honda Motor, it is possible to see the origins of the sui generis personality traits that would come to distinguish the company in decades hence. From the very start, Soichiro insisted that people working in his companies "never imitate." He termed this principle nonnegotiable. Obviously, as an absolute standard, it was too lofty to achieve all the time; despite his words, even Honda knew that it was more aspiration than certainty. But when his engineers failed to fulfill this ideal, Honda never outwardly softened; instead, he showed his utter dissatisfaction either by heated condemnation or cold silence.

That was certainly the case during the design period for the first motorcycle produced by Honda Motor. Soichiro asked his engineers to draw up a distinctive two-stroke engine, unlike anything that had yet been produced, a difficult task because these motors are relatively primitive and simple by design, leaving scarce room for creativity. And some of Honda's employees wondered why novelty was even necessary in this instance: motorized bike purchasers in Japan had limited expectations of what they would get for the little they would have to pay. "We could have done fine by simply making copies of the engine for the Mark 6 wireless radio that Honda had used in his first bikes," said Kiyoshi Kawashima, who was the first employee of Honda Motor with an engineering degree. "It pretty much had the performance we needed, after all. But he absolutely couldn't stand to simply make that engine the way it was. He didn't like to copy things."

Looking for a design breakthrough that would differentiate his company, Soichiro was unreservedly disappointed by the blueprints that his engineers placed before him. "What part of this is new? What part is different from other makers?" he asked, shaking his head in disbelief. And as he crumpled the papers, he told them to leave and think about whether they should even be working in an engine factory.

Honda took out his pad and began to scribble some ideas. One stood out—and although no drawings or prototypes of this engine remain, it is legendary within Honda Motor. It was called the "chimney engine" because instead of relatively uniform dimensions, the top half of each cylinder and piston was extremely narrow and the bottom half plumped out like a potbelly. This structure allowed the fat end of the piston to more forcefully drive the crankshaft during the down or power stage, while the slim side of the piston was lighter and cycled through the piston's phases more smoothly and efficiently.

Compared with the typical two-stroke motors at the time, Honda's chimney engine was not only a daring design change but apparently would have altered performance expectations. Working mostly from oral recollections, in 1996 Honda engineers built a replica of the chimney engine for a company exhibition. To test the motor, they recreated the operating conditions that existed in the late 1940s, using oil, gas, and speed specifications that were typical then. The engine easily outclassed the other two-stroke motors of that era in both horsepower and fuel consumption. Although it is believed that prototypes of the phantom chimney engine were created, production plans were abandoned, apparently because the machining equipment available then could not produce the tolerances required by the engine's intricate multidimensional design.

Plan B for Honda Motor's first motorcycle engine would be less inventive but nonetheless unorthodox. Although a far cry from the look of the chimney engine, the Honda A-Type motor, as it was called, deviated from the norm in at least one significant way—and thus, incrementally produced gains in engine performance while minimizing fuel usage. In the A-Type, the air and gasoline mixture entered the engine through a rotary disk valve attached to the side of the crankcase instead of through the more traditional intake valve on the pistons. This enabled the engine to more precisely regulate the amount of gasoline entering the cylinder, matching as best as possible fuel needs with fuel usage.

But perhaps an even better, more striking illustration of Soichiro's belief in originality and of his conviction that independence and self-reliance are mandatory skills for a successful company can be seen in the manufacturing processes at the fledgling firm. Unlike other motorcycle makers in the United States and parts of Europe, Honda Motor did not have money to spare. Its financial backing was limited and Japanese consumers were compelled by events to be penurious. Yet Soichiro adopted an assembly technique for the company's factory that was more typically used by large manufacturers—including some of the automobile makers—although none of the top U.S. and European motorcycle companies were yet among them: he chose die casting rather than sand casting for constructing engines as well as components like tie rods, crankcases, and valve seats.

Simply put, in die casting, which is commonplace today in manufacturing, molten metal is squeezed under high pressure into so-called dies (similar to molds) that have been machined into a certain shape—for example, an engine block with cylinder holes. Dies can be reused repeatedly, literally from one moment to the next.

Sand casting, by contrast, involves pouring sand and then a hot metal, such as aluminum, over a mold (often made of plastic) in a large plate. The combined sand and metal mixture adheres to the mold, producing the finished product. Because molds, unlike dies, can only be used once, sand-casted items are built individually, although now automated equipment can speed up the process. And the excess sand and metal must be thrown away as waste.

By all business measures, sand casting should have been the obvious choice for Honda Motor at its debut, because initially the number of motorcycles that the company would manufacture daily was relatively low. Generally, die casting is more applicable for high-volume assembly lines. The dies and die-casting equipment are extremely expensive to purchase, and without a lot of output to spread the costs over, it could take a company months and even years to earn back the outlays.

However, Soichiro was drawn to die casting because it was efficient and less wasteful than sand casting. It would enable his fledgling factory to make engines and other components directly from raw materials, reducing the number of necessary processes involved and yielding a more consistently attractive and uniform product with minimal excess or waste.

Still, Soichiro's preferences notwithstanding, Honda Motor didn't have the money to purchase die-casting equipment. One die fabricator told Honda's brother-in-law Takeo Isobe, who worked at the firm, that it would cost as much as 500,000 yen to produce each die. That was well beyond the company's budget. So Honda asked his employees to make the dies themselves by hand. He said this would teach them how to work with the die-cut equipment better and also give them the skills to design proprietary dies suited to Honda Motor as its manufacturing processes and models changed, giving the company an advantage over competitors.

As Isobe recalls Honda saying at the time: "In a country that doesn't have resources, people shouldn't do work that generates shavings. And if we have to meet hardships, we might as well get it over with first. Take your pains with the front-end processes. If we can get the precision we need at this stage, then we won't need the time and labor and machinery later, will we?"

The plan worked; Honda employees made the dies, saving a substantial amount of money while allowing the company to speed up the production line as sales improved without having to add a lot of additional equipment. Within a few years, Honda Motor would upgrade its die-casting systems by purchasing state-of-the-art machines to improve its metal molds. But the company's early adoption of die cutting—especially making its own dies—provided a base of knowledge about a critical production capability that few other manufacturers would amass for another decade or more.

Moreover, Honda's success with dies became a critical precedent. For much of its history, Honda has designed and developed most of its advanced production equipment, like robotics and other automated machines, a practice still unusual in the auto industry. Manufacturing experts believe that this skill set alone gives Honda unique advantages in factory flexibility, costs, and processes.

Although just a start-up and located in a country prefecture, Honda Motor rapidly became one of the more desirable places to work in Japan for engineering talent. Applications with cover letters pleading for a chance poured in by the dozens. Soichiro's reputation was a bit uneven: people said that he was a hard-charging, cranky, and demonstrative boss. But they praised the organization he had created. It was far different, less rigid, than most other Japanese companies, notable for its emphasis on collaboration and respect for a job well done, no matter how menial the task. Indeed, Honda Motor workers never fully got used to seeing Soichiro spending more time on the factory floor or in the draftsman's room than in his office, wearing a white mechanic's coat, telling jokes and sharing personal stories unselfconsciously. Nonetheless, employees warmed to Soichiro's presence, fondly calling him Oyaji, which means Pop, and toward the end of his life, Honda recalled those days with affection. "We thought together, suffered together, celebrated together," he said.

And in the first half of 1949, Honda Motor had something to crow about. The company debuted its first bike, made from top to bottom in its factory. By this point, Honda Motor, which named its engines by ascending letters in the alphabet, had just completed its D-Type motor and named the bike the Dream Machine. Since then, at Honda, which religiously (at times overly so) plumbs its history and especially the choices made by Soichiro to endow strategic decisions, the word *dream* (as in Honda's corporate motto, "The Power of Dreams") has taken on metaphorical significance, symbolizing mobility, creativity, individual empowerment, and passion for work and play.

The D-Type motorcycle was not particularly groundbreaking; its engine was basically an offshoot of the C-Type, a three-horsepower, two-stroke, 96-cc motor. But it no longer had the look of a bike with an engine attached. This was a real motorcycle complete with a fully integrated power train, a rarity in Japan at the time as the big international motorcycle manufacturers like the American companies Harley-Davidson and Indian avoided the market and its few customers who could afford their products. And the Dream Machine had three Honda innovations: frames made of fabricated channeled steel tubes instead of solid steel piping, which made the motorcycle lighter and more inexpensive to produce using Honda's die equipment; two-gear manual transmission without a clutch; and it was maroon, one of Soichiro's favorite colors, rather than black.

The manufacturing system that Honda used to make the D-Type bike was perhaps the most impressive aspect of the Dream Machine. A first-ever conveyor-belt mass-production process for motorcycle manufacturing was layered on top of the extraordinary capabilities that Soichiro somewhat quixotically promoted in his nascent factories—and the result would foreshadow Japanese manufacturing prowess to come in the ensuing decades. An article in a now-defunct prestigious Japanese science magazine, *Kagaku Asahi*, summed up well the accomplishments of Honda's Dream Machine factory: "There is a company that has achieved a production increase unthinkable in our time, producing 876 units in fiscal 1950 out of the national production total of 3,439, and then leaping to 700 units a month in fiscal 1951. As the reality of free trade approaches, the first thing people talk about is the cost problem. But costs are difficult to cut in any sector, and the greater difficulties faced by larger companies are well known. It is not easy to streamline a business without taking some kind of special measures. This is what the Honda Motor Co. has been exploring in actual practice. With a mere 150 employees, they have been using die-casting methods not found even in European motorcycle engineering, and manufacturing all their own engines. Perhaps the key to increased unit production is to be found in this direction."

The Dream Machine sold relatively well when it first hit the streets, but its success was short-lived. Within months, Japan's fragile economy crashed again as the United States imposed a monetary policy known as the Dodge Line, crafted by American envoy Joseph Dodge. Intended to curtail inflation by fixing the Japanese exchange rate at 360 yen to the U.S. dollar, a level that initially made Japanese manufactured and mined products more expensive than the international standard, and by ending uneconomical bank loans, this program forced the Japanese to cut costs in order to compete globally. On the heels of this plan, Japanese companies fired nearly a million workers and small businesses went bankrupt in droves.

With potential customers suddenly at a premium, Honda's sales slowed to a trickle. The Japanese economy was not the only reason for Honda's woes. It turned out that after an initial burst of enthusiasm for the Dream Machine's unorthodox clutchless manual transmission, motorcycle riders decided that they did not like the idea after all.

Soichiro had added that touch hoping to attract inexperienced motorcyclists. Rather than a clutch lever on the left handlebar, pressing down and forward on the gear change pedal with the front of the foot would put the bike into first gear; by letting go, it would return it to neutral. Using the heel of the foot to press down and back on the pedal locked the transmission into second gear.

"It was extremely popular at first as a very easy-to-ride motorcycle," said early employee Kiyoshi Kawashima. "But then, after a while, people started to complain. The problem was that in order to stay in first gear, you had to keep your foot pressed down on the change pedal. If you were going up a long uphill road, for example, your toes would get tired. That was why the sales suddenly dropped. We just got too far ahead of ourselves with the idea of what would be good for the customer. Coming on top of the economic slowdown, this was real trouble."

Honda Motor was on the verge of going under. The company fell behind on payments to suppliers, and employees were often told to wait a few weeks for their paychecks. At age forty-two, Soichiro believed that if the company failed, there was probably no fourth act for him. He was desperate not to lose the business. He found it impossible to focus on engineering and designing new motorcycles, the only way out of this morass, when his financial problems were so overwhelming and consumed so much of his time.

"I solemnly said to myself: If I give up now, everyone will die of hunger," Honda recalled. "And I imagined the pathetic state of all those people who were depending on me."

As a result, Soichiro made a decision that he never thought he would be faced with or would have to seriously consider. He sought a partner, a moneyman to bring in funding and manage the fiscal side of Honda Motor. A last-gasp gamble, it was far from certain of success. Soichiro was fiercely independent and demanding; he would not take easily to someone vetoing or second-guessing his conclusions or questioning the validity of his ideas for new products. Somehow, providentially, he found an individual who perfectly suited him, his alter ego, his mirror image—a person whose beliefs and ideals were in perfect accord with Soichiro's and with the principles that Soichiro envisioned for Honda Motor, but whose personality could not have been more different. As a result, Soichiro's new partner, Takeo Fujisawa—a tall, regal, bushy-haired man (physically, too, Soichiro's opposite)—amplified his genius and attenuated his flaws.

Fujisawa was born in 1910—he was about four years younger than Honda—in what is now Bunkyo-ku, Tokyo, a center of education and literati in the capital city. But he wasn't cut out for academia or pedagogy; his grades were mediocre and he repeatedly failed teacher-licensing examinations. Uncertain about what career to pursue, Fujisawa chose sales, saying that he had an intuition that it was the right path to follow.

He took a job in a small steel outfit as a traveling salesman and quickly rose to be the top performer at his firm. Fujisawa's success resulted from two characteristics that also illuminated his stint at

Honda: he always told the truth and was rigidly frank—for example, giving customers honest reasons for late deliveries and, in turn, gaining their trust and loyalty—and he was an investment wizard, a master speculator who took advantage of volatile steel price swings to squeeze the best profits out of his orders. Indeed, Fujisawa became so adept at navigating commodities markets and managing customer expectations that when the company's president was drafted in 1937 at the outbreak of the Second Sino-Japanese War, Fujisawa was given control of the company.

Two years later, Fujisawa opted to go out on his own, raising 100,000 yen in a difficult wartime business environment for start-ups, to launch the Japan Manufacturing Research Institute, which made blades for cutting tools. A principal client was the Nakajima Aircraft Company, a large Japanese defense contractor, which also bought pistons from Soichiro Honda's company, Tokai Seiki Heavy Industry. Hiroshi Takeshima, a Nakajima procurement officer, paid visits to Honda and Fujisawa, frequently checking on the quality of the parts in their shops.

As World War II worsened and the firebombing of Tokyo intensified, Fujisawa moved his family out of the city. At the end of the conflict, he remained in the countryside, running a small lumber company to provide wood for the rebuilding effort. But he was bored and still had aspirations of striking it rich with another business in the city. To that end, Fujisawa visited Tokyo often, rummaging through the black markets in Shinjuku, at the time a dark and wretched area of homeless living in cardboard boxes or in huge craters in the streets left behind by the steady pounding of American B-29s.

Downtrodden and depressed, Shinjuku was an unlikely place for Fujisawa to find a kernel of business activity that would germinate into a major opportunity. Yet there was an odd sense of entrepreneurship among the ruins. Indeed, journalist Robert Whiting, in an intriguing book about Japanese mobsters, *Tokyo Underworld*, reproduced an ad from August 18, 1945, flogging the prospects available in Shinjuku to the industrious:

> **Urgent notice to enterprisees, factories and those manufacturers in the process of shifting from wartime production to peacetime production. Your product will be bought in large quantities at a suitable price. Those who wish to sell should come with samples and estimates of production cost to the following address:**
>
> **Shinjuku Market, 1-8-54, Tsunohazu,**
> **Yodobashiku, Shinjuku Tokyo.**

In Whiting's words, "It was surely some kind of record for speed. Three days after the end of the war—and a full ten before the first American soldier set foot in Japan—the newspaper advertisement appeared for what would be the nation's first postwar black market. One of the very few paid announcements in print at the time, it was a call to commerce hardly anyone expected so quickly, given the wretched, bomb-ravaged condition of Tokyo."

Perhaps that "call to commerce" drew Fujisawa to the Shinjuku, to watch the business activity, enjoy it vicariously, if not to participate. On one of these many trips, though, in the summer of 1948, he finally found out, as he was to say later, why he was compelled to travel that route so often. In the local Ichigaya train station, he bumped into Hiroshi Takeshima, whom he hadn't seen for some years. Takeshima had left Nakajima Aircraft to take a position as a technology official in the Ministry of International Trade and Industry (MITI), the Japanese agency that set industrial policy and investments.

During that chance meeting, Fujisawa told Takeshima that he had recently acquired forests in Fukushima, 150 miles north of

Tokyo, to provide building materials for the postwar construction boom. But the timber business was far from the bustling business world in the capital and Fujisawa missed being near the center of commercial activity. Takeshima advised him to move back to Tokyo and promised Fujisawa that he would try to connect him to some business opportunities in the near future.

A year later, the fledgling Honda Motor had hit hard times and desperately needed funding if it was to keep making motorcycles. Hearing of Honda's plight, Takeshima wondered whether Fujisawa, who had followed his suggestion and moved back to Tokyo, might be able to help Honda raise capital and place his company on a more stable course. Takeshima contacted Fujisawa, suggesting that he meet with Soichiro Honda. He told Fujisawa that Soichiro, with whom Takeshima kept in touch from time to time, was a gifted and creative engineer. The unique features on the bikes he had made—the breakthroughs in engine design and frame design—and the patents he held, as well as his manufacturing acumen, attested to that. But he was nobody's idea of a great businessman. He needed a partner, Takeshima said.

"Count me in," Fujisawa said immediately. "You can rely on me to get Soichiro Honda whatever he needs."

Some months later, at Takeshima's home in Tokyo, Honda and Fujisawa met. It was a relatively short meeting, with the loquacious and gregarious Soichiro drinking a lot of sake and going on about his vision for the future of individual transportation and factory process. Fujisawa drank as well, but his mien was severe and he spoke little. He watched Honda closely, impressed by his vigorous mind, the way he piloted through numerous fresh ideas at the same time with the confidence of a master juggler. And when Honda said to him, "If we form a partnership, I'm the engineer and I don't want you meddling in decisions about what to make. But in return I'll leave everything about money firmly in your hands," Fujisawa heartily agreed that this was the right arrangement.

"Understood," he said. "I'll take full responsibility when it comes to money, and I'll leave you to your work. I'm only interested in creating the best possible working conditions for you."

But Fujisawa added, to implicitly warn Soichiro that he must be disciplined, as an engineer and as a manager, and do nothing rash or illogical that would harm the company: "I will work with you as a businessman. But when we part I am not going to end up with a loss. I'm not talking only about money. What I mean is that when we part, I hope I will have gained a sense of satisfaction and achievement."

The pair struck a deal that day in late 1949 to be coleaders of Honda Motor. For the company, it paid off immediately. Within a couple of months, Fujisawa had raised a million yen, including 500,000 yen of his own money, to keep the company afloat. And he also had established a sales team of high-fliers out of Tokyo, extending Honda Motor's market into new population areas (the company's headquarters shifted to the capital as well, although many of the manufacturing facilities remained in the countryside).

Fujisawa exhorted his salesmen to go out and meet customers—retailers, distributors, and motorcycle riders—face-to-face, the initial discernible appearance at the company of a principle that has guided Honda Motor ever since: *sangen shugi*, which holds that effective and profitable decisions can only be derived from firsthand presence and knowledge. He gave salesmen travel budgets that equaled almost half of their annual salaries, which would keep them out in the field for months upon end, promoting Honda's bikes and Soichiro's genius at town meetings; spending long hours at motorcycle retailers, often working in the shops for a day or more; and even making ad hoc sales calls by the side of the road when they saw bicyclists pedaling up long hills. If a shop owner agreed to carry

Honda motorcycles, the salesman would ask for a small up-front payment and use the money to fund his continued road trip. Within a short time, Honda was selling as many as a thousand bikes a month.

Through much of the 1950s, Honda Motor was on the upswing—with occasional cyclical valleys. Virtually every new motorcycle model leapfrogged the technology and features of prior versions as Soichiro freely molded the company into an imaginative engineering shop—and could do so without significant financial concerns. In 1951, for example, Honda surprised motorcycle makers by introducing a breakthrough four-stroke engine with double the horsepower of the competition. And in the ensuing years, Honda produced two of the more inspired motorcycles of the era: the Benly, which was a practical, low-cost, scooterlike machine, and the Super Cub, which was larger than a Benly but smaller than a full-sized bike.

Among other things, the Benly was notable for where its engine was mounted. In most bikes, the motor is placed on the main frame—that is, the area in front of the seat. But in the Benly, Honda attached the engine to the swing arm, which is the primary component in the rear wheel suspension intended to hold the axle firmly and help absorb bumps in the road. This eliminated engine vibration from the frame, providing Honda customers with a much smoother ride.

And for the Super Cub, Honda radically redesigned the so-called step-through part of the motorcycle, where the rider straddles the bike. If the fuel tank was placed in the step-through, as was the case with most bigger motorcycles, Honda's potential customer base for this slightly larger-than-moped bike would have been inconvenienced, so he came up with the idea, since then imitated by many other companies, to put the tank under the seat.

"This isn't a motorcycle that you ride from behind with your leg raised," Honda said. "This is a bike that you sit down on from the front. We want customers wearing skirts to buy this. We can't put the tank where it gets in the way."

But it wasn't only the endless stream of new bikes and new ideas that were the hallmark of Soichiro's creative vitality during this period. Honda's factories and design teams were also innovation laboratories that he constantly tinkered with, seeking to simplify, improve worker productivity, cut costs, and add efficiency. Soichiro would experiment with new materials, such as polyethylene or lighter sheet metals, to reduce development budgets and the weight of the motorcycles.

These moves, in turn, compelled the company to embrace novel production methods like injection molding and electric welding that no one else in the motor vehicle industry had yet tried. Although it was not yet clear that Honda Motor would be a major manufacturing force—after all, motorcycles had the reputation of being simple to build—anyone visiting the company's factories in the 1950s would see that in many critical ways (materials, processes, design procedures, worker participation, and productivity) Honda Motor was far ahead of other industrial companies.

Honda prodded and cajoled his employees to invent and think differently, to find new ways to transform old processes. One lean-manufacturing expert described the evolution of Honda and Toyota during the 1950s as "one company saw chaos, change and restless advancement as the tools of simplification and improvement, while the other saw rigor and rules and systems. Both didn't fail at what they set out to do."

Soichiro expressed the same sentiment this way: "Action without philosophy is a lethal weapon; philosophy without action is worthless."

By the beginning of the 1960s, a mere ten years after its founding, Honda Motor had become the largest motorcycle maker in the world, producing about 1 million bikes a year for numerous major markets around the world. A significant part of Honda's global popularity was due to its newfound international reputation as a preeminent engine maker. Honda gained this celebrity when Soichiro audaciously entered Honda bikes in the Isle of Man Tourist Trophy (TT) Motorcycle Races in England, the planet's most demanding bike competition.

In 1954, Honda had initially announced his intention to enter a motorcycle in Britain's grueling and dangerous race—a thirty-seven-mile on-road, mountainous course with a breakneck series of bends, stone walls, manhole covers, bumps, leaps, and telegraph poles, taken at more than 100 miles per hour. At the time, with Japan viewed as an industrial and technological basket case, Soichiro's ostensible folly was laughed at by the Europeans. Nevertheless, five years later, Honda Motor made its first appearance at Isle of Man. No Japanese manufacturer had yet entered a single international motorcycle race, and European and U.S. companies presumed that the Japanese couldn't produce engines capable of competing at such a high level. Indeed, continental newspapers reported that the Japanese worked Saturdays and Sundays, suggesting that their productivity and efficiency levels were insufficient compared to the world's manufacturing giants.

But Honda, who had raced motorcycles decades earlier and never lost his thirst for competitive racing, viewed such assumptions as a challenge that once vanquished would alter the perception of his company forever. Success in a closely watched global tourney, he knew, could bring instant legitimacy.

He wrote to his employees: "Since I was a small child, one of my dreams has been to compete in motor vehicle races all over the world with a vehicle of my own making, and to win. . . . Now that we are equipped with a production system in which I have absolute confidence, the time of opportunity has arrived. . . . It goes without saying that the winner of this race will be known across the globe. . . . I see that Germany, though like us defeated in the war, has many industries that are reviving, and feel more than ever that our Honda Motor Co. must, above all, enter this race and complete it. . . . We must gauge the true worth of the Japanese machine industry, and raise it to a point where we can display it proudly to the entire world."

The first obstacle was tightening the torque of Honda's engines to 10,000 rpm to equal the other bikes in the race. This was triple the speed of Honda's motors at the time. Honda achieved this goal, but at the expense of horsepower. Which turned out to be the reason that at its Isle of Man debut in 1959, Honda's bikes placed sixth, seventh, and eighth in the 125-cc class. But two years later, the company was more prepared; by then, its engines could cruise along at 15,000 rpm, faster than aircraft motors even today, and simultaneously Honda tripled engine horsepower. The Europeans were stunned by the machines Soichiro sent over to the races—and they were soundly beaten in the competition. In 1961, Honda's motorcycles took first to fifth in the 125-cc and 250-cc categories.

Suddenly, every industrialist around the world—and potential consumers who were followers of the motorcycle races—were forced to view Honda Motor in a new light. As the British newspaper the *Daily Mirror* wrote at the conclusion of the 1961 races: Honda engines are "the best in the world"; they are like "fine watches."

With Honda Motor riding the crest of global approbation, Soichiro and Fujisawa felt that they had limited time to take advantage of this newly gained celebrity and achieve a much larger ambition for the company that had been on their minds for a couple of years—to become an automobile manufacturer. During its short existence, Honda Motor had learned all too well that motorcycles (especially smaller ones like those that the company sold in high volume) tended to be faddish—in and out of fashion depending upon whether practicality or immoderation was in vogue. By contrast, cars are never out of favor. Certainly, models come and go and gas prices dictate the appropriate sizes of vehicles and engines, but a good automaker can manufacture cars for all salient preferences and never face a crushing drop in sales across the board.

Entering the auto industry is an extremely risky undertaking because of the high costs and the quality of the competition. A Detroit maxim, shared with some relish among auto industry insiders, holds that the last successful new U.S. car company was Walter Chrysler's in 1925. Since then, entrepreneurs remembered only as nostalgic nameplates on cars—Packard, Kaiser, Tucker, and the latest, DeLorean—tried and failed to join the ranks of American auto companies. Indeed, in Japan, Nissan and Toyota both debuted in the 1930s; it had been many years since anyone else had tried to follow in their footsteps.

Notwithstanding the low odds of success, Soichiro and Fujisawa believed that as the leading global motorcycle company, Honda Motor had skills and resources that other would-be automakers lacked. The company already knew how to manufacture stellar engines and had substantial knowledge about assembly lines. Plus, the ready cash flow from the motorcycle business could subsidize the initial automobile operations.

In addition, there was no time to waste; the window appeared to be closing because of Japanese domestic politics. Under U.S. pressure, in 1961 Japan took the first steps toward liberalizing trade, allowing a larger number of foreign products—even automobiles—to be sold in its domestic markets more freely. To dull the impact of these new policies—chiefly to better compete against General Motors, Ford, and Chrysler both at home and around the world—the Japanese Ministry of International Trade and Industry announced that it had decided to consolidate the auto industry in Japan. Nissan and Toyota would be designated international players and be the primary bulwark against the U.S. Big 3. As MITI envisioned the plan, those two companies alone would be allowed to sell autos outside Japan. MITI also proposed legislation that would bar new companies from making four-wheel vehicles, mostly to minimize competition among Japanese manufacturers.

There already was bad blood between Soichiro Honda and MITI well before these new plans were enunciated. In 1950, when Honda opened his first factory in Tokyo, MITI accused Soichiro of padding his monthly production numbers—the agency said that no company could produce three hundred motorcycles a month—in order to wheedle higher gasoline rations out of the government.

And when Honda motorcycle sales ballooned in the mid-1950s, Soichiro mocked MITI's protectionist trade policies, taking an unusual position for an industrialist who would have been expected to support fewer imports. In a public utterance also seen as belittling Toyota's, well, manhood, Soichiro said: "Japanese motorcycles were able to conquer the world market mainly because industry was not protected by the government. If the government steps in with some kind of far-reaching industrial policy to profit corporations, it is going to have the exact opposite effect. The best way to tackle the liberalization of trade is open competition. The auto industry has been crippled ever since the end of the war and why? Because of government restrictions on importing foreign cars. Companies need to hone technology through competition."

Given this history, MITI's latest policy gambit in the early 1960s was viewed by Honda as a personal attack, an attempt to impede his company's growth prospects and ambitions while the agency was once again showing favoritism to the firms of the Japanese *zaibatsu*, the government-sponsored industrial conglomerates of imperial

Japan before World War II, of which Toyota was one. Soichiro made no secret of the fact that he intended to ignore MITI's rules and would produce a car for public sale before the Japanese Diet could consider the recommended measure to stop new companies from entering the auto industry. "If you want to control us, you will have to be a shareholder," Honda told MITI. "Only our shareholders have the right to dictate to the management of this organization. Only then will we listen to you."

At least in theory, Honda Motor had already taken a meaningful first step toward designing and developing a car some years earlier. In 1957, Fujisawa had raised concerns that the company's technological advances, which were the very lifeblood of Honda Motor's success, could be stunted by the organization's structure. Chiefly, he worried that the research and development team might be influenced, even tacitly, by financial and sales issues affecting the company and that its research choices would be swayed by market considerations. If that happened, Honda Motor would be just another company, following the herd passively rather than leading the pack aggressively, Fujisawa believed.

Hence, Fujisawa made a decision that was dictated by the company's situation at the time, but which, taking a broad view of Honda Motor's history, is responsible for the unique character of the company and for its standing as a technological giant among industrial firms. He persuaded the company's board to authorize spinning off the R&D division into an entirely separate and independent subsidiary of Honda Motor, and he gave the new unit total autonomy to develop its own research agenda and strategic direction—its mission driven solely by potential long-term gains in innovation, divorced from short-term profit goals. In practice, R&D would be segregated from the manufacturing side of the company but have as its sole client Honda Motor. Project development teams in manufacturing could choose from among all of R&D's output to embellish new vehicles and new models.

"It is important for a research center to allow its individuals to work to their full capacity and concentrate on the task of research," Fujisawa told a group of Honda managers when he first proposed the new R&D setup. "However, this is not likely under a conventional, pyramid structured management system."

To further ensure that R&D had few constraints, Fujisawa eliminated rank among the engineers, assuming that a mostly flat organization would encourage researchers to try out new ideas without fear of being rebuffed outright. "Within Honda R&D, we have an expression that all engineers are equal in the presence of technology," said Frank Paluch, president of Honda R&D Americas.

No other company had ever undertaken such a radical move to propel continued technological breakthroughs—and indeed, none have since. Fujisawa earmarked more than 5 percent of revenue to fund the new R&D team, and Honda Motor has maintained that level virtually every year since 1957; in 2012, the company's R&D budget was 6.5 percent of sales, more than every other automaker and even greater than companies that principally rely on innovation, like IBM and Samsung. Indeed, the R&D team has become so essential to Honda Motor's trajectory that it has produced every CEO since Soichiro.

Fujisawa would call the R&D spin-off "the most important decision I ever made; the turning point for the company." Indeed, he was so certain that this was a make-or-break proposition that he was prepared to leave the company if the board had turned down his reorganization request. "There was no doubt in my mind that having this proposal accepted was the only way for us to gain a foothold in becoming a major corporation," Fujisawa wrote years later. "I had made up my mind then to resign had the proposal for an independent Research Center been rejected."

Fujisawa said he was inspired by a satirical novel called *I Am a Cat*, written by Soseki Natsume, which chronicles the mixing of Western culture and Japanese traditions during the Russo-Japanese War at the turn of the twentieth century. In the book, while the conflict raged outside, a young scientist sat in a basement laboratory, oblivious to the noise and tumult, studying the electrical characteristics of frog eyeballs. Fujisawa wrote in his autobiography that he realized that Honda Motor's "engineers would benefit from the scientist's isolation—a place so serene that they can conduct their research even when society is in an uproar around them. That way, the engineers can focus on their work without worrying about anything else."

The R&D team was fiddling with ideas for a car almost as soon as the unit was formed. But most of these concepts were relatively inchoate, in large part because the group's attention was focused on new motorcycle drive trains, particularly to better compete in the Isle of Man race. Thus, when MITI's threats compelled Soichiro to speed up the company's automobile development efforts, there was sufficient engine and component research already completed at the company to design and manufacture a car relatively quickly, but not enough to produce a vehicle worthy of the Honda Motor nameplate. Nonetheless, Soichiro's hand was forced by the tight deadline. And in October 1963, Honda Motor released its first automobile, the S500, a diminutive roadster that Japanese journalists disparaged as being "just a four-wheeled motorcycle." Nonetheless, this admittedly rudimentary vehicle was legendary for an advanced miniature engine that generated remarkably high speeds and good gas mileage.

Despite the car's reception, Soichiro had made his point. He wasn't going to follow MITI's dictates and he was essentially daring the Japanese government to padlock his business, a move that he knew wouldn't go over too well with Japan's new friends among liberal capitalist democracies. As a result, the government backed down. Under pressure from Japanese leadership, MITI decided to let the auto manufacturers navigate trade liberalization on their own. And the Diet never even voted on the bill to bar new companies from making cars.

Honda Motor exported the S500 and its sequels to the United States and Europe through its existing motorcycle distribution channels but sales were slow. Consumers in countries with developed automobile industries were not ready to give cars made by Japanese companies the level of respect that they afforded domestic firms, despite Honda Motor's reputation as an extraordinary motorcycle and engine maker. A car was much more complicated, with many more moving parts than a bike, or so the common perception was at the time.

But Soichiro saw an opening, a way to get around this view, in a new U.S. law that would give his company the chance to prove that it could outdo GM, Ford, Chrysler, and all the other established players in the auto industry. In 1970, Sen. Edmund Muskie, a Democrat from Maine, sponsored an amendment to the 1963 Clean Air Act that would require automakers to reduce exhaust gas hydrocarbon emissions by 90 percent in five years. This bill was attacked by the Big 3 U.S. automakers as a job-killing and anti-industry action, but environmental concerns were paramount at the time and Congress easily passed the amendment.

To be sure, this legislation appeared to present a significant hurdle for U.S. automakers; they were not prepared commercially or technologically to so radically alter the motors in their cars. But Soichiro saw the new rules as simply another engineering challenge—in other words, his turf. He excitedly told his staff: "Now is the chance for Honda to take over the world marketplace. Every manufacturer is facing the exact same problem. You can't buy the technology. This is a rare chance . . . for Honda to pit our ideas and technology against a score of world-class contenders. When it comes to developing new technologies we can't lose."

Over the prior two decades, that had certainly been true. But this latest exercise was to expose a notable shortcoming in Honda Motor's corporate culture that, left untouched, would have made it impossible for the company to achieve the immediate emissions reduction goal set by its founder—and, just as important, to fully manifest in the ensuing years the unique characteristics that have distinguished Honda from other companies.

Although Soichiro certainly was sincere in his frequent demands that his employees be imaginative and original in their thinking—that they avoid imitating others—he was simultaneously headstrong and not shy about imposing his will on them, whether a new idea was feasible or not. In any organization, those two conditions—employee creative license and top-down management control—are mutually exclusive. And at Honda Motor the conflict between these opposing principles finally climaxed over the Clean Air Act engine.

The disagreement centered on whether the new engine should be air or liquid cooled. Up until then, Honda Motor vehicles had been air cooled, in large part because of the company's origins as a motorcycle maker. Fully exposed to the elements—such as gusts of swirling wind amplified by the movement of the bike—most motorcycle engines operate perfectly well cooled only by outside air. Not so with automobile motors, which are encased under a tightly closed hood, where heat can build up to ferocious levels—often greater than 200 degrees Fahrenheit. In that environment, liquid cooling can facilitate higher levels of engine output much more efficiently than air. In the late 1960s, Honda Motor vehicles and, famously, the Volkswagen Bug were among the few that were air cooled.

Soichiro favored air-cooled engines primarily for their reliability rather than their performance—although he also believed that there were unexplored gains in horsepower that had not yet been realized that were possible with this type of motor. And he would support his preference by pointing to the dozens of water-cooled cars stranded by the side of the road on any warm afternoon, their hoods opened, smoke pouring off their overheated engine blocks. In theory, that wouldn't happen with an air-cooled engine. "If that kind of inconvenience happens to a customer only once, he will never buy your car again," Honda said adamantly.

The problem was, however, that Honda Motor's R&D team could not foresee a pathway to meet the Muskie standards with an air-cooled engine. In their view, they could reduce emissions and maintain better-than-acceptable automobile performance in two ways: one, by decreasing the torque, which is simply the amount of turning effort transmitted from the pistons to the crankshaft in each gear, while maintaining acceleration speeds; and two, controlling more precisely the air-fuel mixture ratio. Both of these required a liquid-cooled engine.

Soichiro found this position unconvincing and forbade the R&D team from working on a liquid-cooled motor. He was certain that they were just being incurious and would overlook a major breakthrough in air-cooled engines by shutting the door on that approach. But in taking this hardened stance, Soichiro belied the autonomy of the engineers—in effect, he was saying that they had freedom to set their own research agendas as long as he agreed with their choices. And simultaneously, he was gambling with the future of Honda Motor, whose success thus far had been carved out of a culture of individual creativity. Takeo Fujisawa was particularly sensitive to this point and was concerned that this conflict of principles could be lethal for Honda.

It's important to note that the default action for most companies faced with this type of clash between principles and day-to-day management, in which their culture is ultimately threatened, would be to bury the issue—find a compromise or, worse yet, take an expedient course—weakening their values in the process. One of the most obvious examples is Eastman Kodak, which invented the digital camera in 1976 when a young engineer named Steve Sasson was playing around with optical electronic sensors and emerged with an eight-pound contraption the size of a toaster that could capture a black-and-white image on digital cassette tape in twenty-three seconds at a resolution of .01 megapixels. It was crude, yet a digital camera nonetheless.

Kodak management's reaction to this revolutionary device, says Sasson, was "that's cute—but don't tell anyone about it." And so he didn't. It would take until 2001 before Kodak released its first digital camera, a full decade after Sony and other Japanese companies had already conquered the market for these devices and around the same time that digital cameras were initially included as an add-on feature in smartphones. Simply put, Kodak's impressive one-hundred-plus-year record of innovation, an R&D culture emblemized by thousands of patents and iconic cameras from the Brownie to the Instamatic, had been erased by executives who were wedded solely to celluloid film.

A similar theme, if different stories, bedeviled companies like Motorola, Xerox, and Hewlett-Packard, all of which squandered their support for fresh ideas and internal invention in favor of turf wars and silos that stymied communication and unorthodoxy in the organization. And Honda's rival Toyota, which has enjoyed more positive press for the purity of its corporate culture than any other company, found during its 2009–10 sticky gas pedal recalls that it's all too easy to let distractions, like leapfrogging sales targets, enfeeble even the most treasured company principles.

Takeo Fujisawa was remarkably astute in choosing to protect the corporate culture from the founder of the company. If Soichiro Honda could be allowed to browbeat the company's engineers into building an air-cooled engine against their wishes, the unique innovation matrix that Honda Motor's achievements were built upon would topple. Fujisawa knew he had to confront Soichiro about this, particularly after a visit from an R&D technology manager, Tadashi Kume, who told him that a low-emission engine that would meet the Muskie bill benchmark was in sight, but only if it was liquid cooled. "The president believes that air-cooled engines can meet the regulations, but we believe that's 100 percent impossible," Kume said.

Fujisawa decided that his conversation with Honda had to be about more than the merits of liquid-cooled engines or it would devolve into an argument over technology, which Fujisawa would surely lose. Rather, it must have the subtext of giving R&D back its autonomy and, hence, returning Honda Motor to its roots, he thought.

The next day, Fujisawa visited Soichiro in his office at the R&D site in Wako. He told him: "I'm no engineer so I've stayed out of your way. But there is one question I'd like you to ask yourself. Which path are you planning to take, Honda-san? Are you the president or an engineer? I believe the time has come to clarify your position and I'd like to know what you think."

Soichiro knew full well that the R&D staff had prompted this inquiry. But he so genuinely respected Fujisawa's wisdom as a manager that he dropped his defenses and tried to puzzle out why Takeo was keen to take up this issue and make it an ultimatum. He realized that Fujisawa was protecting the company from losing its way. In his heart, Soichiro was dismayed, not at all ready to give up his prerogative to micromanage; but intellectually, he knew that Fujisawa was right in asking for a firewall between R&D and management.

After a long silence, Honda responded: "I suppose I better stay on as president."

"It's all right then if the staff works on water-cooled engines?" Fujisawa asked.

"Yes."

And to put Soichiro at ease that Fujisawa's wishes in this regard were tied solely to furthering Honda Motor's values and not an attempt to grab power from Honda or weaken him in any way, Takeo added: "Honda-san, I want you to know that I'll quit when you quit."

It was a poignant moment, a reigniting of the partnership between the two leaders, a restatement of their roles without embarrassing or diminishing either of them, a reassertion of the importance of cultural principles to Honda Motor's future—and it was a fitting illustration of an idea that Honda Motor has practiced so extraordinarily well: differences—paradoxes, dialectics, arguments, and disagreements—are the essence of continuous improvement.

Within two years, in September 1972, Honda Motor introduced the Compound Vortex Controlled Combustion (CVCC) engine, a radical leap forward in automobile motor design, different from any before it in a mass-production automobile. The conventional wisdom at the time was that to comply with the emissions reduction targets, vehicle designers would have to use an engine that runs on unleaded gas, equipped with a catalytic converter, which had not yet been perfected.

But Honda's CVCC engine defied these expectations. Instead of a catalytic converter to scrub toxic exhaust, the CVCC engine was bedecked with two separate carbureted intake lines per cylinder to feed a rich, incendiary air-fuel mixture into precombustion chambers. The powerful flame produced in these chambers would then set fire to a much leaner combination of gasoline and oxygen in the cylinders themselves, resulting in an extremely potent, efficient, and relatively pure explosion that minimized the formation of unburned hydrocarbon, carbon monoxide, and nitrous oxide emissions. Besides burning cleaner, the early CVCC engine's gas mileage was impressive as well, in excess of 40 miles per gallon, by far the best in the industry.

The engine easily passed Muskie Act emission standards—and shocked the rest of the auto industry. Most of the other automobile makers licensed the new engine design from Honda, conceding that their own engineers would not be able to produce a similar motor by the time the new rules would be in place. Notably, although General Motors was also unable to design a sufficiently clean-burning motor, its management was contemptuous of the CVCC engine. The company's chairman, Richard Gerstenberg, said in 1973: "Well, I have looked at this design, and while it might work on some little toy motorcycle engine, I see no potential for it on one of our GM car engines."

Soichiro Honda took this dismissal as a dare. He bought a 1973 V8 Chevrolet Impala, air-freighted it to Japan, designed a set of CVCC heads to fit the automobile, and flew the car back to the Environmental Protection Agency's facility in Ann Arbor, Michigan, for further pollution testing. The car easily passed the stringent 1975 requirements. Which prompted Honda to say in a *Playboy* interview: "When Congress passes new emission standards, we hire 50 more engineers and GM hires 50 more lawyers."

The 1974 Civic was the first Honda Motor vehicle equipped with the CVCC engine and, with all the publicity surrounding the breakthrough engine, it sold remarkably well around the world; it rapidly became the paradigmatic small car, outpacing the VW Bug. A mere nine years after its initial, somewhat awkward stab at manufacturing an automobile, Honda Motor had become a preeminent global carmaker on the wings of its engineering capabilities. And in less than a decade, with the opening of its Marysville, Ohio, facility in 1982, Honda Motor would be the first non-American auto company to successfully establish a factory in the United States. (Volkswagen had started a plant in Pennsylvania in 1978, but it was unprofitable and short-lived.)

Soichiro Honda and Takeo Fujisawa were no longer in charge of

Honda Motor when its U.S. foray began. About twelve months after the introduction of the CVCC engine, which was certainly the capstone to Soichiro's career if his legacy is the company itself, Honda and Fujisawa announced their retirement; as planned, they would exit the company on the same day, in October 1973. Honda was sixty-seven years old; Fujisawa was sixty-three. The automobile business was entering a new round of transformation—leaving the big models of the 1950s behind for an era of unprecedented experimentation with engine design to improve efficiency and fuel economy, and for a period of streamlining and reimagining manufacturing and supply chain processes.

Honda and Fujisawa felt that this was a job better managed by younger, more energetic individuals than they. Characteristically colorful, Soichiro described their joint departure with these words: "Takeo Fujisawa and I, we're half good each. We're like apprentice Geishas who count as one Geisha together. We wouldn't have made it if either of us weren't there. We're just applying the same logic to quitting. One goes, the other goes, too."

Takeo Fujisawa died on December 30, 1988, of a heart attack; he was seventy-eight years old. Soichiro said at his funeral: "We burned as brightly as we could. . . . I want to thank you for making my life so happy."

Soichiro Honda's death came on August 5, 1991, at age eighty-four, of cancer and liver failure.

Just two years earlier, the U.S. automobile industry grudgingly (and finally) paid homage to the man who as one automobile expert put it "devastated Detroit's most lucrative and muscular era with a non-polluting engine in a tiny car"—by enshrining Honda into the Automotive Hall of Fame in Dearborn, Michigan. He was only the third non-American and the first Japanese to be given this coveted honor in the automobile industry.

3

PRINCIPLE #1: EMBRACE PARADOX

None of the conference rooms were available so the meeting was held in a maintenance closet, a small eight-by-eight room with mops, brooms, and brushes and the smell of cleaning detergent in the air. Ten men and women squeezed into the tiny space. They were all dressed the same, wearing white tops and pants with their first names in red on the upper right side of their shirts, the outfits that every Honda employee, whether pipe fitter or president, wears on the job at every factory or office. The logic behind the uniforms is that they eliminate rank; in the moment-to-moment give-and-take of their daily responsibilities, each Honda worker's point of view or suggestion is equal. You may agree or think them foolish, but their title or position, camouflaged by their uniforms, should not be a factor in drawing a conclusion.

Shoehorned into the room were factory floor managers, assembly line associates (that's Honda terminology for workers), and quality control experts at the Anna, Ohio, engine plant, where Honda has been making motors and drive train components since 1985.

The plant, which was opened three years after Honda inaugurated its first U.S. automobile factory in nearby Marysville, Ohio, produces about 1.2 million motors a year, making it one of the world's largest engine factories.

A serious crisis on the plant floor spurred this spontaneous meeting. A supplier had sent the Anna team dozens of faulty camshafts, a critical part that manages the flow of air and gasoline entering the engine's cylinders. Because of a hairline defect in the way the camshaft was seated, a faint, rhythmic chirping sound could be heard in the Honda motors that contained these components.

This noise, barely audible but disturbing, was discovered at the Marysville plant at the end of the Honda Accord sedan assembly line when workers revved the motors for the first time. Because of the tight conditions under the hood, it appeared that it would be impossible to try to remove the defective camshafts without taking the engines out as well. The factory managers at the two plants drew up a preliminary plan to ship the affected Accords fifty miles from Marysville to Anna, where the engines could be repaired and reinstalled. It seemed like the only viable option, although clearly not a desirable one. The whole process, not counting transportation, could take upward of three hours per car. And financially, this would be a significant drain on labor costs.

When the plan was relayed to the Anna workers, an assembly line employee shook her head, saying: "Let's get off the floor and talk about it." Finally, away from the thrum of the factory, in the quiet, albeit congested, maintenance room, a Honda manager said to the others, "Look, I'd prefer to not belabor this issue because we've got a lot of work to do to get this process moving. And since the fix will be such a time sink, let's not make it worse by losing more time discussing it."

Although most in the room concurred with the manager, one of the workers noted testily: "All I can say is that we're doing something very wrong if a slight problem in the engine isn't addressed until the end of the vehicle's assembly line when we have no choice but to tear the car back down. We should have discovered this problem before."

The Anna factory head was getting impatient. Hindsight and complaining about what should not have gone wrong were useless, and if that's what this meeting was going to turn into—a session to air our frustrations—he preferred that it end sooner rather than later. Yet he knew better than to try to cut off discussion about this too early; you didn't do that at Honda. A balance had to be preserved between hearing everybody's ideas—a good one may yet emerge—and moving people back to their jobs.

The discussion went on with everyone speaking—and petty arguments flaring up with little accomplished—for about twenty minutes. The meeting seemed to be winding down when an assembler suggested a way to replace the camshafts without removing the engine completely and virtually rebuilding the guts of the car: through an overhead pulley system that would lift the motor just enough out of the Accord to give the workers sufficient room to maneuver.

"It's not worth it," one of his colleagues responded. "That's more work than just doing the repairs. Let's just give up and do it the obvious way."

But the assembler's suggestion struck a chord with the quality control expert who had originally called for the meeting. Upon hearing it, she remembered something she had seen a month or so earlier in Marysville, an observation that she suddenly realized could provide clues to a possible solution. "In Marysville recently I was looking at how our engines were fitting just for the hell of it and I noticed that there was a bit of room around the engine that just seemed larger than usual to me," she told the team. "It was just a curious reflection; it didn't mean anything to me at the time or until now. But that small bit of space, I think, will give us enough room to tilt the engine sufficiently to get at the camshaft and, if so, we can then make the fix without any pulleys or a major conveyance system. We can experiment with this and come back together to discuss within a couple of hours."

Indeed, she was right. In short order, the Anna engine line and quality control workers had put together a scheme with "jigs, pictures, and everything else to basically roll the engine, pull the heads off, reset all the taps, put a new camshaft in—and tie up only an hour per vehicle, saving two hours for each car," said Paul Dentinger, the Anna plant supervisor who was involved in that incident.

Dentinger said that he recalled this story so vividly because it was one of the seemingly fruitless moments at Honda when you wish the corporate culture were more like those at most other companies—that is, less sensitive about employees and their ideas and more top-down, letting supervisors' stances carry more weight in the discussion phase than, say, an assembly worker's. But proving Soichiro Honda's somewhat exaggerated judgment that success is 99 percent failure, spontaneous, open meetings may have little value half of the time—and they may, in fact, often appear to be a waste of resources—but on the whole, in Honda Motor's experience, these sessions lead directly to significant gains in productivity, process, systems, and performance that would otherwise have been lost.

"If we had the old style of management at Honda that says do it this way, that there is no other way, follow the blueprint that we created without your input," Dentinger said, "we would be literally and figuratively sliding engines in and out of cars every day, not knowing that there might be a better way that, given the chance, one of our associates would think of. If we don't include our associates in the decision making, we're ignoring potentially our most valuable asset."

He could say the same thing about the meetings themselves. At Honda Motor, these unplanned, shapeless gatherings are ubiquitous and indispensable—and arguably the most inventive, characteristic, and elemental principle of the Honda Way.

The meetings are called *waigaya*, which isn't a word in Japanese or any other language, but rather a name given them by Honda Motor cofounder Takeo Fujisawa (at least according to company lore). He chose *waigaya* because to him the three syllables sounded like babble, the jabber of many people talking at the same time—*wai-ga-ya, wai-ga-ya, wai-ga-ya*; in English, it could be *hubbub*. It is the noise of heated discussion and the free flow of ideas; it represents a battleground of subjective and objective opinions, of chaotic communication, open disagreement, and inharmonious decision making.

An offspring of Soichiro Honda's unstructured management and cultural style—which is best exemplified by his insistence that Honda Motor employees favor unorthodoxy over imitation—*waigaya* comes in many forms. It can be a half-hour meeting on a specific problem that needs to be addressed immediately or it can be a series of sessions that last weeks or months about a new factory under development or a vehicle model upgrade. Every department at Honda practices *waigaya*—from sales and marketing to manufacturing and maintenance. As few as three people or as many as twenty (in some cases, even more) may attend.

Although to most companies and most observers *waigaya* is an odd idea, seemingly too free-form to be productive and lacking a strong enough leadership component to produce real results, these meetings actually have an organizing framework that at least in theory ensures their success. Indeed, the central tenets of Honda Motor's *waigaya* can best be explained by four very straightforward rules:

1. Everybody is equal in *waigaya*—there are no bad ideas except those that are not aired.

2. All ideas must be disputed and rejected until they are either proven valid or vanquished.

3. When a person shares an idea, he or she doesn't own it anymore—it belongs to Honda and the group can do with it what it will.

4. At the end of *waigaya*, decisions and responsibilities are generated—a precise list of who is to do what next and by when.

As one Honda executive put it: "*Waigaya* to me means perpetual dissatisfaction. At our company, self-satisfaction is the enemy."

Or, put another way, *waigaya* is the antithesis of the status quo. Which was made clear in one of the most quarrelsome interactions at a series of *waigaya* leading up to the development of the third-generation Acura TL. A midsize luxury sedan, the original TL was introduced in 1995 and immediately became Acura's bestselling model and the second bestselling automobile in its category in the United States, behind the BMW 3 Series. Since then, new entrants from Lexus, Audi, and Mercedes have made this vehicle class—essentially, the $30,000 to $50,000 sedan—among the most competitive, and TL sales have suffered somewhat. But the TL is still one of Acura's most popular cars and has largely held its own against its rivals.

A decade after its debut, the TL's boxy design had become a liability; more often than not, potential customers viewed the car as old-fashioned and stuffy. Like a Buick—practical, reliable, but not eye-catching and certainly not worth the price. Sleekness, catlike quickness, and nimble responses to road conditions were increasingly the expectation for cars in this corner of the market. It was clear that a design overhaul for the TL was absolutely necessary.

In 2004, Honda put together a team of designers, manufacturing experts, and sales, marketing, and engineering specialists to come up with the new model, one that the company hoped would radically alter the perception of the car and revivify its fortunes. The *waigaya* would be the channel through which the reinterpretation of the TL would be initially crafted. Ten people took part in this meeting, which was frequently adjourned and went on for months.

After a lengthy early discussion, a catchphrase to conceptually characterize the car was agreed upon: "the Ultimate Athlete." (Honda uses such adlike slogans in the design stage for all of its vehicles to give the development team a coherent and common ideal to strive for.) Inspired by this term, the car's chief designer envisioned a single individual as the manifestation of the new TL.

"I'm a big Bruce Lee fan," said Jon Ikeda, who has since been promoted to head of the Acura Design Studio. "So I saw the car, this athlete, as if it were a metallic version of Bruce Lee, flexing his muscles, its tendons tense and outsized, its body ready to pounce and move quickly unimpeded in any direction it had to go."

The *waigaya* proceeded generally as expected. Each participant had ideas for what he or she believed the car should look like and for the type of engine, interior design, and components that would fit within overall cost boundaries and still give the TL a facelift that could reanimate its potential customer base. As these recommendations were argued over, Erik Berkman, the large project leader—the title given to the overall manager of each Honda development group—was looking for points of agreement and areas that perhaps needed more investigation in the next phases of the redesign effort. At the conclusion of the *waigaya*, his goal was to produce initial specifications for the vehicle that the entire team could support, even those individuals who had voiced strong disagreement with a design proposal that made the final cut and were still not convinced of its viability or value.

However, this is not to imply that a *waigaya* achieves consensus through compromise. Quite the opposite; it would be a failure if that were the outcome, a triumph of the lowest common denominator. Instead, the purpose of the *waigaya* is to extract the most sweeping, dynamic, and distinctive ideas from a team of professionals with widely divergent backgrounds, generating previously unimagined recommendations that suit the conceptual, design, manufacturing, and budgetary framework of the vehicle.

"It's not design by committee," said Ikeda. "A good project leader will have a vision of where he wants to go with the car and he will make sure that everybody's ideas that survived the *waigaya* are considered for the final design—but then only some will make the final design; others won't because they're ill suited. After that, he sells the whole package back to us so we can call it our own and begin to think about the challenges of building the car now that we know its specifications."

But the most intriguing moment of the Acura TL's *waigaya*—an instant in which a sudden burst of anger laid bare the full potential of the *waigaya* as a laboratory for innovation, a place to air original ideas that would unlikely be taken seriously in a more typical corporate chain of command—occurred when Ikeda insisted on a radical concept for the car's wheels.

Most of the cars in the Acura TL's category had a relatively conservative tire thrust. Although the individual models had become more supple and vibrant, generally the wheels were conventional, blending into the designs, not particularly eye-catching or muscular. Given his Bruce Lee conceit, Ikeda believed that if the new TL's tires didn't support the athleticism of the rest of the car with their own sheer strength, the vehicle would look awkward and soft, like a man with a powerful torso and flabby legs.

Since the discussions about design elements during the *waigaya* had gone about as he hoped, Ikeda could afford to approach the tire issue with a bit of swagger. He told the team: "I'm going to ask for a lot of stuff or I'm going to ask for one thing; it's your choice. Well, I know you'd rather one thing, so here it is: the tire size must be exactly what I want—17 inches, 235-45, not 16 inches, 215-55, which would be more in line with a typical and less aggressive TL upgrade. I'm going to need the wider, bigger wheels to make a powerful, potent statement on the road—a vehicle that will be noticed for its hard-body physique that can simultaneously deftly turn from a dead stop with the best of any cars. And I want these tires on the base model, not some upper-end version of the TL."

Ikeda's single-demand strategy worked masterfully at first. Although there was grumbling that the tire design would add to the budget and would necessitate modifications to the chassis, suspension, and drive train, most of the other *waigaya* attendees were drawn to Ikeda's idea because it was singular and bold, perfect for a car that few people viewed in those terms anymore. The dynamics engineer noted that the bigger tires would improve performance. The representative from the engine team was a bit less upbeat. He pointed out that the wheels Ikeda had selected would reduce fuel economy but he added that if the design required these specifications, he would be willing to work on squeezing a few more miles per gallon out of the motor. Ikeda was convinced that he had won an enormous victory.

At once, though, a business-side vice president, who represented Honda's Japanese headquarters, spoke up softly. "It's not going to happen," he said. "You don't even understand what you're asking for. The cost of the testing time to make such a change is immense. That's crazy. We're not going to pay for that. I know you guys will be unhappy to hear me say this but this is not a road you want to go down for this car. We're going to do the sixteen-inch wheel and that's that."

Ikeda was fuming; he felt that the vice president had hijacked the *waigaya* by implicitly using his seniority and, worse yet, his access to top corporate executives in Japan to undercut the other opinions in the room. And given the stunned silence as the VP finished talking, Ikeda concluded that the VP had indeed succeeded in intimidating everyone; in the process, he had undermined the ideals of the *waigaya*, Ikeda thought.

Ikeda stared directly at the vice president, his anger visible in his deep-set black eyes. "We're trying to make a dream here," Ikeda said.

(Ikeda admitted later that he chose these words purposefully. The word *dream* has coursed through Honda Motor's connective tissue since the debut of the Dream Machine, the company's first legitimate completely self-built motorcycle in 1949. It was a favorite word of Soichiro Honda, who said, "It isn't necessary to be born a nobleman or rich to succeed in life. There are other qualities which also lead to success. Courage, perseverance, the ability to dream. . . . Honda has always moved ahead of the times, and I attribute its success to the fact that the firm possesses dreams.")

"And you're going to piss on our dreams?" Ikeda continued. "You're going to reject them just like that with some old-fashioned attitude that the new is impossible because it just looks like it is? Dream a little. Isn't that what we're supposed to do? Six months from now, if we are unable to live up to our dreams, then reject us. But not now."

Even as he spoke, Ikeda kept reminding himself that there are no stupid questions, answers, or comments in *waigaya*, that he was not committing career suicide with this passionate but obviously angry rant at a superior. When Ikeda finished talking, the meeting was adjourned; there was a palpable sense of relief in the room. Someone had to say what Ikeda said, the other participants felt.

In the end, Ikeda got what he asked for. The project leader, Erik Berkman, told him after the session that he would include the larger wheels in the design because undoubtedly it was the right choice for this car and had the support of the *waigaya*. Although the vice president's dismissal of the idea might have been merely an attempt to play devil's advocate—a fundamental attribute of *waigaya*—and not a reflection of his real point of view, Berkman felt that the VP's stance did not mesh with the overall direction of the new Acura TL that was emerging from the arguments at the meeting. For that reason, it had to be rejected. Dissected from all possible angles—repudiated and then reconsidered—the status quo can survive a *waigaya*, but only if the unconventional is clearly a worse option.

When you ask people at Honda about their most memorable *waigaya*, individual dramatic incidents like the way the faulty Acura camshafts were replaced in Anna or the iconic TL tires were agreed upon are often recalled. After all, these were explicit, identifiable moments when out of the ashes of desultory discussion—blah, blah, blah, *waigaya, waigaya, waigaya*—something truly useful emerged; a simple, quiet idea was thus hatched out of noise.

But *waigaya* are so second nature to Honda, so prevalent each day throughout the company in every one of its manufacturing facilities, research labs, design centers, and offices around the world, that the most enduringly valuable sessions are frequently too routine to be remembered. This is particularly true of the many *waigaya* that occur daily but are continued over a period of time—that, in effect, take the place of watercooler discussions. Just as it's hard for most of us to separate one casual workplace conversation from another, Honda employees may find it difficult to distinguish between who said what yesterday or last week at ongoing, unfinished *waigaya*. Yet that's when *waigaya* have their greatest impact: once woven into the fabric of day-to-day activities, *waigaya* become increasingly spontaneous, candid, fearless, and unselfconscious—the very characteristics that Honda believes are necessary for practical, new ideas to blossom.

In fact, many of Honda's most significant manufacturing improvements have been the result of *waigaya* lasting a year or even years, held each day, sometimes for five minutes if the discussion lacks spark and other times for an hour or more when a robust argument ensues. In those cases, breakthroughs may be infrequent but they inevitably happen. For example, at the Marysville, Ohio, factory, a daily *waigaya*, which took more than twenty-four months to complete, drove a quality control effort that increased the factory's "direct pass" output—the percentage of cars leaving the assembly line without any defects—to 95 percent from about 70 percent. (The direct pass in most auto factories industry-wide is actually well under 70 percent.) In this case, the meetings were intended primarily to isolate better ways to engage employees so that they take responsibility for the total quality of each car on the assembly line, rather than treating certain process or product flaws as not in their department and, hence, not their duty to pay attention to.

The *waigaya* wended from identifying seven key attributes of Honda's culture that all plant workers must embrace—among them, teamwork, questioning extant processes, finding solutions even before problems arise, individual leadership no matter what job you hold, and taking personal responsibility for the company's success—to concluding that many employees had become myopic, viewing their small part of the manufacturing operation through the tiniest, most opaque lens. To change this attitude, a portion of the *waigaya* addressed working conditions and job descriptions for each position in the factory. It's important to note that while some statistics were used in this analysis, the discussions were predominantly anecdotal, showing a critical bias in *waigaya* for visceral responses to conditions rather than data-driven assumptions.

"What people say and how passionately they say it can be more illuminating than a set of dry numbers," said Pat Gillen, Marysville plant quality leader, who participated in the quality improvement campaign. "You never know what valuable observation about a specific factory activity is being obscured by the statistics."

Indeed, if data about defects and flaws in separate parts of the assembly line were the primary tools to determine where and why direct-pass percentages were lagging, the real problem at Marysville would have been buried in an onslaught of numbers. Instead, emerging from the stories told during the *waigaya* was the uncomfortable revelation that few employees in the Ohio factory knew or cared much about what their colleagues did up or down the assembly line. Worse yet, they criticized mistakes made in other departments and showed no inclination to help find solutions. These sentiments were unusual for Honda Motor, so antithetical and indifferent to the company's kinetic, participatory culture that it took the top brass at Marysville aback.

"It was management's fault; we had obviously relaxed the environment to the point that employees had become dangerously uninvolved in their jobs and in the company," Gillen noted. "We had stopped listening and observing well enough."

As a remedy, employees—some of whom had worked at their current positions for two decades—were given new assignments in parts of the factory they had little knowledge of. Welders moved to assembly, assemblers to paint, and painters to weld. Quality control experts were sprinkled throughout the assembly line. And on-the-floor training emphasized to employees in new roles that they should attempt to understand how the job has usually been done while thinking of ways to do it better, particularly to collaborate with other parts of the assembly line more effectively.

"By doing this, we were able to innovate our thinking," said Rob May, a twenty-seven-year veteran of Marysville, who at the time of the marathon *waigaya* was a manager of the assembly department.

"I think we all get wrapped up in being one-dimensional and seeing everything from one perspective, and we left people in positions, quite honestly, probably too long. That was a significant change, in just being able to understand that the way I've been thinking is very one-sided. I need to be part of the solution, not just point the finger and push it off on someone else."

Concrete evidence that this effort was bearing fruit in changing the way employees perceived their jobs and their responsibilities came in a *waigaya* interaction that is now affectionately (and legendarily) known in the Marysville plant as the "weld-splatter breakthrough." For months, an unhealthy standoff put the weld and paint departments at odds. Metal shavings and dust from welding doors, fenders, bumpers, and the like would mar the frame of a small number of vehicles as they streamed into the painting section. It was hard to avoid and is an endemic problem in automobile factories, accepted by many manufacturers as a by-product of the assembly process. And because only a few cars were affected, the Marysville painting team ignored the weld splatter and focused solely on coloring the body. The paint department's reasoning was that the defect would be corrected when the car reached in-line quality control (toward the end of the assembly process), adding cost and time to the manufacturing process, but since the paint team wouldn't be blamed, why tackle the problem?

As jobs were rejiggered on the assembly line, such institutional conflicts seemed all the more ridiculous to new people placed in these departments. Nobody could even remember how this weld-splatter impasse started, but more important, nobody could come up with a good excuse for continuing it. However, resolving this issue still took up many hours of *waigaya*, during which wild arguments would erupt among old antagonists over why weld failed to control its splatter and why paint believed that it had the right to neglect it.

In the end, the relentless discussions about this relatively banal topic revealed one obvious truth, something that it should be noted might never have been exposed were the adversaries not forced to debate this subject over and over ad nauseam: this weld-splatter disagreement was pointless, the kind that is typical of human nature but poison to an organization.

Finally, it ended—surprisingly, with little fanfare. Suddenly, in a quiet moment during a *waigaya*, Jim Hefner, the paint team manager, said: "All right. Splatter's ours. We'll stop it. We're not going to send it through anymore." Hefner said later that he couldn't justify prolonging the obviously senseless argument.

"That was a big day. That was a big breakthrough," said Gillen, the relief still visible on his face well after the event. Without this agreement, achieving the upper quadrants of the direct-pass goals was out of the question.

Moreover, by taking responsibility for this previously intractable problem, and explicitly merging his department's performance with the overall goals of the factory, Hefner deftly purged a chain of troubling and costly dynamics at the plant. In so doing, he motivated others to do the same. In fact, in the wake of Hefner's pronouncement, the welding team initiated an extensive reevaluation of its own quality control measures, which ultimately led to fewer and fewer vehicles splattered during bonding.

■

Although they have their most obvious impact as a basic day-to-day tool, *waigaya* are essential to the support of a much larger cultural framework that governs the way Honda fashions information and ideas, assumptions and conclusions. These combative meetings are best understood as the inspiration for an eccentric approach to innovation and decision making that places Honda among very few companies capable of continuously churning up new and useful knowledge to supersede existing beliefs.

The value of this system to a multinational organization is immeasurable. Nothing is more important for global companies today than having the dexterity to be simultaneously local and international, to swiftly respond to regional preferences while scaling operating tactics and manufacturing improvements around the world. And as Honda's success in the international arena demonstrates, this capability is directly linked to unremittingly reexamining with every new automobile model—more broadly, with every new undertaking large and small—and, for that matter, in every new market—what is already believed to be true.

F. Scott Fitzgerald famously wrote in *The Crack-Up*, a book that originated as a 1936 series of essays for *Esquire* about celebrity and insanity, that "the test of a first-rate intelligence is the ability to hold two opposed ideas in mind at the same time, and still maintain the ability to function." For many companies, though, that condition is precisely what they hope to avoid. To them, contradictions—for example, uncertainties in strategic plans or a new market destination without a full-fledged road map—are weaknesses that reveal confusion and lack of leadership and purpose.

Yet whether they choose to recognize and address it or not, organizations live with paradox continuously—especially now. In an environment influenced strongly by technology, social change, and global cultural upheaval, opposing concepts are routinely altering the business equation: centralization versus decentralization; worker empowerment versus productivity; multinational control versus indigenous autonomy; invention versus risk; disruptive innovation versus cannibalization of existing product lines; creativity versus discipline; proprietary versus open source; robotics versus humans; and on and on.

Most companies are afraid of these dualities, which are deemed too perilous to even entertain. Once you begin considering conflicting possibilities, you must be prepared to continue doing so unendingly and to constantly weigh whether there is a contrasting point of view that has not been given full measure in the current strategic posture. In their hesitance to do this, corporations are like people: individuals resist self-examination and pure, selfless, unvarnished attempts to understand whether there are opposing choices that they should be making, so why should companies be any different?

Indeed, the annals of U.S. commerce are peppered with once mighty corporations that failed to acknowledge the threat from rivals ascending on the strength of a novel approach that was about to turn the business sector's assumptions upside down: companies such as General Motors, ITT, the American railroads; Eastern, Pan Am, United, and American Airlines; Sun Microsystems, Digital Equipment Corp., Blockbuster. All of them and dozens and dozens more have been forced into temporary bankruptcy or outright liquidation because they erred on the side of inertia, failing to scrutinize whether there was a potentially more effective alternative—a set of options better synchronized with current conditions—than their own product, labor, service, innovation, and organizational practices.

In an article in *The Atlantic*, business blogger Megan McArdle argued persuasively that most companies get used to acting in a certain way and believing their own assumptions—and are too risk-averse to modify their fundamental habits. "Change is risky, after all, since it definitionally involves doing something that isn't already working—and even product lines that have grown lackluster still have *some* customers," McArdle wrote in "Why Companies Fail." "Firms that are prone to frequent large changes will probably have more opportunities to kill themselves off with bad choices than firms that resist big changes."

Charles Handy, who has written extensively on organizational resistance to duality and self-analysis, chose an apt metaphor to describe the fear and opportunities that seemingly contradictory business considerations represent. "Living with paradox is neither comfortable nor easy," Handy wrote in his well-regarded book *The Age of Paradox*. "It can be like walking in a dark wood on a moonless night. It is an eerie and, at times, a frightening experience. All sense of direction is lost; trees and bushes crowd in on you; wherever you step, you bump into another obstacle; every noise and rustle is magnified; there is a whiff of danger; it seems safer to stand still than to move. Come the dawn, however, and your path is clear; the noises are now the songs of birds and the rustle in the undergrowth is only scuttling rabbits; trees define the path instead of blocking it. The wood is a different place. If we can bring light to the paradoxes, then the world could look different and less threatening. In fact, that is what successful companies are doing."

Well before Handy wrote those words, Honda had already enthusiastically embraced that concept. Throughout its relatively short history, Honda has welcomed paradox as an opportunity to continuously reassess the status quo and shape new responses to ingrained expectations. Certainly, the notion that all wrong answers are useful and that failing to question conventional wisdom is unacceptable is strung deep in Honda's DNA, the logical by-product of Soichiro Honda's enduring respect for mistakes and what can be learned from them.

As Richard Pascale, the business theory specialist who studied Honda in *The Art of Japanese Management*, and also wrote *Managing on the Edge: Companies That Use Conflict to Stay Ahead*, put it: "Honda's success did not result from a bold insight by a few big brains at the top. On the contrary, success was achieved by senior managers humble enough not to take their initial strategic positions too seriously. They think more in terms of *strategic accommodation* or *adaptive persistence,* underscoring their belief that corporate direction evolves from an adjustment to unfolding events."

That is, the best strategies are fluid and are practically obsolete from the moment they are voiced; their value is maintained only by assiduous reevaluation. This philosophy propelled a pivotal episode in the history of Honda Motor in the late 1950s, when Soichiro Honda was desperate to peddle the company's motorcycles in the United States. Although sales of Honda bikes had grown rapidly in Japan throughout the decade, the company had still not made significant inroads around the world. Soichiro had always envisioned his firm as a global player—the Japanese market was too small to support the continuous technical advances that an engineering-heavy company had to make, he believed—and getting a toehold in the United States was critical to Honda Motor's future.

To do this, the company sent a trusted executive, Kihachiro Kawashima, who eventually became president of American Honda, to the United States to come up with a plan to enter the market. He was given no guidance, no market research—just a goal: sell some bikes in America. Kawashima traveled to Los Angeles with a couple of Honda colleagues, a few large bikes that would seem to fit the U.S. preference for big choppers that can be driven comfortably over long distances (these were samples for motorcycle retailers), and a small, lightweight 50-cc Super Cub to get around town.

As it turned out, Honda's choppers were a flop. They were less expensive than most other motorcycles of their size, but virtually nobody—dealers or customers—was willing to take the chance on a Japanese nameplate in such a high-style, high-performance product sector. Harleys were macho and virtually unbreakable; whether the assessment was fair or not, Hondas were perceived as a low-cost, low-rent imitation of the real thing.

Kawashima's dire assessment of the challenge Honda faced in the United States both in overcoming the prejudice against its motorcycles and in gaining a stable distribution channel only deepened upon venturing coast to coast. "My first reaction after travelling across the United States was: How could we have been so stupid as to start a war with such a vast and wealthy country?" Kawashima told Richard Pascale. "My second reaction was discomfort. I spoke poor English. We dropped in on motorcycle dealers who treated us discourteously and in addition, gave the general impression of being motorcycle enthusiasts who, secondarily, were in business. There were only 3,000 motorcycle dealers in the United States at the time and only 1,000 of them were open five days a week. The remainder was open on nights and weekends. Inventory was poor, manufacturers sold motorcycles to dealers on consignment, the retailers provided consumer financing; after-sales service was poor. It was discouraging."

Clearly, the big-bike strategy was a nonstarter, so Kawashima and his U.S. team took to the streets and hills of LA with their Super Cubs—going dirt biking off-road and zipping in and out of congested car lanes in the busy downtown shopping district and highways. That got the attention of Los Angelenos. The media wrote articles about the strange Japanese company that set up shop in a tiny loft, invading the city's avenues and back roads with these convenient and seemingly dependable motorized bikes—so unlike those made in America—that cost only $250 and delivered 200 miles per gallon. TV stations showed the Super Cub at street fairs and farmers' markets.

And potential customers were charmed. Clamor arose for these unusual but oh-so-convenient minibikes from people who had never considered buying a motorcycle before: newly minted professionals, homemakers, straitlaced teenagers and young adults (not the Wild Ones depicted by Brando and his cohorts), and even middle-aged commuters. Honda couldn't keep up with the orders coming in. As a result, starting from a flat line, by 1961 American Honda was selling about forty thousand Super Cubs through more than five hundred dealers, who now, some months after Kawashima and his team had first arrived in the United States, were more than eager to fund inventory and consumer purchases. This sudden popularity was enhanced by Honda's stunning wipe-out of the European competition in the Isle of Man TT motorcycle races that year, taking the first five places in both the 125-cc and 250-cc categories. With that, the reliability and performance of Honda's engines were no longer suspect.

In the wake of its unexpected success, American Honda inaugurated one of the most famous and longest-running sponsorship campaigns ever: Grey Advertising's "You Meet the Nicest People on a Honda" print ads. This lighthearted full-page promo, showing housewives, young couples, rich matrons and their dogs, delivery boys, and even Santa Claus, among many others, riding a Super Cub, was ubiquitous in mainstream magazines like *Life*, *Look*, and *The Saturday Evening Post* in the early to mid-1960s—and legitimized the little Hondas (and all motorcycles, for that matter) as a means of convenient transportation for regular folks.

("You Meet the Nicest People" is so iconic and linked so closely to the gestalt of the decade that the TV show *Mad Men* used Honda's search for an ad agency to popularize its 50-cc bikes across the country as a plotline in its fourth season. The firm in the show, Sterling Cooper Draper Pryce, is courting Honda, but essentially loses its chance when one of the ad agency's partners, a World War II veteran, expresses his displeasure about working with the Japanese in colorful terms.)

Taking the broad view, Honda's unlikely triumph in the U.S. market turned out to be a decisive, even lifesaving moment in the company's history. Had Honda's attempt to win over American customers foundered in the early 1960s—indeed, had Honda stubbornly and vainly marched ahead with its original tentative plan to compete with Harley and other big bike makers in the country—more than likely the company would have run out of money and been forced to reconsider its fortunes. Indeed, the ability to "adjust to unfolding events," as Pascale described it, or to use failure as an opportunity to view opposing possibilities, allowed Honda to avoid facing the brink.

"We could have gone about this differently—and come up with nothing," said Kawashima. "I think most companies would have spent years trying to sign up U.S. dealers for our big bikes from our Japanese headquarters and only after putting together a distribution network sent executives over to the U.S. In our case, we would never have succeeded in getting a distribution network if we chose that plan. Instead, by sending me and my team to the U.S. with a half-baked idea and a blank slate and a few motorcycles—and the admonition that we were not to imitate others, that we should think as others aren't thinking—we were able to react to what we saw on the ground and ultimately prevail. Don't forget this was a critical initiative for Honda-san; he was absolutely adamant about us becoming a big player in the U.S. Yet he didn't force any preset ideas or strategies upon us."

Years later this same fixation with examining (and even favoring) the mirror image of what would seem to be the obvious or more commonplace choices led Honda to one of its most imaginative engineering achievements: the development of the Ridgeline, Honda's first (and only) North American truck. Although every major automaker in the U.S. market has a pickup in its portfolio, Honda approached this venture differently from most of the others. First, the company determined that the Ridgeline would not be a global car, but rather one specifically made primarily for American customers, part of Honda's continuing emphasis on local markets. Second, Honda opted to dismiss established design and structural ideas for pickups, asking instead, "What kind of truck would we build if we rejected the traditional?" In antithetical Honda fashion, the company would design a pickup truck with few characteristics in common with how a child, for example, would draw one.

Honda could adopt this clean-slate tactic because the Ridgeline's potential customer base bore little resemblance to owners of lumbering Ford F-150s or Chevy Silverados. Rather than hoping to attract cowboys and hard hats, Honda chose to target people who were transitioning out of passenger cars, minivans, and SUVs into trucks, looking for the adventure, utility, and freedom that a pickup promises—it can haul boats and ATVs, trees, camping supplies, furniture, and wood—while still planning to use the truck for carrying groceries, kids, grandkids, and dry cleaning. Which meant that Honda needed to devise a vehicle with the stability and comfort of a car and the muscle of a pickup.

Armed with these opposing standards as the ideal, the Ridgeline's development team examined each aspect of the vehicle they were designing for how well it met the criteria. As a result, the Ridgeline, which debuted in 2006, would radically depart from the typical truck in some extraordinary ways. There were relatively simple differences: the Ridgeline has a full-sized, carlike storage trunk below the bed; it has four doors and two rows of seats in the cab. And also some striking innovations. The most dramatic one to the naked eye: the tailgate opens both vertically and horizontally to conveniently load cargo in the bed or the trunk.

This dual-mode tailgate was particularly challenging from an engineering standpoint. Not only would the tailgate have to swing open horizontally without a closed ring around it for support—that is, absent a rectangular frame as, say, a similar horizontal tailgate in an old station wagon would have—but in the more common vertically opened position the tailgate would have to be capable of bearing much more weight than other pickups in the Ridgeline's vehicle class. At that time, there were numerous complaints from pickup truck owners about tailgate cables snapping under loads of as few as 150 pounds; Honda was determined that the Ridgeline's tailgate would instead hold the weight of a motorcycle or ATV—explicitly, hundreds of pounds—as it was being placed onto the truck bed. And to make matters more difficult, the Ridgeline tailgate would have to shoulder this weight without the help of a supporting cable on the right side, which had to be eliminated so that the tailgate could open horizontally as well.

"Everything stemmed from the decision to not make just another pickup truck but rather to make a hybrid truck and car," said Gary Flint, who was the Ridgeline's large project leader and is now division director of Honda's Proving Center operations. "As long as we weren't questioning that decision, we were compelled to figure out a new tailgate design that would let people both place everyday items easily into the back of the truck and haul big equipment or materials in the truck also. Until then, no other automaker had been moved by its own design requirements to engineer such a fundamental change in the traditional truck tailgate."

The solution, one of the most time-consuming and ingenious aspects of the Ridgeline's development program, was to craft an asymmetrical, cantilevered design projecting from the two vertical support bars in the tailgate; the left bar is connected to a tremendous amount of weight-bearing material—"the thing is literally a fortress," Flint said—and the right bar contains the locking mechanism. The bottom rail is buttressed with additional beamlike supports and the tailgate is made of steel-reinforced composite with twice the strength of traditional metals used in pickup beds.

But if the unique movements of the tailgate are an engineering hallmark of the truck, the Ridgeline's overall frame and support architecture is its most unorthodox feature. Honda thoroughly broke with pickup truck tradition and selected a *unibody* platform for the Ridgeline, an assembly method in which the exterior of the automobile and the chassis are welded essentially as one piece. Most cars are built this way, but virtually no trucks are. Instead, trucks are assembled using what is known as a *body on frame* design, in which the chassis and body are bolted together but otherwise are separate sections. (To get a picture of what body-on-frame looks like in action, drive down a bumpy road in a pickup and through the rearview mirror watch the truck bed bob and weave completely independent of the cab.) Truck makers believe that the two individual parts in the body-on-frame architecture can each be made stronger than a unibody, and hence that this technique is better for vehicles that will be towing, plowing snow, and carrying heavy materials down uneven, rock-strewn paths.

However, in seeking carlike stability for the Ridgeline, Flint and his development team were forced to take unibody construction seriously, although they knew full well that the Ridgeline would be viewed as an outlier in the truck sector if they chose that architecture. A yearlong engineering and cost analysis ensued. At the end of it, the Honda team concluded that a unibody truck would provide 20 times more torsional firmness and 2.5 times more ball joint rigidity (which governs wheel suspension and road balance) than a traditional body-on-frame pickup. This meant a huge performance improvement that was, in fact, more than sufficient to give the pickup the on-road elegance of a car. And in a surprise discovery made possible only by Honda's willingness to explore the feasibility of unibody design for a truck, Flint's team found body and chassis materials that allowed the automaker to claim that the Ridgeline had the load-hauling capacity of a typical pickup.

"I think we surprised a lot of people by disproving long-standing attitudes about the towing and carrying strength of unibody designs," Flint said.

Indeed, *Car and Driver* wrote that the Ridgeline "turned conventional thinking on its ear. . . . Up to that point, pickups were, by definition, body-on-frame workhorses for lugging gear and towing. The fact that . . . trucks were increasingly being used as family cars was irrelevant when it came to the frame. Then Honda did the unthinkable. It engineered a pickup on a car platform, with a clever in-bed trunk. And the industry watched to see if the public would buy into the heresy."

As it turns out, the public mostly did. In its first year, the Ridgeline won *Motor Trend*'s Truck of the Year Award. And since then, although sales in the overall small-pickup category have been volatile, mostly in response to gas prices, the Ridgeline has continued to post respectable numbers; for example, up more than 20 percent year-over-year in 2012 compared with 2011. Nonetheless, the Ridgeline has never been able to repeat its record volume of more than fifty thousand sold in 2006. In an attempt to bolster sales again in what has become a very difficult sector of the auto industry, Honda plans a Ridgeline redesign for 2016.

Still, the market difficulties notwithstanding, the truck remains one of Honda's most profitable vehicles. The chief reason: despite the Ridgeline's many novel features, the multiyear development effort came in at under $250 million—primarily due to Honda's meticulous frugality in research, engineering, and manufacturing—less than half the amount that General Motors, for example, would normally pay for a new vehicle.

▪

Honda's unusual ability to indulge paradox—to employ opposing forces and ideas as fulcrums for strategic and operational choices—

is dependent chiefly on organizational spontaneity. Examined more closely, that conclusion, in itself, advances yet another business paradox: although most executives give lip service today to the importance of split-second flexibility in altering product, strategic, and development decisions to meet shifting market demands, the trajectory of modern industry over the last 150 years has been marked by efforts to eliminate disorder and spontaneity in favor of seeking perfection through data-driven systems, rules, and procedures. The messier approach—Honda's method—of using conflict and contention as a philosophical underpinning and a means of creating practical knowledge to influence seat-of-the-pants corporate decisions is decidedly against the grain.

From Frederick Winslow Taylor's nineteenth-century time and management studies, in which workplace tasks were observed and precisely measured to determine the most efficient production methods for each job, to Henry Ford's assembly line, the goal has been to increase yield while minimizing variation. In more recent times, computers, information technology, robotics, and assorted forms of data automation have sought these same measurable results. Arriving on the scene in the 1980s, lean manufacturing was an attempt to eliminate the factory waste and inefficiency that Ford's production ideas failed to address. And even more recently, a lean-derived concept known as Six Sigma has become extremely popular because it is essentially a paint-by-numbers, fill-in-the-blanks statistical technique for gauging and managing factory throughput, worker productivity in everything from assembly to research and development, and production defects.

All of these concepts have one tangible goal: to reduce deviation in the quality and quantity of output that the presence of humans in the workplace organically introduces. In other words, to eradicate ambiguity and derive order out of potential chaos. But in attempting to achieve this extremely difficult outcome with rule-bound systems and processes, organizational agility suffers and innovation may be squelched.

Numerous case studies prove this point, but one of the most instructive involves 3M, which in the late twentieth century had enjoyed a well-deserved reputation as one of the most creative multinationals in the world. On the wings of such products as masking tape, the Post-it note, Ace bandages, Thinsulate, Scotch tape, and numerous essential industrial materials that end up in everything from the iPhone to automobiles to sporting goods, in its heyday 3M drew at least one third of its sales from products released in the prior five years.

In late 2000, James McNerney, an acolyte of General Electric CEO Jack Welch, was named to the top job at 3M, the first outsider to lead the company in its one-hundred-year history. McNerney brought with him a devotion to Six Sigma, which Welch had made virtually a religion at GE. McNerney introduced Six Sigma protocols throughout the organization; everywhere you turned employees were filling out forms and justifying their productivity. Adhering to Six Sigma rules, they were asked to define, measure, analyze, improve, and control.

As is often the case with lean procedures, jobs and capital expenditures were slashed and the balance sheet improved. Wall Street and 3M's board fell in love with McNerney. But not so in 3M's R&D warrens, which have consistently been the backbone of the company's success. Essentially department agnostic, Six Sigma introduced a layer of accountability into the research unit that was anathema to invention. In order to take some of the uncertainty out of R&D—to make it more orderly and productive—a tightly controlled phase review process was implemented, in which 3M scientists had to justify the value of their work on a weekly or monthly basis and provide a time line for moving experimentation quickly into the new product pipeline. As a result, before long, small research gains with immediate revenue potential took priority over possible groundbreaking advances. "It's really tough to schedule invention," Craig Oster, a thirty-year mechanical engineer at 3M, told *Fortune* a few years ago.

Not surprisingly, by 2005, when McNerney abruptly left 3M to become CEO of Boeing, sales from five-year-old or newer products had dropped to 21 percent of revenue. 3M had already lost its leadership position in new product and materials ideas and it was in danger of slipping further into irrelevance, increasingly known for inventions that were decades old. Replacing McNerney, George Buckley, an electrical engineer, continued many of the Six Sigma initiatives in the company's factories but freed up the researchers to think blue-sky again. And his effort paid off. Exploring new avenues of inquiry in more advanced technologies like radio frequency identification systems, optical films, composite materials, cloud storage, and biometrics, 3M has rebounded from the recession and is again drawing 30 percent–plus revenue from newer inventions.

This was an absolutely necessary change in approach, Buckley said, because breakthroughs by definition challenge the quotidian and they can't be fit into a system whose sole purpose is to eliminate deviations from the statistical norm. "Invention is by its very nature a disorderly process," Buckley said. "You can't put a Six Sigma process into R&D and say, 'Well, I'm getting behind on invention, so I'm going to schedule myself for three good ideas on Wednesday and two on Friday.' That's not how creativity works."

To Honda, the story of 3M's recent troubles is a cautionary one, which can only be avoided by welcoming paradox, rather than trying to eradicate it with systems like Six Sigma and other lean practices. Honda has not specifically codified its approach to innovation;

doing so would run counter to the company's view of originality as an organic by-product of two-sided, argumentative discussions. But some academic observers have described Honda's method as a theory of dialectics, in which, as the influential Japanese organization guru Ikujiro Nonaka and a coauthor wrote, the "combination of thesis and antithesis (are synthesized) into a higher stage of truth."

Nonaka, who is professor emeritus at Hitotsubashi University Graduate School of International Corporate Strategy in Tokyo, added that as a fundamental operating principle, dialectical strategic thinking is a neglected but critical skill for the modern corporation. "Firms that can manage contradictory forces, such as competition and cooperation, integration and disintegration, and creativity and efficiency, are the ones that will survive and prosper," he wrote.

In simpler and practical terms, Honda's protocol for exploring opposite sides of a given challenge is to assess and deconstruct its absolute and relative values—and make sure that the two are aligned throughout a project. The absolute value encompasses the company's overarching ideals—such as respect for the individual and promoting dreams and aspirations—as well as the goals for a specific project; for example, to make a pickup truck that people will want to drive all the time, dressed up or dressed down. Absolute values are fixed and not affected by outside conditions. The relative value is fungible; it addresses a task through the lens of the current business environment, evaluating the strengths and weaknesses of competitors, suppliers, internal resources, and factory capacity as well as the conditions of the marketplace and the targeted customer base.

Honda's contrarian decision to build a business plane, known as the HondaJet, offers an easily comprehensible glimpse into the distinction between absolute and relative values. Although companies have been shedding their private planes for the past decade or more, often as a necessary cost-saving measure or a way to raise cash—and accelerated these sales during the 2008 recession—Honda chose to investigate in the early 2000s whether a profitable plane could be built that met the corporate market's needs and mitigated its constraints while offering a desirable flying experience. Most other companies would not have contemplated investing in such an obviously floundering sector; brand names like Learjet and Cessna were either sold off or struggling to make ends meet, and there were few signs that anything else but a fundamental, permanent collapse of the market had occurred. But Honda was confident in its ability to logically entertain the paradox of pumping millions of dollars into a soft sector.

Former Honda president Takeo Fukui provided a thumbnail sketch of the absolute values that stood on one side of this analysis in a speech at the end of 2003. "Mobility is a basic desire, right and joy for all people," he said. "Honda continues to pursue mobility from all dimensions. Mobility in the third dimension, the sky, was a dream we have had since shortly after our company was founded. The words of our founder, 'Do not imitate others,' are burned in the minds of everyone at Honda. We have no interest in following."

To wit, mobility and uniqueness are the primary absolute values that Honda is attaching to the project. The relative values are more granular, starting from "What will be the cost and the return on investment of pursuing the sky; what are the new features that Honda can offer to build a better flying experience at the right price point for customers; who are the customers for the HondaJet?" and so on. The answers to each relative value question will be judged by whether they satisfy the ideals inherent in the absolute values.

For any project, as Honda weighs absolute and relative values independently and then against each other, often during multihour *waigaya*, three levels of questioning are frequently employed—known inside the company (from top to bottom) as A00, A0, and A.

The top-line query (A00) is the most essential and the most existential: What is this engine for? A0 delves a little more deeply into the undertaking: What is the conceptual basis of the engine; what do we think it will feature, from a broad perspective; what other engine can it be compared with? And the A-level question gets down to the critical minutiae: What should the horsepower of this engine be?

The power of this three-tier script lies in its lack of complexity. When a problem cannot be solved, Honda designers go up a level. For example, if an argument ensues over the appropriate horsepower rating, the discussion will move backward to revisit the engine design again; perhaps by changing the engine's conceptual principles, the horsepower debate will be resolved.

Some Honda employees offer a slightly different perspective on harmonizing absolute and relative values, preferring to describe this process as the synthesis of idealistic and realistic exigencies. "Idealistic is sound theory; realistic is what people want," said Ridgeline developer Flint. "The two have to coexist in the same vehicle or we shouldn't make it."

For example, in the case of the Ridgeline, the target customers demanded a truck that handled like a car; that was the realistic, or relative, value—the goal that Flint's team would design around. And the volumes of engineering manuals containing unibody construction ideas, calculations, physical properties, and recent advances held the sound theory, the absolute values that Flint and his team could tap into to ultimately achieve the realistic goals. Given this exercise, "Honda engineers can't just come up with pie-in-the-sky diagrams and drawings," said Flint. "They have to design parts that solve problems."

Honda has devised a raft of ad hoc and formalized techniques for reconciling opposing ideas and generating realistic if untried applications from this process, in large part because even in organizations wedded to spontaneity, procedures for managing the many ways employees confront one another's points of view are critical to avoid disorder and ensure timely decision making. And in that effort, the role of Honda supervisors and middle managers in fostering a free flow of what is known as tacit knowledge—which has been described by Honda observers as something that is not easily visible and expressible, something that is highly personal and hard to formalize, something that is gained through the use of metaphors or pictures, and something deeply rooted in an individual's action and experience—is vital.

Through *waigaya*, ad hoc and informal discussions, extending free time to employees to work on original applications for improvements and new products, placing inspired employees near one another to spark original ideas and numerous other techniques, Honda supervisors are expected to, in Nonaka's words, "manage creative chaos within the organization." The supervisors are, in essence, charged with articulating the company's vision while frontline employees use their day-to-day experiences to respond with what is actually possible, given the great latitude that Honda offers in defining that term.

The HondaJet was green-lighted in 2005 after a two-year study found that the opening in the corporate jet market that Honda could exploit would, indeed, perfectly meet the ideals of innovation and practical, enjoyable mobility. The plane, which is now in full-scale production after passing a series of test flights, is a compact, lightweight, six-person aircraft with an avant-garde engine design that places the two turbofan jets directly over the wings. This reduces drag and enables the HondaJet to maintain a cruising speed of 483 miles per hour. The cockpit has the animated feel of a video gamer's playhouse, and the aircraft is 15 percent more fuel efficient and 20 percent roomier than comparable jets. The HondaJet's price tag is about $4.5 million, about one third the cost of the competition.

Still, it's an enormous gamble. Even at a discount, demand for corporate jets may remain sluggish at best. But it's precisely the type of risk that Honda enjoys taking; it represents a controverting bet made palatable because in each of the project's relative values—price, speed, size, comfort, fuel use, and design—Honda engineers were able to substantially improve upon prior corporate jets of that size, to reimagine or revivify the model. And in achieving these goals so adroitly, the plane's designers inevitably honored the promise of the aircraft's absolute values.

And perhaps the most telling nod to Honda's fascination with paradox occurred recently when Honda Aircraft Company president Michimasa Fujino was discussing the first orders that Honda had received for the plane and predicting profitability within six years. Rather than purposefully ignoring his rivals or making claims about the superiority of the HondaJet, Fujino went out of his way to welcome the competition in the market. Echoing Soichiro Honda's unusual demand in the 1950s that the Japanese government allow foreign cars and motorcycles into the country to encourage improvements by domestic manufacturers, Fujino said: "We want to evoke new demand to make the pie bigger for all. As the pie becomes bigger, we'll all be motivated to sharpen our competitiveness, which will in turn attract more new demand."

Funny thing is, if he said that during a *waigaya*, he'd get an argument from someone telling him in no uncertain terms why he was wrong.

4

PRINCIPLE #2: REAL PLACE, REAL PART, REAL KNOWLEDGE

Soichiro Honda was known for his quick temper and impatience with people, traits made worse by perfectionism. But even conceding the most disagreeable aspects of Honda's personality, one story about Honda Motor's founder stands out as being truly perplexing and even bordering on sadistic.

The incident occurred in 1964. Fresh off triumphs in the Isle of Man Tourist Trophy motorcycle races a few years earlier, Soichiro Honda audaciously undertook an activity most automobile makers to this day prefer to avoid: he fielded a racing team in the Formula 1 circuit, the non-U.S. version of NASCAR. This was a particularly bold move because his company had made only one car to that point—the S500 roadster, roundly criticized as little more than a motorcycle with doors, seats, and four wheels. Nonetheless, Soichiro was still basking in the praise Honda Motor had earned for winning the Isle of Man—and he was enjoying the instant credibility as an engine designer and the huge gains in worldwide motorcycle sales his company had reaped in the wake of those victories.

Surely, he thought, a win or even a representative showing in an F1 race would immediately catapult Honda Motor into the vanguard of the automobile industry. In addition, Soichiro believed that the mere presence of Honda Motor on the international stage would permanently undo the Japanese Ministry of International Trade and Industry's hopes of stymieing the company's global car-making ambitions. Like so many of Honda's new initiatives, the Formula 1 gambit was a top company priority the minute it was announced. And ultimate success, Soichiro made clear, was the only outcome he would accept.

As with the Isle of Man races, victory would have to wait. Honda Motor's initial Formula 1 entries often failed to finish the course. There was a vast difference between building a 50-cc motorcycle engine designed to drive a bike that weighs a couple hundred pounds and engineering a high-performance 1,500-cc motor that can propel a half-ton, single-seat racing car at speeds of 200 miles an hour. And among the handful of Honda Motor misadventures in the 1964 F1 races, the most sensational occurred in the English race, where the company's entry overheated and caught fire, making for a jaw-dropping combustible sight as it jackknifed off the course.

Back home in Japan, Soichiro was at his wit's end. Publicly, he was humiliated. Privately, he was concerned that his company was not yet ready to make a great automobile. He ordered the charred car brought back to Japan, where it could be analyzed for why it failed so miserably. Soichiro led the investigation himself.

The problem was obvious the instant he looked at the engine: the piston rings were ashen and disfigured. Looking at the engineering team standing around him, Honda demanded: "Who made these piston rings?"

Shoichiro Irimajiri, a twenty-four-year-old designer who had graduated from the University of Tokyo with an aeronautical engineering degree and was in his fourth year at Honda Motor, said that he did.

Honda laughed, nodding his head knowingly, as if this callow youth was just who he would expect to shame the company with such a flawed product. "Did you design them to burn?"

"None of my calculations indicated the rings would burn," Irimajiri answered. "Perhaps there may have been other factors at play."

Even as the words came out of his mouth, Irimajiri knew that he sounded impertinent and disrespectful—especially because by that point he was aware that his engineering equations, no matter how complex, sophisticated, and elegantly symmetrical, were useless to Honda since Irimajiri had not verified his results on high-stressed automobile engines, but only on motorcycles.

Not surprisingly, Honda's anger only worsened. "I'm an expert in piston rings," he yelled. "Before the war I ran a company that made nothing but piston rings. I've got patents on piston rings. And you're trying to lecture me? This is why I can't stand university graduates. Your heads are all swollen but you still don't know a damn thing."

Honda told Irimajiri that as punishment he would have to apologize to everyone on the F1 team individually "for his stupidity," and Honda added that he would walk with him as he did so.

Mortified but prepared to take the blame, Irimajiri, holding a burned piston in his hand, walked slowly through Honda Motor racing headquarters, bowing and saying quietly to each member of the engineering group, "I apologize for the trouble my mistake caused."

Honda stood next to Irimajiri, a look of complete satisfaction on his face.

To Western eyes, this episode certainly has a disturbing quality. The punishment seems too strict and purposefully humiliating for the young engineer's misstep. However, now—decades later—it remains among the most apt anecdotes to explore the value to the company of a business principle that few other industrial firms are able to follow with the rigor or success that Honda Motor does: a Japanese concept known as *sangen shugi*, one of Honda Motor's three most treasured principles.

Although there is a lot of confusion—even among Japanese speakers—about what *sangen shugi* means literally, at Honda Motor *sangen shugi* is defined as going to the three realities (sometimes called actualities) before making a decision. The three realities are:

Gen-ba. The real spot: go to the factory floor, the showroom, the backyard, the parking lot, the driver's seat, the back row, the truck cab and bed—wherever you must—to get firsthand knowledge. (This is also anglicized as *gemba*—most prominently by lean guru Jim Womack, whose recent book about observing how people work together in factories is called *Gemba Walks*.)

Gen-butsu. The real part; use the firsthand knowledge to focus on the actual situation and begin to formulate a decision or recommendation.

Gen-jitsu. The real facts; support your decisions with actual data and information that you have collected at the real spot. Or, as one Honda executive put it: "Make decisions based on reality."

Sangen shugi can be seen as a tautology. *Gen-ba* is where knowledge begins; after maturing during *gen-butsu* this knowledge serves as the footing for *gen-jitsu*, where decisions are arrived at based on firsthand understanding. In turn, the facts that emerge during *gen-jitsu* organically inform the blossoming of new information at future *gen-ba*.

Sangen shugi is not original to Honda, although many manufacturing observers say that Honda's distinctive adaptation of *sangen shugi* is arguably the most effective and directly impactful use of the principle. Other Japanese companies generally link *sangen shugi* to lean manufacturing implementations. In fact, for many companies, including Toyota, *sangen shugi* is a proxy for modern-day Frederick Winslow Taylor–like factory efficiency studies or Six Sigma quality and productivity analyses. It is used as a tool to derive statistics that can dictate the most optimal assembly-line configurations and benchmarks. In these applications, the last of the *sangen shugi*, *gen-jitsu*—collecting facts to support data-driven decisions—is given undue weight.

For Honda, the scale is tilted in the opposite direction. While *gen-jitsu* is still practiced at Honda, *gen-ba*—going to the spot—is perceived by the automaker as the most critical aspect of *sangen shugi*. It is relied upon daily at Honda to assess everything from a small glitch on the assembly line to the features in a new vehicle or upgraded model to the company's globalization strategy. No decision is made at Honda without firsthand information, and no Honda manager or employee would dare try to offer a point of view, make a recommendation, or challenge an existing process or system unless he or she had "gone to the *gen-ba*," a term that is heard at Honda factories and offices everywhere in the world, no matter what language is spoken locally.

"They chase women out of supermarkets in California and scare them out of their wits, following them to their cars, trying to figure out how they can make it easier for these potential customers to load grocery sacks in a CR-V or Pilot," said Sean McAlinden, chief economist at the Center for Automotive Research. "All through their factories, you'll see meetings pop up anywhere on the line where they're all looking at one rivet or screw. They have to see it firsthand or it's not real."

In that light, Soichiro Honda's reaction to the burned Formula 1 piston rings makes more sense. Shoichiro Irimajiri had not only failed to test his engine under harsh automobile racing conditions, but he had also neglected to talk to engineers and drivers on the circuit and to dissect their motors for stress points and failure history. All of Irimajiri's calculations were conducted in the laboratory, where, in Honda's view, he was isolated from the real information he would need to design the engine.

(Ironically, Irimajiri's oversight echoed Soichiro Honda's own piston fiasco in the early days of his career, well before Honda Motor existed, when Toyota rejected nearly all of the rings Soichiro made because their tolerances were skewed. To overcome this failure, as mentioned earlier, Honda went back to school to learn every facet of metallurgy, although he ignored the exams, and toured dozens of factories, where he interviewed engineers about their manufacturing and machining techniques.)

There is another dimension of *gen-ba* as well that the piston ring incident illustrates. Soichiro and his partner, Takeo Fujisawa, worried often about how the company would endure after they had left it. Their influence on the business was pervasive. Soichiro's peripatetic engineering genius, his enthusiasm for individual innovation, and his hunger for excellence, and Fujisawa's diligence, fiscal prudence, and rectitude completely colored the company's culture. But the degree to which their industrial and business beliefs had actually taken root and would continue to be practiced when they were no longer at the company was difficult to measure.

As a result, Soichiro maintained that his responsibility (and that of other Honda supervisors) was to confront deviations from the company's bedrock principles immediately and directly; a Honda manager fulfilled his duty to go to the *gen-ba* by continually teaching with example and discipline the value and significance of *waigaya*, *gen-ba*, and other tenets that the company held dear, as Soichiro did with Irimajiri.

The importance of this management obligation was captured in an intriguing koanlike interchange between Fujisawa and a

Japanese plant manager that fully reflected Fujisawa's concerns about the durability of the culture that he and Honda were attempting to implant. This conversation took place during an idle moment when Fujisawa and then factory chief Kiyoshi Kawashima were relaxing at the end of a day.

"Do you think Honda will last forever?" Fujisawa asked.

"Of course. It'd better or we will be in trouble," Kawashima said, at first thinking that Fujisawa was being flippant.

But Fujisawa's seriousness became clearer as he pressed the point. "Do you really believe that, though? If corporations grew forever, Japan would be swamped with them before long."

"Does that mean you think that corporations have a life span?" Kawashima asked.

"Put that way it would seem Honda is destined to die," Fujisawa responded. "I want you to think about how we can avoid that."

Later, reflecting on this exchange, Fujisawa explained that if Kawashima, who at the time was being groomed for the top spot at Honda Motor after Soichiro retired, explored this question seriously and exhaustively, he would ultimately reach this conclusion: only companies with strong, immutable, homegrown values passed from one generation of workers to the next escape dissolution. Furthermore, to make certain that these fundamental principles are perpetuated, a company must place a premium on individual responsibility—managers' and employees'—to preserve and embody these tenets. "Competition in the business world is incredibly fierce," he wrote. "Honda Motor must rely on itself, not other people or other things to flourish."

Since the debut of Honda Motor in the late 1940s, *sangen shugi* was among the company's primary operating principles. The types of roads and climate Soichiro's wife and her friends encountered as they biked into town to purchase food and sundries in postwar

Japan inspired the design of Honda's first motorcycles. In later models, features like mounting the fuel tank under the seat away from the step-through so that women in skirts could demurely get onto the bike were developed by sending out squadrons of people to observe how the motorcycles were used in the real world and by whom. On the manufacturing floor, Soichiro's prescient decision to have Honda Motor make its own dies—a radical choice for a start-up company—was spurred by his belief that intimately understanding the process of cutting and stamping by actually engineering this equipment would give the firm a competitive edge in skills and knowledge. And Honda Motor's successful entry into the United States with small bikes was only achieved by sending a team to Los Angeles to set up shop in the country, rather than working through a network of distributors, to determine firsthand which part of the market Honda could legitimately aspire to. In all of these instances and substantially more, *sangen shugi* served as a guy wire to anchor the company's most meaningful decisions.

Additionally, Honda Motor's long and rewarding connection to motorcycle and automobile racing—which far surpasses the involvement of any other vehicle manufacturer—is itself a testimony to the company's deep commitment to *sangen shugi.* Since the 1960s, Honda Motor has stood at the top of the winner's circle in hundreds of F1 and bike races. Recently, the company joined the IndyCar series and between 2006 and 2011, Honda Motor powered the entire thirty-three-car starting field at the Indianapolis 500, the only period in Indy 500 history that not a single driver dropped out of the event with an engine-related problem.

Soichiro Honda, who built his first motorcycle racing engine in 1928 when he was twenty-two—a converted Curtiss-Wright aircraft motor that set a Japanese speed record of 75 mph—believed that racing was an exceptional training ground for engineers and designers; the pressures and pace challenged people continuously, forcing them to find fresh solutions and quick, accurate responses to problems they'd never faced before. Racing perfectly encapsulated what was meant by going to the *gen-ba*, he thought. What spot could be more valuable for observing firsthand vehicle engineering than a site that tested engines, bodies, tires, transmissions, and brakes under the harshest circumstances?

"In a race a split second can define the entire competition, one tire length will decide whether you are a winner or a loser," Honda said. "You cannot disregard even the smallest improvement because in a race you must be ahead or be left behind. If we're going to build the best vehicles in the world, the best place to learn how to do that is at the highest level, where the demands and rewards are the greatest."

Although the F1 piston ring debacle was humbling, Irimajiri later said that Soichiro's message was well taken. "I got the point," he said. "I didn't go to the spot at all, and he was right, because of that I was too ignorant to build an engine that would succeed in a race against the best in the world."

Irimajiri would not make that mistake again. The Formula 1 engine he designed for the Mexican Grand Prix the very next year, developed after hours of on-road testing and performance analysis aided by experienced race car designers, surprised the rest of the field by coming in first. About a decade later, Irimajiri was named president of Honda of America, a position he held until 1992, spearheading Honda Motor's transformation from a small Japanese automaker in the United States into a bestselling brand. In the 1980s General Motors recruited Irimajiri for a top executive position because of his success at Honda. But Irimajiri chose to stay with Honda.

Sangen shugi has had its most indelible influence on Honda Motor as the ideology behind Honda's lucrative globalization strategy—or, in Honda's case, a postmodern globalization approach that could better be called localization. The hype and decline of globalization—the reasons why the internationalist strategies of most multinationals have floundered—and Honda's deft gamble on a business environment not governed by a flat, boundary-less commercial landscape but rather by homegrown self-contained markets will be covered in some detail in chapter 9. However, it bears pointing out here that Honda's strict adherence to the principles of *sangen shugi* led to the decision more than two decades ago to defy the skeptics and establish autonomous footholds in each major global region that could independently develop products locally for domestic customers and to a lesser degree for exports.

That approach alone enabled Honda to avoid many of the globalization missteps that other manufacturers took, primarily through ill-advised and hasty plant openings in countries where they were not yet prepared to operate and through plans to manage these manufacturing operations with R&D, engineering, and design located miles away at corporate headquarters. By avoiding these tactical errors, Honda's profit margins in virtually every global market that it invests in are higher than the auto industry average.

The precepts of *sangen shugi* militated against the possibility that Honda could consider any alternative to decentralizing its global operations. After all, the meaning of going to the spot is corrupted if you merely observe something from a distance and then try to interpret what was seen from yet a greater distance away—which would have been the case had Honda attempted to concentrate control in Japan of its regional affiliates' operating and product decisions. Rather, *sangen shugi* demands a more tactile, rapid, and localized response.

Although Honda may be on the receiving end of jokes from experts in the auto industry who find the whole idea a bit eccentric, Gary Flint, the chief designer of the Ridgeline, did in fact sit for hours in Home Depot parking lots on Saturday mornings to watch people clumsily load purchases into their cars and trucks before he decided that the two-way tailgate, despite its cost and design hurdles, was the obvious, if unorthodox, choice for the hybrid car-pickup.

And Flint and his team experienced firsthand what it was like to own a truck in the United States by taking competitive vehicles, such as the Chevy Avalanche, Ford Explorer Sport Trac, and Toyota Tacoma, on camping, white water rafting, and shopping trips. The radical choice of unibody construction grew out of these excursions. Because of the added expense and complexity of these features, Flint argues that had Honda's corporate chiefs in Japan not trusted the Ridgeline's U.S. developers with relative autonomy to make the truck that they believed would best exemplify a Honda vehicle in the U.S. market—that is, had the company not paired *sangen shugi* with global decentralization, "no matter what our in-person observations were, they would have been vetoed."

Told of Flint's assessment of the value of local independence at Honda and the implied criticism of corporations with centralized command-and-control structures, one top Honda executive said that it was a frank but accurate appraisal and then offered a simple predicate to explain why *sangen shugi* dictates localization:

> knowledge emanates from local conditions; and
>
> decisions are outgrowths of knowledge; hence
>
> operating tactics and strategies from one region to the next should be determined chiefly by local preferences and characteristics, rather than a corporate template.

In Honda's factories, the impact of *sangen shugi* is seen in a unique plant layout that places a number of pivotal industrial functions under the same roof, blending in a single central spot operational activities that manufacturers would typically isolate. For example, in Lincoln, Alabama (and more recently in other Honda plants), Honda's engine and automobile assembly lines are situated side by side.

This approach allows for precise, visual inventory and production oversight because soon after the engine is built it is meant to be installed in the skeleton of a car twenty feet away. Any slippage in engine stock will be immediately apparent to the plant workers, who can alleviate the imbalance by manufacturing buffered cars (which are partly built vehicles held aside to fill the output gap when the regular assembly line needs to be shut down) while the engine makers replenish the supply. Moreover, when an engine flaw is discovered after the vehicle is completed and ready to roll to the test track—the first time that a Honda motor is actually turned on and revved up—the engine team can address the problem at the factory without the need to send the cars or engines to a separate site for repair.

In sharp contrast, most auto companies don't build their engines from start to finish anymore, as Honda does. Instead, they assemble the motors from third-party components in a factory at a distance from the main assembly line. It is commonly believed that combining engine and automobile assembly would make it difficult to keep track of parts shipments and oversee worker skills development for each activity. But Honda has found the opposite to be true. In fact, according to Honda data, by integrating engine and auto assembly Honda has enjoyed gains of 10 percent or more in the pace of skills training, quality control, manufacturing speed, and factory utilization. Moreover, exorbitant logistics costs and the risk of damaging engines in transit are avoided by not having to ship the heavy motors hundreds of miles by truck or rail.

Also in walking distance to the assembly line at Lincoln is a twenty-person team of design engineers. This group, part of Honda Engineering, an independent subsidiary with units embedded in plants in every region of the world, builds proprietary industrial tools, jigs, dies, robots, hardware, software, and machining equipment that addresses specific local needs. Broadly speaking, the engineering unit's many creative industrial design advances are primarily responsible for Honda's unequaled flexible factory techniques that enable the company to seamlessly produce multiple autos on a single assembly line and switch a line over to a newly designed vehicle faster and more dexterously than the competition.

"In-house engineering is one of our secret weapons, important for new model development but also for day-to-day running of the plant," said Chuck Ernst, who designed the Lincoln plant and is currently chief engineer of the Powertrain Function at Honda's North American Engineering Center in Marysville, Ohio. "If we have technical issues big or small or if we have to make capacity or flexibility changes—like moving a product from Line One to Line Two or changing to a completely new vehicle on Line Two—having an engineering team on-site is invaluable. We can make big changes on the fly."

While virtually all car companies now house their designing engineers in centers near the corporation's home office, prior to World War II, well before Honda was even a company, dedicated engineering teams were commonly linked to automobile factories. At that time, most auto plants were in relatively close proximity to one another—for example, GM and Ford had practically all of their factories in the Detroit area—so a group of engineers could be assigned to multiple locations. Moreover, the engineers could be asked to handle a variety of tasks because unions had not yet won agreements limiting autoworkers, including designers, to specific jobs and salaries by title. In the postwar period, workforce flexibility declined significantly and many North American plants were shuttered, replaced by international factory networks. As a result, on-site engineering became a much more expensive and much less desirable option for traditional automakers.

"But in abandoning that practice, these companies lost some of their ability to respond to regional differences and local factory requirements," said John Casesa, a veteran auto industry analyst who is currently senior managing director at Guggenheim Partners.

Honda produces more of its own factory equipment than any other manufacturer in any industry. The local plant-embedded design engineers routinely create interchangeable welding jigs and new stamping equipment, among other heavy tooling devices, that have helped Honda rewrite traditional standards for factory flexibility and productivity. For example, new welding robots designed recently in Lincoln can determine on their own which jigs are appropriate for the specific vehicle approaching their zone—this could change at a Honda plant from one car to the next—and within seconds reequip themselves without slowing the assembly line down. This automated retooling process eliminates one of the most unwieldy and time-consuming aspects of automobile assembly. Ernst recalled that it used to take "two or three body positions or five to ten minutes to manipulate these big monolith blocks of steel into position for changing the welding system to a new model on the line." (Lincoln's welding system is described in more detail in chapter 6.)

But in-house engineering also solves factory shortcomings with less-heralded improvements. To illustrate, Lincoln's engineering team recently built a machine to assist workers doing quality inspection on transmissions by lifting the enormous casings and flipping them over in exactly the same fashion each time so that extra coolant falls into a precisely placed pan. Previously, when assemblers handled the transmissions manually, the coolant often seeped out onto the factory floor.

And in another instance, engineers designed a robot "the size of Mark McGwire's forearms when he was juicing," as one employee put it, to work on V6 engines, installing critical bolts on the cylinder heads that if not sufficiently tight could lead to engine failure down the road. Quality is improved while a difficult task for Honda employees is eliminated.

Although the creativity of these and many other engineering improvements is unmatched and a point of pride for Honda, they would likely be met with much less enthusiasm if they were devised from afar without local input and support. After all, many engineering advances come at the expense of workers' jobs; as a result, frequently employees are threatened by a new machine that they were unaware of or uncertain about why it was needed, so much so that they might sabotage or at least resist its implementation.

"I've seen situations where you're told to install some device invented by engineering at headquarters," Ernst said. "There are strict specifications for the equipment with strict rules and strict guidance, and it can takes months to figure out how to install it to the specific dimensions of a local factory. And then it takes months to train everybody and months to get over people's resistance to having been told that they must use the equipment as is without their input. Doing it as one team in one factory, where we have to look each other in the face every day, overcomes these obstacles."

And viewed from a higher plane, for Honda Motor *gen-ba* manifested by on-site engineering satisfies a larger corporate objective first articulated by Soichiro Honda, when he demanded that his engineers learn how to make their own dies and stamping tools. As a Honda executive put it: "When you buy technology it remains frozen, a foreign thing that is not part of yourself, and in the end you don't know its full possibilities and where to go with it."

Which is precisely why Honda has also employed *sangen shugi* to compel individual workers—that is, not only engineering and research teams—to take personal responsibility for on-the-job improvements and even for patentable inventions; to avoid nine-to-five passivity in favor of, in essence, customizing their corner of the factory or any part of the plant, for that matter. In a letter written about a decade ago, distributed throughout the company, then Honda CEO Takeo Fukui provided clear notice of the connection between *sangen shugi* and the company's expectations vis-à-vis its employees.

"(At Honda) there is . . . extensive delegation of authority, which indicates that this is a company where each and every person is the main player," Fukui said. "This is why and how the enthusiasm, energy, and actions of each individual combine to create the company's values. . . . There has been a focus on . . . (fostering) a workplace environment where each individual can exercise the maximum level of positive energy; and pay respect to the importance of working at the spot, or the actual workplace, and make decisions based on the real situation. This means, in other words, efforts to reinforce the actual spot in the workplace. . . . It is important for each individual on the spot to think and act on their own initiative. Innovation and value creation are the culmination of each associate's passion. In other words, it is each individual's effort to practice the Honda Way."

Honda workers, sometimes in near cultlike fashion, have routinely heeded that message. Virtually all of the automaker's employees that I have met are remarkably invested in Honda's demanding but rewarding culture. And they view designing a new process or a systematic change in a factory as a responsibility, not an option, something that they are required to do in exchange for the paycheck and white uniform that Honda gives them. As Michael Robinet, managing director of consultants at IHS Automotive in Detroit, put it: "It can look to outsiders as if they all drank the Kool-Aid—very wide-eyed and all—but no company is as good as Honda at grassroots innovation. They have mastered a culture in which there is no distance between a daily job and generating workplace improvements."

Many of the myriad employee-driven advances are relatively straightforward, commonsense concepts. For example, with the price of copper rising recently, one Honda worker devised a vacuum-and-funnel system that catches copper shavings during production and dispenses them into a recycling bin where they are reconstituted and ultimately reused. In another instance, a conveyor system was designed in the Marysville, Ohio, factory that rotates vehicle doors, allowing workers to easily and with little physical leverage of their own install locks and window components before attaching the doors to the frame. Chiefly an ergonomic gain, this new system also boosts quality because in most factories frequent touches by assembly line workers are responsible for chips and dents and other imperfections in the doors.

And there was the seemingly obvious but nonetheless inventive brainstorm in Lincoln, Alabama, to avoid end-of-shift gridlock after a second assembly line was added to the factory by slightly widening the two-lane, two-way road that led in and out of the plant. Adding just a couple of feet to each side of the road allowed Honda to create one incoming lane and two outgoing lanes, and eliminate the natural inclination of workers to race away from the job to beat the exiting rush; in turn, productivity rose and quality levels were maintained. Until that concept was floated, the only other option would have been to build a new road and bridge, a cost-prohibitive proposal.

But by far the most fascinating and globally significant breakthrough that I came upon during my research was a mathematical formula devised by a soft-spoken technician in Marysville. Since it was patented a few years ago, this algorithm has substantially reduced Honda's carbon footprint around the world. The genesis of the project was a speech by former CEO Fukui in 2007, in which he identified global warming caused by carbon emissions as a grave problem that auto companies must address both in their manufacturing techniques and in the products they make. Shubho Bhattacharya had felt the same way for some time and viewed Fukui's words as an invitation to do something about the problem.

Bhattacharya, who had been in corporate planning at Honda for about a decade and had a master's degree in mechanical engineering, began to explore factory carbon emissions by breaking down the automobile manufacturing process into energy usage buckets. He found that frame assembly is responsible for 50 percent of the energy consumption during production, and, of that, 60 percent of the energy consumption is linked to painting. Moreover, in the large, rectangular spray paint shops, typically about 150 feet long and 20 feet wide with assembly line belts that carry a steady stream of car frames through the booths, air-conditioning monopolizes power demand.

"For the paint viscosity to be at optimum levels—not runny and not concentrated—these booths must be at a target temperature of seventy degrees Fahrenheit plus or minus five degrees and sixty-eight percent relative humidity plus or minus five percent," Bhattacharya said. "So the very large volume of air in the booths must be constantly conditioned to a narrow band of comfort for the paint."

Under normal circumstances in any venue, air-conditioning is not a particularly efficient process. In the summer, the hot incoming air is first rapidly cooled and demoisturized below targets and then reheated to reach the desired levels. In the winter, the opposite occurs: the cold air is warmed but then needs to be humidified to reach the appropriate range of temperature and humidity.

Given the energy drain of this roundabout climate control process, Bhattacharya set out to write an equation that would take into account outside weather conditions, paint requirements, and the way the HVAC (heating, ventilation, and air-conditioning) system cooled and heated the air to identify in real time the single temperature and humidity point within the paint tolerance range that could be arrived at using the least amount of energy. Instead of a system that constantly sought to provide the same paint booth environment, regardless of the season or the energy consumption, Bhattacharya's approach would seek to produce an acceptable working climate in the paint booth moment to moment that also generated the greatest energy savings.

On paper, the formula seemed logical and surprisingly simple to produce if you understand advanced mathematics, Bhattacharya thought: "And when you look back, you say, well, why wasn't it done before? I can't really answer that. Like all new ideas they seem obvious the moment you think of them."

He asked the Ohio State University mechanical engineering department to program the algorithm in HVAC system controllers to assess whether it could reliably manage climate control systems in real-world equipment, away from the drawing board. And once that was completed, Bhattacharya presented the results of the project to Marysville management. By his estimate, he told them, his Intelligent Paint Technology (IPT) would reduce energy usage in the paint shop by 25 percent. And just as important, it would cost virtually nothing to execute. "My target was zero investment so there could be no reason for the factory leadership to reject it," said Bhattacharya. "That's why I focused on a knowledge-based system that would take advantage of the existing infrastructure and not require new instrumentation or new components."

IPT represented an enormous potential improvement, much

more than could be expected from most worker initiatives. And in early 2008, Bhattacharya received virtually immediate approval to implement IPT in the Ohio plant. Within a few weeks it was obvious that Bhattacharya had indeed achieved something truly remarkable: his system eliminated air-conditioning's hammerlock on factory energy consumption. Bhattacharya met his energy reduction projections perfectly, and the savings in tangible terms, not just in dollars or percentage points, were extraordinary. In the Marysville plant, Intelligent Paint Technology reduced Honda's annual carbon footprint by 10,000 metric tons; that equals the CO_2 emissions of 1,500 homes per year, 417,000 propane cylinders, and 1.1 million gallons of gas. Since then, IPT has been installed in every Honda North American plant and the company has been awarded patents for the technology in Canada and the United Kingdom; patents are pending in the United States, Japan, and China.

Despite the excellent results, Honda management concedes that the company took an enormous gamble in adopting IPT. Most energy reduction efforts in factories tend to focus on non-production-related steps like turning off equipment that isn't in use or installing motion-activated light switches. These are easy to implement, because plant production wouldn't be affected if these initiatives faltered. However, Intelligent Paint Technology was aimed squarely at an energy usage deficiency in one of the most critical functions in an automobile factory. The quality of the paint job in a new vehicle as well as one that has thirty thousand miles on the odometer can impact sales, overall brand reputation, and warranty claims. For most automobile purchasers, paint integrity is more important than engine specs because few people can tell the difference between two different motors unless they are wildly dissimilar.

Consequently, tampering with the painting process is not undertaken lightly. Yet there was no technique for testing IPT in real factory conditions—it would have been impossible to simulate the actual climate control challenges of a room the size of a paint booth with hulls of cars coursing in and out. So, armed only with the projected savings data and Bhattacharya's assurances that his system would not alter the climate in the paint booths in any meaningful way—instead, it would just arrive at an appropriate temperature and humidity via a more efficient route—Marysville managers knew that they had to give Intelligent Paint Technology a try.

Indeed, taking chances—in Honda terms, having a challenging spirit, an attitude frequently associated with the company's racing obsession—is a trait that the automaker demands of its workers. And, if so, then the corollary is true: rejecting employee innovation is difficult to justify. In emphasizing this point, Honda workers often return to a quote from Soichiro Honda: "We push hard as an organization and we push quickly, because we only have one future and it will be made of our dreams if we have the courage to challenge convention."

John Mayberry, the plant manager in East Liberty, Ohio, where the Honda CR-V, Accord Crosstour, and Acura RDX are made, explained that he has a simple aphorism to make sure that he gives this aspect of the culture the respect he believes it deserves. "We can't be risk averse," Mayberry said, "if we ask employees to take risks."

For Bhattacharya, who has since been promoted to a supervisory position in Honda's North American Engineering Center, the algorithmic invention was totally unexpected, the result of being inspired by a CEO's speech and then, as he puts it, "connecting the dots." Beyond that, he added, "there was no project, no initiative from upper management to do this. Just my idea."

An idea, in the primitive and mystical language of *sangen shugi* preferred by Honda, that could only have emerged in the real place.

5

PRINCIPLE #3: RESPECT INDIVIDUALISM

Cordell Fluker is a man who easily commands respect. He's about thirty years old, large and imposing, a former Marine Reserve, but it's not just his bearing that compels people to listen to what he says. It is also his dark eyes, determined and searing. At the Honda plant in Lincoln, Alabama, where he is an inventory control manager, Fluker supervises upward of three hundred people, who log, inspect, and dispatch supply parts into the factory as they arrive in a steady stream by day and night.

Fluker, who is black, grew up in the Lincoln area, in a lower-middle-class neighborhood, and graduated from Auburn University about two hours south of his hometown with a degree in systems engineering. He never expected to work in an automobile factory. Rather, upon finishing college, he envisioned a life as an officer in the Marines, and if he eventually did work in the private sector, it would be in the supply chain of a clean business like Walmart or in a relatively light industry like textile manufacturing.

But that tidy plan changed when he met Honda recruiters at an

Auburn job fair in his senior year. By this point, Fluker was in his early twenties, married, and his wife was pregnant; he was a bit overwhelmed by his responsibilities but felt that his military aspirations would provide a smooth transition into a relatively stable career in which he didn't have to worry about losing his job and his income.

Upon meeting Fluker at the fair, the Honda executives imagined his future differently. The Lincoln factory, the most advanced in Honda's portfolio, would open in August 2001, within the next year, and the automaker was looking for dependable, self-reliant, meticulous, principled, and creatively thoughtful people to work there. Experience in the auto industry—or any knowledge of auto manufacturing, for that matter—was not a requirement; conscientiousness, an independent disposition, and assiduousness were. Fluker had these characteristics in spades.

In a series of interviews for the job at Honda, Fluker was asked about his home life and his goals, his hobbies and his passions, how he would address specific personal challenges at work involving coworkers—belligerence, bullying, undercutting, and tattling, for example—more than he was queried about his knowledge of logistics and supply chains or his unfamiliarity with the automobile sector. As the interviews progressed it became clear to him that Honda would make him an offer that would ultimately lead to a management role.

"I think I got them with my work ethic and my personal story of what I achieved on my own—to be a senior in college, working a full-time job, having a wife, a baby on the way, and being a Marine; and I was honest to a fault with them—I didn't even think I wanted the job so I had nothing to lose," said Fluker. "In fact, it probably would have been easier if I didn't get the job so I could just do the plan I had in mind for myself. Turns out, that's exactly the kind of person they love to hire."

Indeed, Honda's hiring and employee promotion practices, like so many aspects of the company, defy logic—at least of the sort that most other organizations subscribe to. The unorthodox ways that Honda chooses employees—and the unorthodox employees that Honda chooses—stand in sharp contrast to typical auto industry practices. Most automobile manufacturing jobs are filled by people who evince a love for vehicles, some technical knowledge about cars, and the personality to follow directions closely, whether in a lean Japanese factory or a less disciplined American plant—a formula that Honda perceives as limiting and lacking in imagination. Instead, Honda seeks workers who have charted an irregular course, whose path in life has been a bit odd and unconventional. And the farther they've stayed from the auto industry—and are free of the preexisting biases about how automobile manufacturing should be done—the better. "We want independent people, who can see auto manufacturing with fresh eyes, not blind followers," said Honda CEO Takanobu Ito on many occasions.

Ito's comment is a sanitized and more practical version of the qualification that Soichiro Honda said he looked for when making hiring decisions, according to lean expert James Womack, coauthor of *The Machine That Changed the World*. Asked for the single most important attribute that an ideal Honda applicant should have, Soichiro noted that he preferred "people who had been in trouble."

Soichiro was obviously being cheeky but not entirely so. In only a slightly roundabout way, he was articulating Honda Motor's third critical organizational principle: respect individuals and, more precisely, individualism. Since the company's founding, Honda has stood alone in aggressively questioning and then often breaking the rules for how a successful industrial outfit should behave. That contrarian streak has gotten Honda into uncomfortable feuds with, for example, the Japanese Ministry of International Trade and Industry, which Honda defied upon making and then exporting its first cars, and with rival Japanese companies in calling for trade liberalization that would permit more imports of products from global rivals. Moreover, that attitude has drawn skepticism (undue, as it turns out) after some of Honda's more outrageous departures from the norm, such as the decision as a start-up to construct its own dies and stamping equipment (and since then virtually all of its factory hardware and software), its longshot entries against established companies in world-class motorcycle and F1 races, or its confidence that it could build an engine that cleared the Environmental Protection Agency's pollution standard before any other carmakers.

Such untempered innovation in ideas and practice can only be achieved with employees who, in fact, wouldn't flourish—who would, in Soichiro's words, be in trouble—in organizational models constructed primarily around rules and structured systems, no matter how progressively or intelligently plotted, Honda believes. Or put positively, an individual who can thrive in paradox and contradiction, who would instinctively explore the way things are traditionally done expressly to contradict them—who, in fact, sees a glass not as half full or half empty, but as twice the size that it needs to be and considers designing a vessel with different dimensions—would be a suitable Honda candidate.

In this, as in many other ways, Honda views itself as the mirror image of Toyota, its oldest rival. In a recent interview with me, Womack recalled a wonderfully humorous conversation he had with Shoichiro Irimajiri, who ran Honda's North American operations in the 1980s, in which Irimajiri depicted the personalities of the two giant Japanese automakers through colorful descriptions of their employees. " 'I will now imitate Toyota man,' " Womack remembered Irimajiri saying. "At which point Irimajiri puts on blinders and then proceeds to walk straight into the wall and fall down. He said, 'Ah,

Toyota man. Very, very good in a straight line. But no peripheral vision, like the Roman legions.' "

Then, Irimajiri said, according to Womack: " 'Ah, now, Honda man.' Without the blinders, Irimajiri's down crouching behind the furniture and he's running around from one side of the room to the other, and he says, 'Honda man, guerrilla fighter. Honda man loves chaos. Toyota man hates, hates chaos.' "

Honda's off-kilter approach to hiring—its belief that each individual must actively redefine the contours of his or her job rather than the other way around—has produced some eyebrow-raising employment policies, starting at the very top. Each of Honda's CEOs came up through the company's engineering ranks. And all of them at some time were former chiefs of the automaker's prized autonomous research and development unit.

That's an extraordinary record: conventional wisdom among multinationals holds that the most effective chief executives are specialists in marketing, sales, or perhaps accounting, anything but engineering. As a result, even CEOs in technologically based industries, like pharmaceuticals or computer hardware and software, tend to know little about designing or manufacturing the products that they sell. Still, that's not considered a disadvantage because the skills that engineers are thought to have most are believed to be the least valuable to a corporation's financial performance.

Engineers are said to be able to solve challenging problems while creating, planning, and building products; they're product oriented. By contrast, a CEO is commonly perceived as being obsessed with profits, focused on taking risks to beat the competition and on finding untapped revenue. In fact, CEOs see themselves—regard their jobs—as moneymakers, peddlers, and promoters of the company's products or services, whatever they happen to be. When I have asked CEOs or other top corporate executives how they motivate themselves, more often than not the response is one of the many clichés about successful salesmen: *A great salesman can sell a refrigerator to an Eskimo.* (That's sounding a bit hoary, a relic of the Mad Men era, but it still pops up now and then.) *A good salesman can sell a drowning man a glass of water; a great salesman can sell a refill.* And my favorite, because it's actually nonsensical, if you give it any thought: *A great salesman can sell toilet water to a plumber.*

Given this non-product-specific portrayal of their jobs, it's little wonder that corporate chief executives unapologetically jump from one industry to another with surprising ease—and too often with distressing results. James McNerney left behind Post-it notes and Scotchgard at 3M to sell 787s at Boeing; Edward Lampert bounced from Goldman Sachs and subsequently hedge funds to Sears; Robert Nardelli skipped from the Home Depot to Chrysler and stayed there until the car company went bankrupt; and, to pick one of the most puzzling examples from an earlier epoch, in the late 1970s John Sculley left PepsiCo for Apple Computer, only to force Steve Jobs out of the company a few years later. None of these CEO interindustry moves—or many others besides these—can be considered successful using any serious measures. (In fact, *Forbes* has described Lampert's tenure at Sears as the destruction of "once the most critical force in retailing.")

The prejudice against engineers as CEOs is not peculiar to just American or European firms. Many Japanese companies also suffer from this myopia. Toyota's CEO Akio Toyoda is a scion of the founder of the company and has an MBA from Massachusetts' Babson College, a fertile training ground for CEOs; he has no engineering skills. And until recently Sony Corp.'s CEO was Welsh-born Howard Stringer, a former TV producer with an M.A. from Oxford University, who presided over the worst losses in the electronics company's history, a period when Sony shed its reputation for producing inventive products. (It should be noted, however, that Nissan and Ford have more recently followed Honda's lead in appointing engineers to the top spot at their companies, Carlos Ghosn and Alan Mulally, respectively.)

Soichiro Honda and the engineers who have succeeded him at the helm of his company reflect a starkly different vision of the executive suite from the one favored by other multinationals. Reared in R&D, Honda CEOs' strengths lie in product and process innovation, primarily in designing new vehicle models and features and in conceiving fresh techniques for building them faster and better. Typically, Honda chief executives are inveterate tinkerers, more at home sketching a headlamp or front grille than exploring the minutiae of a spreadsheet with a roomful of accountants. Their approach to problem solving is dialectical, weighing opposing slices of logic in personal *waigaya*. And their success as managers is measured by how well they cultivate individual creativity in the organization, which Honda believes can distance a company from its rivals better than a new marketing campaign.

Illustrative of how Honda CEOs take unusual pathways to solutions, Soichiro Honda's successor Kiyoshi Kawashima approached business challenges with four possible answers rather than merely the routine binary "yes" or "no," which he deemed inadequate for most complex questions. His four choices were: "yes," "no," "yes and no," and "neither yes nor no." Kawashima used that palette of potential responses to, for example, navigate the difficult decision in 1979 of whether to build an automobile factory in Marysville, Ohio, well before any other Japanese company was yet considering such a move in the United States.

If "yes" or "no" were all he had to choose from, Kawashima would surely have rejected the idea. The cost of the plant would be well over $200 million, and by all projections, the factory would lose money for quite a few years, primarily because developing a Honda-trained competent supplier base around the facility would take some time. Moreover, with the reputation of American cars in decline by then and reliable and inexpensive Japanese imports from Honda, Toyota, and Nissan riding a popularity wave atop two gas shocks in the 1970s, Japanese cars built by American workers were ironically going to be a somewhat tough sell in the United States.

Still, Kawashima knew the right answer was "yes and no." Despite the overwhelming logical, data-driven evidence against the project, Kawashima was not prepared to simply dismiss it. It was too easy to reach that conclusion. And a thought nagged at him every time he was ready to bury the proposal that Honda might be missing a golden opportunity to establish a global localization strategy. By examining "yes and no" for weeks on end, Kawashima knew that ultimately the persuasiveness of either instinct or facts would eventually tilt the scale. And when it did, the answer was obvious, although it flew in the face of what most executives would have decided. "Building an automobile factory is risky," Kawashima said. "But Honda has been known to take big risks at crucial moments in the past."

Two years later, in November 1982, a silver-gray Accord rolled off the assembly line in Marysville, bearing a blue-and-white Ohio license plate, USA 001. The first Japanese car to be made in America, it is on display in the Henry Ford Museum in Dearborn, Michigan. The Marysville factory, which turned a profit within its first two years of operation, "had the most profound effect on the auto industry," said Michael Robinet, managing director of consultants IHS Automotive in Detroit, because it introduced "unique work practices and established new benchmarks for engineering, manufacturing, and quality.

"And Honda showed that American workers could build vehicles as well as other countries."

Kawashima relied on equally uncommon approaches to encourage individual creativity in the organization. For example, in 1978 when he was concerned that Honda's line of compact cars was too dowdy and not attractive to more youthful customers, Kawashima put together a team of the company's youngest designers and engineers, whose average age was twenty-seven, and told them to conceive a vehicle for their peers. He promised that senior managers would not interfere with their decisions. That effort produced the City, a hugely popular, inexpensive subcompact with jaunty lines and a smiling grille, now sold in various iterations in more than forty countries.

Although Honda CEOs are technologists, they are no less interested in financial performance gains than their counterparts at other auto companies. But because they were engineers first and CEOs second, Honda executives approach these metrics differently. To them, outpacing rivals does not necessarily mean being the number-one company in sales. Rather, it signifies earning brand recognition as the automaker with the best products offered at a sufficiently low price point that attracts customers without undercutting the company's reputation for quality. And internally, it means designing and producing vehicles at an expense ratio that yields the highest profit margins in the industry. That's a long-term business outlook—a product-oriented one or, perhaps better yet, an engineer's point of view—removed from the quarter-to-quarter earnings and market share cycles that most business experts agree stanch creativity and durable growth but to which many companies and their shareholders are nonetheless addicted.

Just as Honda Motor has ignored conventional wisdom in its executive appointments, the backgrounds of plant managers are equally eccentric. In case after case, top factory supervisors and department heads on the factory floor had no manufacturing experience before Honda hired them. Tom Shoupe, who ran the Marysville,

Ohio, plant and is now president of all manufacturing operations in Lincoln, Alabama, was a political science major and legislative aide to a pair of Ohio congressmen prior to working at Honda. Susan Insley was a local Ohio attorney before Honda recruited her to become the first (or, at worst, second) female automobile plant manager in the United States. Masa Nagai was a public relations executive prior to being named manager of one of Honda's two factories in China. And Chuck Ernst, who started working for the Honda engine plant in Anna, Ohio, when it first opened in 1985 and went on to design and oversee construction of the Lincoln automobile factory, had no real knowledge of vehicle assembly before Honda offered him a job.

In fact, Ernst wondered out loud during his interview why Honda was even considering him for a position in Anna. Ernst's wife had seen the ad for the Anna job in a local newspaper and he had sent in his résumé on a lark, expecting not to even hear from Honda. "Why are you interviewing me?" Ernst asked Toyoji Yashiki, the manager of the engine plant. "I know nothing about the auto business. I work in a steel mill. As a teenager, I was a motorcycle enthusiast. But I know nothing about mass-producing cars or motorcycles or engines. So why me?"

"You show a passion for motorcycles," Yashiki responded. "We can always teach you how to do things the way Honda prefers."

Actually, it's more complex than that. The company purposely avoids hiring people with auto industry experience because no other automaker has Honda's culture; as a result, Honda prefers individuals who are clean slates, open to on-the-job training and development, independent, jacks-of-all-trades, and willing to plunge into baptisms under fire.

"The person who knows nothing about the job is perhaps the person that should be doing the job," said Akio Hamada, a Honda senior managing director. "They're going to be able to view the job without preconceived ideas. In turn, they will do the job better."

Ernst certainly fit this profile when he started in Anna. The engine plant had not yet been constructed, so he and a small team of other new hires were sent to an old farmhouse adjacent to where the factory would rise to learn how to build motors and draw up the plans for the new facility. The plumbing was bad, the basement often flooded, and the rooms were small, but the group ignored these shortcomings and set out at a rapid clip to meet tight deadlines. To learn all they could about Honda motors, they studied Gold Wing 1200-cc motorcycle engines that were hung on chains from eyehooks screwed into the crossbeams in the cellar. "Our job was to teach ourselves how to deconstruct and reconstruct the engines," Ernst recalled. "There were no tools. I brought my Craftsman set from home."

Just months later, the Anna plant debuted and the original team of motley raw recruits had transformed itself into an expert squad in engine design and assembly and plant operation. Ernst was named a top manager at the factory, which initially made Gold Wing motors and soon expanded to building engines for Honda Civics and Accords. Although it was at first little more than an improvised effort, from the day its doors opened, Anna was among the most vertically integrated and efficient engine factories in the world, combining under one roof seven typically separate plants, from casting, forging, machining, and stamping to manufacturing brake and suspension parts and engine components.

Honda uses the interview process primarily to winnow out applicants whose personalities are a poor fit with the company's culture, not to test their skills. Among other things, job seekers are asked a series of questions about how they would handle certain hypothetical situations. At Honda, the right answers are often at odds with the obvious answers, and an unsanitized response can overcome doubts raised about a candidate by his or her background.

To some degree, that appears to be the case with Cordell Fluker, who at first blush was, in fact, not the ideal applicant for Honda. As a Marine—and heading toward a career as an officer in the Corps—Fluker certainly had and outwardly exhibited a commanding work ethic, but his military record also suggested that possibly he was inflexible in his thinking, too reliant on precedent and procedure and too conformist. However, his description of how he would respond to tense moments in the workplace dispelled any concerns.

When asked how he would manage a scenario in which a talented worker was obstinately resisting the Honda Way by, say, continuing to argue for her recommendation after *waigaya* and consensus was reached, Fluker did not offer a rote solution, such as "I would try to understand her problems and with some empathy ease her back into the job." Instead, without hesitation, Fluker said: "I believe in individual accountability; I would speak to her more selfish instincts because those are the ones that she seems to be displaying the most."

Answers like those got Fluker the job in Lincoln in large part because his response seemed so authentic, pared of pretense and guile. And not long after he became inventory control manager, he faced the very situation that he was asked about in the interview—and the way he handled it was consistent with his portrayal of what he would do.

It was a series of incidents during which one of Fluker's workers complained publicly and often about a goal that his team had agreed to involving the speed of moving essential supplies into the factory. This worker always met the objective but couldn't stop bellyaching about its being too onerous. Fluker didn't want to lose the employee; he didn't want to have to fire him, but it was becoming increasingly clear that the worker was unhappy and that was affecting the rest of the team. Fluker considered taking a hard line with the worker, telling him that it doesn't matter what he thinks, just do the job. But that probably would have made matters worse. Instead, Fluker took him aside and asked him: "How many kids do you have?"

"Two."

"You have a house? You have a mortgage?"

"Yeah."

"An electricity bill? A water bill? Do you pay for oil or gas?"

"Yes."

"How do you plan to take care of all of that? How are you planning to feed your children?"

"That's why I'm coming to work," the employee said, peeved at the persistence of Fluker's questioning.

"That's what you keep in mind when you're here: this is the thing that I'm doing so that I can care for my family," Fluker answered. "Therefore, I wouldn't want to impact that adversely. You're not here working for me; you're working for everything else in your life."

That exchange, which Fluker says he has had more than a few times with other employees as well, offers a very different perspective on teamwork from the one most companies have. It seems so rational and fundamental that groups of peers working together toward a common goal should be encouraged, as most large and small businesses do. But Honda views collaboration from the vantage point of the individual, not the team. As the automaker sees it, the individual is more vital than the group; his or her capabilities, decision making, knowledge, and creativity are the wellsprings from which the group's performance ultimately emerges. In other words, a single person can turn an underachieving team into a model of efficiency and innovation by the way he thinks and what he knows and as an exemplar for people around him. Honda's belief is that the organizational structure must serve to maximize the aptitude and skills of each individual; in turn, the team, the organization, will benefit.

Debbie McElroy, a Lincoln team manager in the paint department who sold underwear and showed horses in Kentucky before she was hired by Honda, recalled an odd incident soon after she got the job that demonstrates this uncommon attitude well. She and a handful of other new recruits were brought into a room off the factory floor, empty except for a car poised in the middle. A manager looked at the wide-eyed hires, who were still trying to get used to the pounding thump of the stamping machines, the pneumatic thrush of the robots, and the tumbling welding sparks in an automobile factory, and told them to tear down the car door.

"So we tore—all of us—the door, the panels, the wires, the glass, everything," said McElroy. "And when we were finished, he said: 'Okay, put it back together.' We just stared at it. We didn't know how to put it back together. We weren't paying enough attention as we tore it apart."

Discussing their failure as a group, McElroy and her colleagues were perplexed by their embarrassing performance. And they looked around at one another for answers: Who was at fault? Who can be blamed? But nothing seemed to explain the group's shortcoming and how it could have been avoided. Until, having run out of other options, it dawned on the recruits working on the disassembled car door that the lesson they should glean from this incident was not "If only we had paid attention to how it was stripped down," but instead, "If only *I* had paid attention."

"You don't know if your neighbor will take notice, so you have to do it yourself; that's your responsibility," McElroy said. "And if everybody looked at it that way, each of us would have known how to put the door back together and the team would've looked golden."

Soichiro Honda had an imaginative metaphor for describing this relationship between the individual and team. "In the ocean you see a bunch of fish and they're going every which way," he said. "And something happens, a stimulus happens where one lines up, then another, and another, until they all line up and they go together in the same direction, perfectly. Later, they separate again to find their own way and nourishment. That's also how successful teams and businesses work."

The profound respect for individualism at Honda was expressed very early in the company's history in a published statement, written by Soichiro Honda, known as "The Three Joys." These principles first appeared in an internal Honda newsletter on December 1, 1951, just three years after the company's founding, and were explicitly offered as a set of commandments, an ethical road map for all of the company's employees.

"I am presenting The Three Joys as the motto for our company," Soichiro began. Later in the notice, he wrote: "I am devoting all my strength in order to bring them to reality. It is my hope that all of you, as employees of the company, will exert every effort so that you never betray this motto."

The body of the memo was a description of each joy:

"The Joy of Producing: Just as the Creator used an abundant will to create in making all the things that exist in the natural universe, so the engineer uses his own ideas to create products and contribute to society. This is a happiness that can hardly be compared to anything else. Furthermore, when that product is of superior quality so that society welcomes it, the engineer's joy is absolutely not to be surpassed.

"The Joy of Selling: Our company is a manufacturer. The products made by our company pass into the possession of the various people who have a demand for them through the cooperation and efforts of all our agents and dealers. In this situation, when the product is of high quality, its performance is superior, and its price is reasonable, then it goes without saying that the people who engage in selling it will experience joy. . . . What sells well generates profits, as well as pride and happiness in handling those items.

"The Joy of Buying: It is neither the manufacturer nor the dealer that best knows the value of the product and passes final judgment on it. Rather, it is none other than the purchaser who uses the product in his daily life. There is happiness in thinking, 'Oh, I'm so glad I bought this.' This joy is the garland that is placed upon the product's value."

Over the years, the Three Joys have morphed into essentially a call for individual innovation and for employees to challenge themselves to spawn ever more novel ideas. And they have emerged as a blueprint for managers and decision makers to consult when setting company policies related to training, developing, and motivating workers.

For instance, the Joy of Producing is now called the Joy of Creating and is no longer centered solely on an engineer's tasks. Instead, the newer renditions of this principle address the need for all employees to build and design products of high quality that "exceed the expectations of customers" and to be "self-fulfilled" and "pursue the leading edge." As Nobuhiko Kawamoto, the Honda CEO in the 1990s who presided over the development of such iconic vehicles as the CR-V and the Odyssey, summed up the meaning of this tenet for the company: "We need to see that we have a culture in which our associates challenge themselves, do for themselves, take chances, and decide for themselves—experience the joy that comes from creating, not merely manufacturing."

Similarly, the Joy of Selling is treated now as a requirement for individual workers to imbue each Honda product with features and levels of reliability that surpass what a customer would expect, rather than a precept for dealers to follow. And the Joy of Buying, too, has been modified so that these days it is less materialistic and not solely directed at a customer's happiness in making a purchase.

Instead, the Joy of Buying is often expressed as a way to inspire inventions that ultimately change society for the better—that delight customers and enhance their lives.

Some of the outward manifestations of the Three Joys at Honda are captured in the automaker's flat and open working environment, which the company deems conducive to individual creativity. Aspects of these workplace initiatives have since been imitated by other companies, primarily high-tech start-ups like Google or Facebook, but they are anomalous in the auto industry.

Perhaps the most obvious example is the way Honda employees—executives to janitors—dress: the white uniforms with no buttons or belts to get caught in machinery or scratch the cars. The employee's first name above the right pocket, written in red inside a red-bordered oval. Above the left pocket is the word HONDA, also in red in a rectangle. If the employee chooses to wear a hat, it would be a green-and-white Honda baseball cap.

The parity among workers doesn't stop there: there are also no offices, just open bullpens with desks, and, of course, the assembly lines; no private dining rooms—everyone eats in the same cafeteria; and no reserved parking spaces—first to arrive gets the spot nearest to the building. In the newer Honda plants, egalitarianism has been taken to such an extreme that the parking spaces are laid out around the building in a pie shape. With this design, the distance to the factory entrance from the same spot in each row is identical.

For most workers, initially at least, there are no job descriptions, just the oft-repeated phrase, "Nobody knows your job better than you." As one engineering division manager told Robert Shook, the author of *Honda: An American Success Story*: "My first boss gave me the best advice I ever received. During my first week I commented on how difficult it was for me to understand what my actual job was. He looked at me silently for a few seconds and said in a low voice, 'Your job is everything.' And that was it! It took me a while to realize what he meant and how right on target he was."

By minimizing job distinctions, Honda has fostered enthusiastic workplaces, efficient and productive with seemingly high morale. This won't come as a surprise to the handful of other companies—generally entrepreneurial ventures, the way Honda likes to view itself—that have chosen similar paths. Indeed, one of the most obvious followers of Honda's approach is Zappos, the largest online shoe retailer, a hugely profitable venture whose revenue hit $1 billion in 2008, fewer than ten years after selling its first pump. Three years later, Amazon acquired the company for $1.2 billion, but the deal stipulated that Zappos be allowed to maintain its autonomy.

That was important for Zappos CEO Tony Hsieh because he had, in fact, set up an operation that even by Honda standards could only be called eccentric and in his own image. In the corporate headquarters in Las Vegas, it goes without saying that there are no offices. But that's the least of it. Each set of cubicles has a motif—the 1950s, cowboys, space aliens, and more. There's a nap room for employees to unwind and there are bells and whistles, literally, at every turn. Some employees are working hard but there are others who are playing catch and gossiping over coffee. One customer service representative spent nearly nine hours on the phone with someone who couldn't decide which pair of shoes to buy; she finally sealed the deal—and she got a bonus, Hsieh said.

And in January 2014, Hsieh eliminated job titles and managers at Zappos, replacing the traditional corporate flowchart with a self-governing *holacracy,* in Hsieh's terms. "Instead of a top-down hierarchy, there's a flatter 'holarchy' that distributes power more evenly," Aimee Groth wrote on the Web site Quartz. "The company will be made up of different circles—there will be around 400 circles at Zappos once the rollout is complete in December 2014—and employees can have any number of roles within those circles. This way, there's no hiding under titles; radical transparency is the goal."

Hsieh is not attempting to out-Honda Honda, he said before announcing the new structure; he's obviously got his own very original approach. But he added that the two companies have certainly learned the same thing: that the more opportunities people are given to enjoy their work and the more they are trusted to be self-reliant and responsible, the better the outcome will be for the organization. Hsieh estimates that because of Zappos's flat and lenient culture, workers are 20 percent to 100 percent more productive.

"There are higher levels of communication among workers and people help each other out because they are helping friends, not just coworkers," Hsieh said. "Our number one priority is company culture, and we believe that if we get the culture right, then everything else that we have to do—provide great customer service and build a great brand that people want to shop at and show loyalty towards—that will just happen naturally on its own."

That sentiment was largely repeated by dozens of Honda employees whom I spoke to in facilities around the world. Except for a handful of workers who "find the freedom oppressive and phony," as one put it, the response to Honda's open-workplace policies has generally been that they are refreshing. Most Honda workers said that these rules, set in motion by the Three Joys, enhance their ability to work efficiently and amplify their desire to take it upon themselves to improve their part of the operation.

Virtually everybody had a story like the one told to me by a Honda brake installer in Ohio who some months earlier had been having difficulty connecting a rubber line to a nut; they were askew by the slimmest of margins. He asked his team leader to take a look, and the two men were examining the part when another man came by to peer over their shoulders.

"It was a Japanese man; his name on his uniform was foreign to me so I paid no attention to it," said the brake line installer.

The Japanese man said to send the part back, but the brake line installer glanced at him sharply and said quickly that that wasn't necessary. There is no need to shut down the operation for this; it's not so dire that it can't be fixed, he said. And the Japanese man left, shaking his head and smiling.

"Well, you probably guessed the punch line by now: that was Hidenobu Iwata, the big boss of the factories in Ohio at the time; his shirt said HIDE. Who knew?" the brake installer said. "But he was wrong; I was right. It wasn't that big a deal. I just needed to adjust a screw on the brakes itself and the line plugged right in. Took me ten minutes to figure out. But imagine if Iwata-san wasn't in uniform, if he had a suit on, and I didn't feel on equal footing with him. I would have been intimidated into doing what he said—maybe he would've said just do it and stop talking about it—and our factory output would have suffered for no reason."

Although Soichiro Honda originally bathed the Three Joys in absolutist colors, it appears that he never meant these principles to be rigid and unyielding. Instead, he perceived the Three Joys as ideals to aspire to, probably always out of reach. After all, the Joy of Creating does not exist in a single moment, nor once experienced is it permanent; rather, it comes and goes, iterating over time, influenced by temporal conditions, but doesn't endure without interruption. More practically, a workplace, like any other facility populated and managed by people—each with different likes and dislikes, personalities, and ways of interpreting the physical world around them—will evolve as individuals devise improvements, but there will never be a moment when no more progress can be made.

That Honda understood this can be seen by his emphasis on continual employee-conceived initiatives and enhancements, which virtually by definition paint a mutable picture of what is new and possible. In Soichiro's mind, the Three Joys were a purposely unreachable but essential set of ideals for his company to follow in pursuing beauty, perfection, and respect for the individual in a world where the meaning of those terms is always in flux.

It is assumed that Honda was stirred to write "The Three Joys" by a Zen Buddhist concept known as *wabi-sabi*, which defines existence as bearing three marks: "imperfect, impermanent and incomplete," according to the writings of West Coast design philosopher and Nipponophile Leonard Koren. More recently, *wabi-sabi* has been adopted by artists who have taken it out of the metaphysical realm, reinterpreting it to mean finding splendor in flawed simplicity—a petrified log, a tangled tumbleweed—while gaining inspiration to produce gratifying and beneficial works of art from natural shapes and rhythms. Molding these ideas to his own life, Soichiro Honda maintained that his responsibility—the responsibility of a creator—was for his products to revere nature by adding beauty to the landscape and for his company to be a fruitful global partner that, in the company's words, "society wants to exist."

In a telling passage from the early 1960s, Soichiro Honda described his design aesthetic in language that echoed the difficulties and the desire to replace imperfection with individual fulfillment that he first implicitly articulated in "The Three Joys."

"Suppose there is a man standing, irreproachably dressed, with neat hairstyle, wearing gold-rimmed spectacles and shining shoes," Soichiro wrote. "How do we think when we see him? We will have a feeling that he is lacking a touch of humanity. . . .

"There is no obvious distinction whether he is a human or an ornament. In such case, he will suddenly become alive only by showing a part of his handkerchief out of his pocket without much care, or by wearing spectacles of tortoise-shell instead of gold rim. He can give an impression of liveliness and warmth by doing so. This is what we call the disharmonized harmony. . . .

"Disharmony is a factor (that) converts into harmony. Man is not interesting without some imperfection, and the purpose of designing is to elevate their imperfection up to beauty."

Honda often studied the most perfect forms he could find as inspiration for new vehicles he was about to design. For example, before engineering the Dream C-70 motorcycle in 1957, Honda spent ten days at the Buddhist temples in Nara and Kyoto "in order to get the spirit and essence."

He wrote: "If we see these historical designs through the screen of modern eyes, there are several excellent points to be applied to modern design. For example, the beauty of the line from the eyebrow to the bridge of the nose of Buddha is so remarkable that such a beautiful line does not seem to be in existence anywhere else. I designed the fuel tank edge-line having the line of the Buddha image in my mind. The knee-grip tried to express a soft feeling by using a somber finish. . . .

"The design of the motor vehicle must be a symphony appreciated visually. As the symphony would be unbalanced by only a single unordinary tone of the trombone, the design must be considered one by one without breaking the balance, such as tires, steering handle, and others. Moreover, each part within the balance has to express its respective unique design."

These contemplative and even profound ruminations by the founder are a continuing inspiration to Honda Motor, as important to the company's culture as its more public displays, such as *waigaya* and white uniforms. In Soichiro's language can be found a respect for natural and divine forms and colors and a desire to comprehend and explore dissonance in order to find harmony—ideas that have reshaped the Three Joys into a set of principles compelling the automaker to not only create to market but also to improve and perfect the environment in which Honda customers live. The Joys of Making, Selling, and Buying are all potentially realized by this über-ambition.

Motivated by this goal, Honda has had an enviable record of producing products and conceptual prototypes that aggressively attack existing environmental concerns or explore the exigencies of human mobility to fashion technology that can serve people's needs without contributing in any meaningful way to the carbon footprint or global warming. Although cynics may find this a bit sanctimonious, recently Honda's CEO Takanobu Ito described the automaker's strategy for the current decade as providing "good products to customers with speed, affordability and low CO_2 emissions and to realize the joy and freedom of mobility and a sustainable society where people can enjoy life.

"Providing the joy and freedom of mobility has been Honda's aim in the development of personal mobility products since the company's founding. The joy of mobility is not just the pleasure of driving your own car or motorcycle. It's also the excitement of making discoveries and realizing dreams through the freedom mobility provides."

Whether Honda reaches this ambition cannot be predicted, of course, but the company's prior environmental achievements should be enough to at least discourage the doubters. That aside, though, from an operational standpoint Ito's statement is significant. Deftly, Ito is purposefully linking Honda's most cherished tenets—the Three Joys—to the organization's current business model. Using the term *joy* repeatedly, Ito draws from Soichiro Honda's original declaration of the company's ideals and pays homage to their evolution over the ensuing years in response to changing consumer preferences and global conditions.

And by explicitly articulating Honda's direction for the next decade in this way, Ito is conveying that the Three Joys must not exist in a vacuum. The ways they are demonstrated in the company—the flat organization; respect for individual innovation, quality, and imaginative products; the focus on satisfying customers; placing employees in positions that recognize their instinctual, untapped skills, to name a few—should be in service to Honda's goals: presently, abetting personal mobility in a pristine planet.

Most companies have failed to grasp the lesson in this. That is, corporate culture cannot solely be a series of ideas, living in their own well-intentioned realm, but never actually connected to a company's day-to-day goals, strategies, tactics, and operational framework. Detached as such, a company's principles—no matter how high-minded—will have little meaning or consequence to employees because the principles are unmoored from worker performance, salaries, or the nature of their jobs. Nor will managers enforce these precepts. And, worse yet, often the company's actions will bear scant resemblance to its cultural ideals and, hence, belie their importance. In these circumstances, the organization will forfeit any opportunities for gains from its ostensible corporate culture, as it is not precisely affixed to the activities of the business. Simultaneously, the company places itself in perilous reputational risk should an accident or a similar public failure unmask its principles as little more than window dressing.

Toyota suffered this fate during the sudden acceleration debacle in 2009–10. As a window into the automaker's operations, that incident showed that while lean manufacturing methods might have still been prevalent in Toyota's factories, they were no longer a priority for management. As noted in chapter 1, employee attempts to raise quality issues were welcome only as long as this fundamental lean principle did not slow down Toyota's drive to become the world's number-one automaker. In the wake of this debacle, consumer perception of Toyota plummeted in a poll by brand and marketing consultancy Prophet, to 139th out of 150 companies in 2011, from 17th the year before. (Honda came in 30th in 2011 and crept up to 29th in 2012, when Toyota rebounded somewhat to 79th. Apple, Kellogg's, Kraft Foods, Johnson & Johnson, and Walt Disney were the top five companies in this survey.)

But perhaps the poster child for the hazards of letting the corporate culture diverge from the company's business model is British Petroleum. In a now-famous misstep, BP kicked off the new millennium by proclaiming that it was the "green oil company": the company's initials would stand for "beyond petroleum," and the oil giant's executives promised that they would focus on protecting the environment by "thinking outside the barrel." A new logo with a sunburst of green, yellow, and white—a paean to alternative energy and environmental concerns—was unveiled.

Although a well-crafted PR and advertising campaign, it was pure fantasy; it didn't reflect BP's real corporate culture to any degree. The company's investments in alternative energy were minimal at best, and published reports and official investigations revealed that executives were well aware that environmental and safety policies were being ignored even as the oil firm was publicly claiming quite the opposite. A 2005 explosion at a BP refinery in Texas City, which killed fifteen workers, and the 2010 blowout in the Gulf of Mexico, the largest ever offshore oil spill, exposed BP's hypocrisy—at a heavy cost to its treasury and its brand name. And, of course, any possible revenue or marketplace advantages that the company had hoped to harvest from being the green BP were sacrificed as well.

By sedulously aligning and recalibrating its short- and long-term strategic goals with the company's basic, long-held principles, Honda is able to maintain a consistent, well-defined corporate culture over many decades and to ensure that the culture is continually advancing the company's goals. Put another way, for Honda, the corporate culture is a fundamental aspect of doing business, rather than a potential impediment.

In a particularly candid remark about this facet of Honda's operations, one of the company's top executives said: "It's important to remember that the Three Joys are a part of our business model; they are not altruism. We believe in what we say we believe in, but we're in business to make money. By focusing on protecting the environment, we expect to generate revenue while doing the right thing. But if there wasn't money in it, we couldn't take this course for very long and survive. We've been fortunate that our corporate culture and the goals for every worker Honda-san developed and instilled were also a pathway to profits."

Indeed, Honda has directly benefited from environmental advances more than any other automaker, beginning with its maiden voyage in the United States, when in 1972 the then three-year-old automaker surprised the industry by becoming the first to meet strict U.S. Clean Air Act emissions standards.

Honda's radical CVCC (Compound Vortex Controlled Combustion) dual-carburetor engine deflated the claims of every other car manufacturer that the new pollution rules could not be met economically enough to maintain vehicle pricing at a reasonable level for consumers. A 1975 version of Honda's CVCC-equipped Civic had a sticker price of about $3,500, or $15,000 in today's money, clearly an inexpensive car.

Since then, Honda has produced a steady line of products in the same vein. For example, the heir to the CVCC engine was the VTEC—for Variable Valve Timing and Lift Electronic Control—a motor that *Import Tuner* magazine, which covers souped-up retrofitted non-American cars, called "four letters that practically started a revolution." Without getting too granular, VTEC was the first mainstream motor in which each cylinder's intake valves are placed in and out of operation depending on the speed of the engine. At low speeds a lean air-fuel ratio is achieved by limiting intake, and at high speeds the engine is opened up wide to be allowed to breathe and deliver more torque.

Subsequent to the VTEC's introduction in the 1980s, Honda has designed many variations and upgrades with any number of different and more complex combinations of automated intake valve adjustments. But viewed in total the VTEC motor has produced meaningful gains in gas mileage (as much as a 20 percent improvement in some cars) and horsepower—for a time, it was the only four-cylinder engine to top 100 hp—with significantly lower CO_2 emissions.

In 1998, VTEC was the first gasoline engine to be certified by the California Air Resources Board and the U.S. Environmental Protection Agency as meeting the Ultra-Low-Emission Vehicle (ULEV) standard, a designation given to engines that emit 50 percent fewer pollutants than the average for new cars released that year. A year later, Honda produced what it called a Zero-Level Emission Vehicle (ZLEV), which had one tenth of the emissions of the ULEV standard. One non-Honda auto engineer described the ZLEV motor as being "cleaner than the air the vehicle drives in."

Additionally, Honda introduced the first gasoline-electric hybrid vehicle in the United States in 1999, the Insight, rated at more than 60 miles per gallon on the highway and ranked as the most efficient gas-fueled vehicle ever by the EPA. At various times in its history, Honda's marketing acumen has left much to be desired—perhaps a deserved criticism of some of the company's engineer CEOs—and by 2001 Honda had ceded global hybrid leadership to Toyota's Prius.

Honda also makes the only consumer car that runs on natural gas, the Civic GX. And Honda's seven-year-old fuel-cell car, the

FCX Clarity, runs on hydrogen, emits no pollutants, has a driving range of nearly three hundred miles, and is the sole street-legal car of its engine type in the United States. Currently, the FCX is leased to customers in regions with hydrogen filling stations, such as parts of California, but many auto industry experts anticipate that fuel-cell vehicles and their offshoots will become in the next decade the most popular alternative to the internal combustion engine.

And more recently, Honda said that it would reduce CO_2 emissions by 30 percent from 2000 levels in all of its global products by 2020. As of 2010, the carbon emissions of Honda's entire fleet of vehicles in the United States was 13 percent below the industry average while fuel economy was 13 percent above, according to the EPA.

But although ambitious, Honda's environmental agenda is taking a bit of a backseat these days, at least measured by the curiosity of industry experts, to a set of related but distinctly separate initiatives that the company's R&D teams are engaged in. Building on the concept of providing the pleasure of mobility that grew out of the Three Joys—and often extending the notion of mobility well beyond its traditional meaning—Honda has begun to develop a series of unlikely prototype products and services, many of which are decidedly nonvehicular. And what intrigues Honda watchers most about these efforts are the potential revenue streams that they represent, which other auto companies do not have.

"Honda has a knack for growing out of its skin every once in a while and expanding the scope of its products, always based on some novel idea they come up with but never ranging too far from the company's DNA," said Sean McAlinden, chief economist at the Center for Automotive Research. "They made bikes with motors; then they made motorcycles; then they made lawn mowers and tillers; then they made cars; now they're making planes. And who knows where the new R&D is going to lead. But it does give Honda possible new ways to make money."

The HondaJet, the lightweight, six-person, fuel-efficient aircraft with the irregular design that places the two turbofan jets over the wings, is, indeed, the latest mobility bauble that Honda hopes to entice customers with. But there are also products without wheels—like the ASIMO, perhaps the most entertaining and athletic robot yet designed.

At four feet three inches and 119 pounds, this white, bubble-headed machine can run at nearly four miles an hour, arms pumping like a track star and feet leaving the ground between each stride like a human; hop on one foot; kick a soccer ball; use its fingers to open a thermos lid and pour a drink; sidestep in two different directions; and climb stairs. It can avoid obstacles as it moves through any environment. ASIMO (which stands for Advanced Step in Innovative MObility) is an extraordinary technical achievement, a physical machine with thirty-four separate computer-driven motors that continually monitor its surroundings and adjust its movements.

Once ASIMO is perfected, Honda hopes that the robot could assist the handicapped in getting in and out of wheelchairs or bed and serve as a helpmate for the more active elderly or, for example, the blind. Honda also hopes to be able to send ASIMO into danger zones—fires, toxic spills, earthquakes, and the like—as a first responder. And there's the possibility that ASIMO may find itself behind the wheel of a car eventually; the term *mobility* is a very big tent. "ASIMO, jet planes, automobiles, they are all going to converge at some point," said Frank Paluch, president of Honda R&D Americas.

There are many obstacles to overcome before that day, or even before ASIMO responds to a simple request like "turn on the light." Artificial intelligence—machines that can think and learn—is a seventy-year-old discipline that has attracted some of the most respected names in computer science, such as Alan Turing (Kings College, Cambridge), Marvin Minsky (MIT), Seymour Papert (MIT), and Roger Schank (Yale), but still has not yet been able to create a computer with anything more than rudimentary knowledge development skills.

So it's not surprising that in a recent presentation for reporters, ASIMO failed to figure out the difference between people raising their hands to ask questions and someone holding up a cell phone to take pictures of it. In addition, ASIMO can't actually understand questions that it is not programmed to answer and got stuck in an embarrassing loop in which it incessantly repeated the same query: "Who wants to ask ASIMO a question?"

However, these intelligence shortcomings notwithstanding, ASIMO has outperformed virtually all other robots in the world in its physical dexterity and awareness.

Perhaps Honda's most far-reaching mobility project is a green house campaign recently begun in California. Honda is bankrolling the installation of solar panels and other alternative energy equipment for homeowners, who need not be Honda customers. The impetus for this effort was the realization that as consumers purchase plug-in electric vehicles, whether fully electric or natural gas–powered with electric backup engines, they are shifting their carbon footprint from their cars to their homes.

The usage numbers break down this way, according to Steve Center, vice president of the Environmental Business Development Office at American Honda: About 30 percent of the CO_2 output of an individual living in an energy-efficient house in California and driving a traditional automobile comes from basic household electricity needs—lights, air-conditioning, TV, appliances, and the like. Another 30 percent is connected to heating the home and making hot water. And a whopping 40 percent of this person's energy use is from gasoline for transportation.

"If we completely revolutionized transportation and deleted gasoline from the equation—and everybody plugs their cars in at home—we've reduced the carbon footprint of that customer by only 20 percent because now the utility grid through the home will have to make up for the gasoline," said Center.

In fact, in some states, like Wyoming and Indiana, where coal is the vastly predominant source of energy, a plug-in electric car will produce more greenhouse gases than an automobile that gets about 45 miles to a gallon of gasoline (currently, hybrids recharged by the car's engine such as the Toyota Prius and Honda Civic). By contrast, the plug-in electric will minimize carbon footprint best in states that rely heavily on nuclear power, like Connecticut, or on hydropower, like Idaho or Washington, as well as states like California with strong environmental regulations.

However, by retrofitting a home for solar power, the California homeowner could offset all of his electric usage with alternative energy, including the amount to recharge his vehicle. "Five kilowatts of solar will cut the homeowner's CO_2 emissions by 70 percent, because he would still need energy for heat and the like. That's a significant difference."

The smart home, like many of Honda's new environmental initiatives, is still in the experimental stage and will certainly evolve over time. More to the point, some of these projects will survive and some won't. Some will be replaced by fresher ideas. But in searching for potential new avenues for revenue, Honda only appears to be casting out an increasingly wide net. In reality, Honda is adroitly meshing a somewhat archaic but nonetheless robust internal concept of joy and an abiding respect for the individual with what actually makes employees and customers feel good about themselves today.

6

A UNIQUELY HONDA FACTORY

If there were a more apt symbol than Richard George of Honda Motor's presence in the tiny hamlet of Lincoln, Alabama, you'd be hard-pressed to find it. George, now sixty-eight, is a lifelong resident of the town, born into a family that worked on a large farm with other sharecroppers in the then segregated community. He grew up with no running water and a little outhouse for relief. By the time George was eighteen and acquired his first jalopy, he was regularly stopped by the local police, physically and verbally harassed for imaginary driving infractions.

"It was 'boy' this and 'boy' that," George said. "And you never could understand what you did wrong because you did nothing wrong. They just wanted to make you feel like you did and punish you for not being white."

George is a sizable man, well over six feet tall and at least 230 pounds, but he shrinks right before your eyes when he speaks of the iniquities of segregation. "You knew something was wrong—it wasn't one of those things where you don't know any better so it doesn't bother you," George said. "There was a free life and our life. But you dare not say it to anyone in the street. You'd be beat up or, worse, put away for a long time without any recourse."

Or described another way, Lincoln, with a population of only a few thousand then, was too small and provincial, too sleepy and idle, for young blacks not to be targeted for trouble. George said he decided that if this was the life he was dealt, he would just work hard, live honestly, and raise a family. He took a job at the nearby Anniston U.S. Pipe foundry and stayed there for more than twenty-five years. In the mid-1990s, George left the factory to open a country store that sold canned goods and hardware. He expanded the site to include a barbecued ribs and chicken restaurant next door.

George's new business was located on an anonymous slice of out-of-the-way property in Lincoln that had been his grandfather's and that he had inherited from his mother. And in 1999, with no warning, Honda chose 1,350 acres across a narrow two-lane road from his store to build a $600 million, 1.7-million-square-foot factory. George owned 40 of those acres. They were part of the same tract as the store and he had been using them as a hunting ground for area sportsmen. He sold this land to Honda for more than $1,000 an acre—a very nice payday for little effort.

"The store was doing okay—just okay—and people liked my food and I expected life to just keep humming along that way," George said, still smiling as he recalls how delightfully wrong his expectations were. "Then Honda picked the spot across the street out of all the places they could have picked in Alabama and anywhere else in the South; it's like someone pointed randomly to a spot on the map and there we were—no, there I was."

During the building of the factory, an eighteen-month period, George in essence became Honda's first tier-one supplier in Alabama. Construction workers and Honda engineers bought work gloves, shoes, shirts, sundries, and food supplies at George's store. But the real attraction was his grilled ribs; at lunch and dinner time, George's restaurant—a dark and funky, bedraggled tin room with old tables and chairs that would have fit well in the dining nook of a 1930s backwater home—was packed with Honda employees. George cooked over wood in an open pit adjacent to the kitchen and gregariously kept a running conversation going with the patrons through a small island that separated the two rooms.

"I'll put my ribs up against anyone in the United States," George would boast, and no one would disagree. "There isn't a cook that makes ribs over wood the way I do. You have to watch it all the time, keep turning the ribs and make sure they don't burn. You need to know just the right time to turn them and just the right temperature that you are working with; you do that and you'll keep them moist."

Honda management was impressed by George's entrepreneurial spirit and acumen; he was offered a job at the new factory. But he turned Honda down. George enjoyed running his store and restaurant too much. And he added that "Honda may be better than most companies and much has changed since I was a boy, but racism is not gone in Alabama. If I keep to my own business I can control my own life and not have to deal with a boss who may or may not like my skin color."

Over the years, George's involvement with Honda has expanded to include catering Honda executive meetings and employee events as well as landscaping the factory's property. George won't say how much money he has made from having Honda as an unexpected neighbor but offered, "We both are happy."

Certainly, Richard George's improbable intimate relationship with a Japanese company that rose out of the ruins of a world war—occurring a mere stone's throw from where he was born in the Deep South—is the culmination of profound racial, ethnic, global, industrial and cultural changes in the past fifty years. It is as removed from George's upbringing in Lincoln as a Chevy without fins and chrome.

For Honda, George emblemizes what the company was hoping to find when the automaker surprised even Alabama state officials by choosing Lincoln as the site of perhaps the most advanced automobile factory in the world: diamonds in the rough—hardworking, independent people with plenty of natural skills and common sense. "Richard George and Honda are cut from the same mold: great work ethic, quick on our feet, enthusiastic about accomplishing great and new things, a bit of a loner in liking to go our own way, outspoken, with the skills to think creatively," said the Lincoln plant designer Chuck Ernst, only partially tongue in cheek.

The path to Lincoln for Honda began in early 1998 when the company's West Coast attorney contacted Harry Henshaw, a director at the commercial real estate firm Colliers International in Cleveland. Honda's lawyer told Henshaw that the automaker was looking for an ample tract of land for a greenfield factory in the South—and that no one was to know that Honda was involved in this search until they had to, not even government or development officials from the southern states.

Some sixteen years earlier, Honda had become the second foreign automaker with a factory in the United States when it opened its Marysville, Ohio, plant. In the ensuing period, Honda had built a second factory in East Liberty, Ohio, and other non-U.S. car companies had followed suit—including Nissan in Smyrna, Tennessee; Toyota in Princeton, Indiana, and Georgetown, Kentucky; BMW in Spartanburg, South Carolina; and Mercedes-Benz in Vance, Alabama.

Since Mercedes had recently opened its plant in Tuscaloosa suburb Vance, investing only $300 million of its own money in exchange for $253 million in tax breaks and other incentives from the state—a huge package that added up to $169,000 per job created—Henshaw thought Alabama might be a generous partner for his new client. Henshaw reached out to Ted vonCannon, who headed up the Birmingham, Alabama, Metropolitan Development Board. In the 1980s in Tennessee, vonCannon had worked for then governor Lamar Alexander and was involved in the efforts to bring General Motors' ill-fated Saturn factory to Spring Hill and Nissan to Smyrna.

A few weeks later, vonCannon offered Henshaw a 1,000-acre lot on Birmingham's I-59 near rail lines and a plentiful, intelligent labor force. A team of Honda executives came down to look at the property—that was when vonCannon learned the name of the automaker involved in this deal—and almost immediately turned it down and went home.

"It was too metropolitan, too near a big city, which most companies would love but not Honda," said vonCannon. "Cities offer good places to eat and entertain and put up visitors, nice places to live for the executives. But Honda saw it differently: 'We want something more quiet, out of the way, where we can do our work out of the urban spotlight,' they said."

In response, vonCannon suggested a tract in Gadsden, Alabama, about fifty-six miles northeast of Birmingham. But even Gadsden, with a population of thirty-six thousand, was too cosmopolitan for Honda. And to be sure, Honda was unnerved by the protracted labor strife at the Goodyear tire plant in the city. (This was the same plant that employed Lilly Ledbetter, who quit in 1998 and sued Goodyear for paying her less than her male colleagues. After the U.S. Supreme Court ruled that Ledbetter's legal action was taken too late, Congress passed a law bearing her name making it easier for women to sue for pay discrimination.)

Running out of choices, vonCannon fell back on a site that he never thought he'd get anyone to bite on enthusiastically. Some months before vonCannon received the call from Henshaw, Lincoln's longtime mayor Carroll "Lew" Watson had invited vonCannon to look at some property in town that Watson's cousins owned, a capacious, flat, broad stretch of land that had once been farmed but was relatively fallow by then. VonCannon admits that he was just being polite when he told Watson, " 'Nice property. Maybe one of these days.' What I really meant was don't expect anything too soon."

Suddenly, that rough-hewn parcel in a rural backstretch of a town with the population of a New York City high-rise was vonCannon's best hope for bringing Honda to Alabama. All of the usually desirable sites didn't interest Honda; perhaps this unlikely one would, vonCannon thought. On a Friday in March 1999, vonCannon asked Watson to quickly obtain options on the Lincoln property so he could present it to a global company that might be interested in it as a turnkey deal with no ownership complications to sort out. Following the rules set down by Henshaw, he didn't tell the mayor that the potential developer was Honda.

Sensing a huge possible gain for his little-known community, Watson, who is a real estate assessor, worked through the weekend to get approvals. The mayor's cousins owned most of the property, but because he was on less than good terms with them, the negotiations were testy at times. But by Tuesday, Watson had clinched the deal. His cousins were to get between $3,000 and $10,000 an acre, depending on the location and quality, for about 1,500 acres that had mostly gone to seed.

With this in hand, vonCannon urged Henshaw to bring the Honda team back down to Alabama to look at Lincoln. The executives inspected the site two weeks later and were instantly infatuated with the property and its location. This obscure community, bucolic and frayed, an unobserved pair of exits on I-20 between Birmingham (48 miles to the west) and Atlanta (105 miles to the east), was perfect; it had rail connections, excellent roads, and a lot of unemployed industrious people who had last been seen maintaining aging Deeres and Cats on their now defunct farms or working day and night shifts in now shuttered textile mills. Moreover, Lincoln was home to the Talladega Superspeedway, one of the most popular tracks on the NASCAR circuit. And although Honda doesn't participate in NASCAR—the high-performance motors of Formula 1 and global motorcycle courses are more Honda's speed—any mention of racing inside the company gets everyone's attention.

During the half year or so that it took to find a suitable property for Honda, vonCannon and other local industrial development officials were working separately to piece together an incentive package for the automaker. Only county development boards and private sector firms, such as the banks and utilities, were invited to these deliberations. Purposely excluded were state officials and executives from the capital city of Montgomery. In 1998, Alabama was in the middle of a gubernatorial race, and vonCannon and his colleagues knew that if the candidates made Honda's plans a campaign issue, good or bad, the company would recoil from the attention and turn its sights toward another southern state.

While most companies would have been tempted to use the prospect of a new plant as a marketing opportunity, Honda's reticence was an outgrowth of its distinctive global strategy. Rather than build a plant in a fresh site and support it primarily from corporate headquarters or from a large operational center in Japan, Honda's localization approach typically involves establishing a self-sufficient cluster of satellite operations—R&D, engineering, a robust supplier and logistics community—around the biggest of its factories.

This wide-ranging but geographically circumscribed industrial ecosystem is the biosphere in which Honda's culture is expected to blossom. The concept of *sangen shugi* or going to the spot is, by definition, dependent on local observations, experiences, information gathering, and knowledge. So is a belief in the joy of making a product that customers—ideally, nearby car buyers whose preferences are known—actually want and need. And similarly, the success of Honda's manufacturing model relies upon homegrown innovation, worker autonomy, and factory efficiency and scale.

Implementing this strategy is a complex undertaking, requiring substantial coordination among the separate plant units, an extensive local hiring effort, and ongoing training of the many businesses—suppliers and other vendors—that will be under the factory's spacious umbrella. It also requires a vast amount of support from the neighboring community in order to recruit the best talent and to secure an ongoing commitment to such a comprehensive industrial effort.

For that reason, Honda is particularly mindful of how its actions are seen by people in the areas that it plans to move into. Specifically, Honda prefers a low-key approach and avoids trumpeting its site searches in a way that would create the perception that the local community should be honored to have Honda in its midst, not the other way around. In short, the automaker believes that it must go beyond being solely an economic contributor to a region if its holistic localization strategy is to thrive. With so much invested in each new facility that it constructs—and in the need to cultivate a deeply rooted relationship with every factory that it builds—Honda cannot afford to be viewed as an outsider or insensitive to local norms and attitudes.

The dissimilar way that Mercedes and Honda responded to the Alabama tornados in April 2011, which killed as many as sixty people in a half-dozen counties, offers a glimpse into each company's relationship to the people in the area. Daimler AG, the parent of Mercedes, donated $1 million to relief efforts in Alabama. Not quite as well-heeled as its German counterpart, Honda contributed $150,000 to the cleanup fund. But Honda also went an important step further. With the Lincoln factory's output slowed by a parts shortage after a massive Japanese earthquake the previous month and committed to maintaining full employment during the downtime, Honda sent hundreds of its idled workers into affected areas to clear debris, provide food and water, and sort supplies—a sea of white uniforms with the red Honda label that earned the Japanese company a remarkable degree of goodwill.

A mayor in a town near Lincoln told me that "Daimler's million dollars will go a long way and I'm not in any way trying to undermine it. But when you see a squad of workers all in the same outfit representing a single company, out there to do good, and then maybe next week you see a few of them in white working with kids at some youth ministry camp and then a week later, there they are in white at a children's hospital—after a while it catches up to you that this company is actually in the community, not just making money from it."

A few moments later, he added: "If Honda needs a permit to build a new road or needs help with a water treatment facility or just good word of mouth praising their cars or help recruiting the best workers in the area, no one is going to turn them down around here."

Given the depth of Honda's sensitivity about its relationship to local communities, vonCannon and his colleagues made it their mission to keep the automaker's search for a factory hush-hush, well out of the reach of the state's gubernatorial candidates and other politicians. But in devising an incentive package they faced an even more significant obstacle. There had been and continues to be criticism of the huge handouts in the form of tax breaks and infrastructure improvements that are routinely doled out to foreign automakers to establish factories in the United States. This is a particularly divisive issue in the South, where tax receipts, even without the corporate giveaways, tend to be on the low end, and services, most especially public schools, rank among the worst in the country.

To be sure, economists generally assert that the arrival of a major manufacturer can produce a financial and lifestyle bonanza for a community. "Every job in an auto plant supports two to three other jobs in the local economy among suppliers and transportation and other indirect sources," said Keivan Deravi, an Auburn University professor and a leading economic forecaster in Alabama. Moreover, Deravi and others point to the ancillary gains in real estate values and expenditures on retail, hospitality and dining, airlines, trains and autos, and health care and financial services. Still, while these optimistic forecasts are not inaccurate at all, if the incentives are too high, decades may pass before the state or local communities earn back what they gave away to the manufacturers, during which time area residents will have to shoulder the cost of decreased services.

That troubling, drawn-out return on investment scenario was a contentious topic in Alabama about the time that Honda was planning its factory there. The $253 million that Alabama had ponied up for the Mercedes plant some six years earlier had become an embarrassment for the state government, especially when it was revealed soon after the ink dried that education funds were being earmarked to pay for the factory. A November 1998 article in *Time* magazine portraying the tangible effect of this diversion on Alabama's public schools—and describing the incentives as "corporate welfare"—was particularly damning. "Go to the Vance Elementary School, located a football field or two from the (Mercedes) plant," wrote Donald L. Barlett and James B. Steele. "Of course, you cannot actually see the school building. That is because it is surrounded by portable classrooms—seventeen in all. They are being added at the rate of two a year. Inside the school, the results of crowding 540 pupils (expected to be 700 to 800 within the next two years) into a building designed for 290 are readily apparent—a marked contrast with the roominess of the $30 million training school the state built for Mercedes."

When it became untenable to use education dollars for the Vance factory, Alabama officials decided to borrow the money from the state pension fund. But Alabama's balance sheet was in such disarray, in large part because of industrial development handouts to dozens and dozens of firms, that the pension fund demanded a punitive annual interest rate of 9 percent; in effect, that worsened the terms of the Mercedes deal. Even the most ardent supporters of state investment in industrial development reluctantly arrived at the conclusion that the incentives given Mercedes were overly generous. "The package was horrendously oversized," Deravi said. "We just wanted to get the deal done. We had no automakers at the time and we couldn't believe that Mercedes would come to Alabama. We were beside ourselves and we didn't want to be left behind and left out."

Given the backlash toward exorbitant incentive packages, Honda executives told vonCannon and the others that they weren't looking for anything too extravagant and, most important, they didn't want any public criticism. The automaker primarily sought help with purchasing the land and recruiting and training local workers, as well as some infrastructure and utilities improvements and tax abatements. That downsized request made it possible for the industrial development boards to put together a funding plan themselves, backed by the five counties that would benefit the most from a factory in Lincoln. Although the state government had to eventually approve the incentives, this was the first time in Alabama that local communities alone produced a financial plan for a new factory. In the end, Honda received about $150 million, 60 percent of the Mercedes package.

"We didn't want to be seen as greedy or arrogant so this package was more than enough," said Tom Shoupe, president of Honda Manufacturing of Alabama. "We already had a strong regional presence in Ohio and we wanted to do the same thing in the South. If we made waves or came off too full of ourselves and demanding, our long-term plan, to have a big presence in the Lincoln area, would have been compromised."

In May 1999, two weeks after Honda executives visited Lincoln for the first time, the automaker announced plans to build a new plant in the town, expected to open some three years later. Honda had essentially wedded its future in the South to Lincoln with very little scrutiny of the community, which is not inconsistent with its predisposition for making decisions rapidly based on what it believes to be sufficient knowledge without long-winded research and studies that could result in missed opportunities.

In fact, when Soichiro Honda was asked if he had run a so-called SWOT analysis before entering the automobile business, exploring his company's and his would-be competitors' Strengths, Weaknesses, Opportunities, and Threats, he responded with a characteristically cocky but telling answer. "If our team had run a business analysis, we would never have ventured into the car business," Honda said. "I simply made a list of the weaknesses of the world's biggest carmakers—and that list was quite long."

In other words, trust your instincts and don't dally.

A Honda executive offered that story about the founder to argue that Honda might not have known much about Lincoln, but, in fact, the company knew enough. "It's incorrect to think we didn't do our homework," he said. "We had gone to the spot, seen Lincoln, seen the property. And we knew immediately that there wasn't much to Lincoln to know; it had become a blank slate. That's what we liked about it—a place so scoured out that we could easily embed the Honda Way."

A blank slate. That's an apt description of Lincoln at the time. Once a thriving agricultural community and a feeder town for jobs in textile and defense plants throughout the region, by the late 1990s, Lincoln's farms had mostly stopped producing and local factories had been shuttered, victims of Pentagon cost cutting and globalization. Few young people in Lincoln had jobs, and few of those who left town to go to college came back unless they had no other options.

Lincoln had only about two thousand residents at the time, not enough to support an acceptable school system or training complexes for skilled jobs in areas like biotechnology, health care, or aerospace, which are booming industries in Alabama cities like Huntsville and Birmingham. Still, a tidy amount of outside money poured into the community from the Talladega Superspeedway. This huge, tri-oval track with prominently steep banks built on the grounds of the former Anniston Air Force Base turns Lincoln into a NASCAR bacchanalia on race weekends. At those times, 175,000 stock car fans pour into the tiny community, leaving behind memories of drunken brawls and motel rooms wrecked. Of course, there are also a lot of families who bring their Winnebagos to the Superspeedway for some clean fun, but their presence is certainly less evident.

Lincoln's other significant attraction in its pre-Honda days was Logan Martin Lake, which is a reservoir of the Coosa River built by Alabama Power in the 1960s. Logan Martin's two dams are a prime source of hydropower in the state and the lake itself lures tourists for fishing, boating, and swimming. Property values around Logan Martin are the highest in Lincoln, although many of the lake residents are retired or using their houses there as weekend and vacation homes.

With the money generated by Talladega and Logan Martin, Lincoln was able to maintain the semblance of an expanding community, but this growth was mostly unplanned and only on the surface. The quality of schools, real estate prices (except near the lake), and town services was mediocre at best. Meanwhile, Lincoln itself lacked a center—literally. As you drove through Lincoln's flat and characterless twenty-one square miles, separate commercial areas—just outcroppings of a few stores and offices—seemed to appear every mile or so. Which somehow made Lincoln look as if it were prospering, if disconnected, when each of these little shopping areas was barely staying afloat.

The old downtown—four stores, three of them shuttered, including a Depression-era bank with a classically cinematic brick façade—had long ago ceased to be the core of the community and was perched listlessly on a little-used railroad track; Lincoln's City Hall, a nondescript office building as flat as the four-lane it sat upon, was a mile or so away, not far from a rundown Dollar General store; and a row of a half-dozen motels and fast-food franchises was in yet another section of the community by I-20. And down every gutted road was a different ministry—from Feed My Sheep to Blue Eye Baptist.

Give or take a few of the current retail and lodging outlets, this placid, somewhat unmoored, lackluster layout is what Honda Motor executives encountered when they came to Lincoln. Alabama officials could not have foreseen it—or perhaps ever understood it given what they are used to hearing from most companies—but for Honda, Lincoln's hollowness was its attraction.

There was another, not so discernible allure as well. Within these muted environs were people whose industriousness could not be in question. They had struggled through agricultural booms and busts maintaining their farm machinery and equipment on the cheap, usually without the help of mechanics, and they had punched clocks in factories with unkind working conditions, the antithesis of Honda's plants. Most people in Lincoln had kept their families together, and the attendance at school was high. They somehow continued to muddle along and survive in a town where the economy had flatlined. The job losses were obviously not their fault and they had long ago proven that they were worthy of the work. Those attributes, not always present in communities without real hope, where bitterness or victimhood become the dominant traits, were qualities that Honda prized.

Honda had a lot riding on the Lincoln plant. Chiefly, this factory was going to be the pivot point for a new Honda subsidiary in the South that would initially supply the popular Odyssey minivan and eventually the Pilot sport utility vehicle, Accord V6 Sedan, and the Acura MDX SUV. Like the Honda auto plants in Ohio, Canada, and Mexico, Lincoln would manufacture cars destined primarily for North American markets, making the southern factory a critical hub in Honda's localization strategy, which has transformed the automaker from a Japanese firm into a predominantly North American outfit, while maintaining its role as a top-selling international car company. More than 51 percent of Honda's automobile revenues come from North American customers. Japanese and Asian markets each contribute a little over 20 percent of sales and Europe about 5 percent.

This breakdown correlates well with the vitality and accessibility of auto markets around the world currently. While China has topped the United States in annual vehicle sales, multinationals' Chinese operations are limited by the joint ventures they are required to form with domestic car manufacturers. As a result, for now the United States has the most available and potentially profitable customer base. Moreover, alone among multinationals, Honda makes well over 90 percent of the cars that it sells in North America locally and has a similar track record in the other regions that it does business. (Toyota's geographic revenue breakdown hews more closely to what would be expected of a Japanese auto company with a centralized business structure controlled by corporate headquarters: Japan, 50 percent; North America, 25 percent; Asia, 17 percent; and Europe, 8 percent.) As global market conditions change, Honda's localization approach should enable the company's sales mix to continue to reflect where the most potential customers are and the products they most want.

But another reason for the importance of the Alabama factory was Honda's plan to introduce a new manufacturing system in Lincoln that the company hoped would generate a level of speed, innovation, cost efficiency, and quality well beyond any other industrial operation. It was a set of ideas that attempted to rewrite a lot of the traditional rules for making cars, some of them having survived barely updated since the days of Henry Ford.

The job of leading the construction of this new factory was given to Chuck Ernst, the engineer who was hired by Honda in 1985 to work in the Anna, Ohio, engine factory, some months ahead of its opening. Although a scion of a family of engineers, Ernst, a mid-fifties, tall, low-key Middle American, never worked in an automobile factory prior to Anna and had never designed a plant before Lincoln.

An Air Force brat, Ernst was born in Michigan and lived in ten cities, as far west as California, by the time he was a teenager. But he spent much of his childhood in Cincinnati, where he was taught the mysteries and brilliance of engine technology by his grandfather, an inventor specializing in experimental aircraft. "His real love, though, was hydroplanes," Ernst said. "And the first time I helped him retrofit an old Fiat aircraft engine into a hydroplane, I was smitten."

By engines and speed. Conceding that he was "a bit crazy," Ernst raced hydroplanes down the Ohio River and even participated in the famed and often reckless Madison Regatta, which takes place in a party atmosphere every Fourth of July weekend out of Madison, Indiana. For a short period Ernst held the freshwater river speed record, juicing his hydroplane to over 200 miles an hour.

Perhaps wisely, considering his daredevil leanings, Ernst's parents forbade him from riding motorcycles as a teenager. But Ernst got around that restriction by fixing his friends' bikes and accompanying them to motorcycle races, ostensibly as a support crew member but more often as a test driver. By the time Ernst finished high school, he had already built two cars.

In 1980, after graduating from Miami University in Oxford, Ohio, with a B.S. degree in applied science, Ernst took a position as a corporate engineer for Ohio-based Armco Steel. He already had some familiarity with the high quality of Japanese products—"I never had to fix Honda motorcycles; they lasted forever," he said—but at Armco he came in direct competition with Japanese companies and saw firsthand how far ahead of their American rivals they had become. Many of the new, more efficient steel minimills of that period as well as the most successful traditional integrated steel suppliers like Nippon Steel and Kawasaki were Japanese, and their selling point was a relentless focus on quality and customer satisfaction.

The difference between Japanese and American companies was clearly evident, Ernst says, in the way they approached manufacturing a master coil, which is a three-thousand-pound hunk of rolled-up steel. Master coils take a long time to make and in order to meet delivery schedules, Armco would sometimes shortcut final product inspection. Not surprisingly, many customers were upset about the coils they received; they complained about damaged edges and bent rolls, and returned the items. "And the attitude of our company was, that's okay, we'll just cut the coils up, melt them down, and do it again," Ernst recalled. "We would say, 'We'll eventually satisfy our customer.' "

By contrast, the Japanese steel companies assessed and rejiggered their manufacturing processes to make sure they could meet demand on time without sacrificing quality control. They refused to let rejections become an acceptable price of doing business. "The way we approached this problem was so discouraging and wasteful, since the attitude of our competition from Japan was to figure out how to get it right the first time," said Ernst. "We knew we had to improve—we weren't blind to that—we just didn't know how to fast enough. Needless to say, we lost a lot of customers."

The enduring irony, of course, is that the quality movement in Japan was an American initiative, begun at the end of World War II when the United States launched a campaign to rebuild Japan's electronics industry so that this sector could supply defect-free equipment to American communications networks in the country. Companies such as Toshiba, NEC, and Hitachi were compelled to take lessons from the U.S. occupiers on statistical analysis of finished products to reduce variation and deficiencies; choosing appropriate, long-lasting raw materials; and following salient design and manufacturing techniques.

Primarily because they were desperate for business, Japanese companies became fast students of the Americans, an educational process that sped up significantly in 1950 when U.S. quality control expert W. Edwards Deming gave a lecture before the Union of Japanese Scientists and Engineers. That speech—which highlighted, among other things, productivity, cost savings, efficiency gains, and customer satisfaction improvements that can result from better quality control analyses—effectively created a nationwide craze in Japan that few companies were immune from. Japanese businesses of any stripe that hoped to sell in global marketplaces adopted the full range of quality control measures with a zealous enthusiasm unseen in the United States or anyplace else in the world. Deming became a Japanese national hero and an award named for him that honors Japanese companies for advances in quality control is his legacy in the country.

As Ernst put it, the weight of the Japanese emphasis on quality was too much for Armco to withstand. And in 1984, when Ernst's wife showed him the classified ad for engineers at Honda in Anna, he decided, "Maybe it's time I join the Japanese, rather than knock my head against the wall trying to beat them."

A year later Ernst was hired by Honda. And four years after that, Armco was essentially dismantled by Kawasaki Steel soon after the Japanese company bought a 40 percent stake for $350 million, the largest investment by a Japanese steel company in the United States to that point.

When Ernst was asked to build the Lincoln factory, he had already moved out of the Anna engine plant to an executive position in Honda Engineering. He approached the task at hand with few preconceptions about the size of the facility or how it would be laid out. He knew that the process of designing and constructing the site would be driven by Honda's company principles—that is, plenty of *waigaya* to bubble up the best ideas and plenty of *gen-ba* to determine what was specifically appropriate for the Lincoln factory and what had worked well at other Honda facilities that could be installed in Alabama.

But from his experience at Anna, he was certain about one thing: his budget for Lincoln would be limited—although he would not have believed this years earlier when he quit Armco for Honda. "At that time I thought I was joining a big, global manufacturing company until the day I reported for work," Ernst said. "I left a big office and eight people working for me [at Armco] for the old, rundown farmhouse on the property where Anna would be built."

In this rustic setting, the children's bedroom in the back of the house served as Ernst's office. And besides having to bring in his own tools to tear down and rebuild the training engines, which were used to teach him and his colleagues how automobile and motorcycle motors were constructed, Ernst often required knee waders to get through the day dry. When the water table was high, the basement would flood. "And we had practical jokers on the team who, whenever they saw me go down there, would go upstairs and flush every toilet in the house to increase the depth of the water," Ernst said.

Ernst didn't appreciate the full meaning of the threadbare working conditions at Anna until much later when he understood Honda Motor better. Over time, he has come to realize that his new bosses were sending an unmistakable message by placing him and the other fresh Anna hires in a ramshackle, barely operational building. Ernst and his colleagues were the earliest American employees for the Japanese company's first U.S. engine factory, built just three years after Honda's Marysville facility, fifty-two miles down the road, debuted as the first Japanese auto factory in North America. In distance and in culture, Anna was a long way from Japan. And Honda wanted these employees to be on notice that their work life was not going to resemble the disengaged, inefficient, and spendthrift approaches found at the Detroit 3 automakers. "We were implicitly being told by our bosses in Japan what they expected of us: be inventive, independent, and don't be too proud to think that any job is below you," Ernst said.

And underlying the tacit directive about individual responsibilities was a broader corporate-wide mantra, also represented well by Anna's primitive digs: cutting costs and waste anywhere in the manufacturing process—from automobile design to delivery, from factory conception to commencement—is an unwavering goal because it leads directly to reduced sticker prices.

"By the time I was assigned to Lincoln," Ernst said. "I was under no illusions that I would have a blank check."

Still, inexpensive or not, Lincoln would be an ambitious endeavor. At the ground breaking in April 2000, Honda officials promised that the first car would roll out of the factory in twenty-four months, a full year or two faster than most automobile plants. But no sooner did Chuck Ernst begin to work on the project than he was told that this schedule had been abandoned in favor of an even more aggressive timetable: eighteen months. Honda hoped to take advantage of increasing demand for the oversized North American version of the Odyssey minivan, which would be Lincoln's first car and until then had been made solely in Canada. By the time Ernst was given this news, he had already hired a contractor, the giant Birmingham firm BE&K, Inc., to oversee the construction. True to form, BE&K had built factories before—pulp and paper plants, for example—but had no experience in the automobile industry.

When Ernst told BE&K cofounder Ted Kennedy about the new planned opening date for Lincoln, Kennedy said that it couldn't be done, particularly to get all of the state and local clearances in time. "I've been in construction thirty-four years in Alabama," Kennedy said, "and what you are proposing is impossible to do. Also, this type of factory is new to us so there could be glitches."

"Wait a minute; you work for me," Ernst replied. "If I have a schedule then you have the same schedule. We chose you precisely because you haven't built an auto plant before and wouldn't load us up with all kinds of reasons why from your experience we couldn't do this or couldn't do that. We hired you to be can-do."

Ernst said he never heard "can't do" again from anyone involved in the project.

As much as the rushed timetable was a bold move, adopting a new manufacturing paradigm in Lincoln—one that would challenge preconceptions about auto factory design and processes—was even more audacious. The first steps toward creating this new system were taken a year or so before the Lincoln plant was announced, when a team led by Honda Engineering senior vice president John Adams began a series of *waigaya* throughout the automaker's network of factories. Employees on all levels were asked to offer up and defend ideas about improving efficiency, safety, and quality as well as cutting costs in the plants.

The most radical concept to emerge from these meetings was a plan to jettison the traditional linear assembly line, in which a car is pieced together serially from one end of a factory to another and then inspected for defects as a finished vehicle before leaving the plant. In Honda's new schema, the factory would comprise five zones, each responsible for both assembly and quality control of a large section of the vehicle. After the paint room, these zones were: underbody, doors and panels, engine and suspension, interior, and exterior. Similar assembly processes—for example, wiring and gas lines, or air-conditioning and power steering—were to be located next to each other in these zones, and workers were expected to become expert in all of the tasks in their sections by rotating among the jobs every couple of hours. In each zone, quality control would be the final process.

Ideally, these compact, self-contained assembly areas would enhance workers' performance by extending their sphere of responsibility and accountability to more extensive portions of the car than single manufacturing stations. And by embedding quality control into the assembly process itself instead of placing the function at the end of the entire factory line, wasteful, laborious fixes—such as having to pull the interior of an assembled car apart simply to rethread deficient wiring hidden under the carpet and seats—could be avoided. In all, significant savings can be realized in the time it takes to produce a customer-ready automobile and in reduced postsale warranty outlays.

"The people inspecting the car at the tail of each zone are right next to those who installed the parts and they can give feedback quickly: 'Hey, you're doing something wrong, the fit is off,' or 'This part is faulty, we need to return them to the supplier and get a new batch,'" said Adams. "And before the whole line is infected with this problem, the issue can be fixed locally."

Although Honda's *waigaya* lit up with excitement at the introduction of this unorthodox idea for an assembly line, the concept also met with a great deal of opposition. It appeared to some at Honda that the idea belied the automaker's prior stated aspirations about quality control. At its core, the quality movement in Japan was based on a fundamental yet unattainable objective: to make products that are so flawless they can be shipped directly to customers without end-of-the-line inspection. Like many Japanese companies, Honda had wholeheartedly embraced this aspiration and, in fact, had come closer to it than many of its rivals.

Possibly the most daring example: In Honda's factories, a vehicle's engine is started up for the first time only when the automobile is ready to be driven out of the building; that is, after final approval in the engine factory, Honda's motors are not checked again for imperfections until they are in a car on a grueling test track, a self-confident but risky approach that few other automakers would attempt. Honda, however, has used its success with this daring production technique to argue that manufacturing defect-free products is, in fact, not out of reach and to inspire its employees toward continuous improvement and excellence.

Yet, in the new manufacturing model that was under discussion, Honda management appeared to be adding extra quality control into the system—even making it more of a centerpiece of the assembly line—rather than ultimately trying to eliminate it. Many employees at the *waigaya* were incensed that Honda would consider moving so far afield from its highest-quality ideals. "The basic concept that we were always working towards was build it right the first time and you'll never have to make expensive repairs at the end," said a Lincoln executive who had been involved in these initial meetings about the manufacturing system. "And if that was our aim, why were we suddenly ready to admit that in our most advanced factories we needed to keep checking our work over and over on the assembly line because, well, we can't build it right the first time?"

Like most paradoxes, this inconsistency channeled the discussion into deeper and more fertile territory. As Honda has adroitly done with other seeming contradictions, the disagreement over the meaning of the company's apparent shift in its adherence to quality control dogma gave Honda an opportunity to reexamine prior sets of beliefs and consider whether and why they may no longer be viable.

The gist of the dispute, continued over many cups of coffee and, if truth be told, jiggers of rye, eventually came down to this: while making perfect automobiles may be a noble ambition philosophically, it's an impossible target currently for a piece of equipment that contains thirteen thousand components. A variation of as little as a micron in a machined part can alter the performance of an entire section of the car. Given that reality, if one alternative was to continue producing automobiles the old-fashioned way in a linear assembly line with hopes to someday phase out quality control but realize no immediate gains, while the other alternative was to radically alter the contours of the assembly line and enjoy instant cost savings and improvements in productivity and speed, the decision was obvious. Expediency trumped idealism, at least in this instance.

"You never give up on the ultimate goal to build a car without flaws, but you have to recognize that occasionally things are going to go wrong when you are making cars and we have to figure out a way to deal with that efficiently," said Adams. "On the one hand you want to deny that you are willing to dilute the 'make it right the first time' ideal—you want to fight it with all your heart and soul—and simultaneously you find yourself saying, pragmatically, we need to. I admit I occasionally landed on the side of 'Why in the hell are we doing this?' "

Chuck Ernst loved the idea of the five-zone factory; he saw it as a stunningly imaginative layout, a chance to redefine typical industrial flow models and to experiment with ways to address issues that bedevil every factory designer but that Honda is particularly sensitive about.

At the top of the list is cost. Perversely, greenfield factories are routinely ranked by how much money a company spends on constructing them, as if the larger the capital investment the greater the return. We've grown used to gushing press reports like these that I found at random through a Google search: "Toyota's new $475 million factory in Nansha, near the southern city of Guangzhou, symbolizes the automaker's ambitions for China," or "Caterpillar's $200 million plant in Georgia is a game changer for Clark, Oconee and surrounding counties." And there were dozens more for each company name that I typed in. But measuring a factory's value by the amount of money it took to build it is akin to assuming that the $436 hammer the Pentagon famously purchased can drive nails more quickly than a $12 Stanley model.

Ernst didn't have the luxury of impressing Honda management by spending a lot on the Lincoln plant. Quite the opposite. So he began to minimize costs by limiting the footprint of the plant. The five zones offered some clues about how to do this. With the linear assembly line abandoned, Ernst had the freedom to use a more economical layout—a looping, rotary line that from a bird's-eye view resembles a paper clip. And with quality control integrated into the assembly process itself, he could trim off excess space at the back end of the plant.

Moreover, the assembly line's coiled shape allowed Ernst to initially place an engine plant in a circular area in the center of the factory; up until then no automaker had yet integrated engine assembly with vehicle manufacturing under one roof. But the potential savings were enormous: Honda could avoid putting up a separate facility for engines and installing an automated conveyor belt to carry the motors from one plant to the other. Eliminating engine transportation costs alone would save more than $1 million; tens of millions of dollars in additional savings could be gained from not having to construct a second building.

This compact factory design dovetails well with Honda's distaste for overbuilding. The company would prefer to lose some short-term sales of a product that has suddenly and unexpectedly captured customer fancy than be hampered by unused capacity and a slew of unproductive construction, operating, and maintenance costs. "You don't want to build a large building, and then have it a third empty," said Ernst. "That's a waste of cash with no possible return."

Ernst found other unusual ways to save money as well, particularly by recycling equipment in the factory that had been used in other Honda plants and subsequently mothballed. Most greenfield auto factories are totally fresh. Part of the reason is a bias of engineers and designers, who are irrepressibly drawn to shiny things and the latest technologies to tinker with and brag about. The chance to construct a factory is viewed as an opportunity to fill in a tabula rasa with the state of the art. In that pristine and au courant view of a greenfield plant, an old machine appears lost and left behind, a relic from a prior industrial episode, like a boulder too cumbersome to move so the plant is built around it.

That wasn't Ernst's perception, though—at least after fifteen years at Honda. He saw the possibility of saving millions of dollars on the Lincoln plant by rummaging through Honda's attic and he enthusiastically seized the chance. He found a ten-year-old casting machine that made engine blocks in the Wako engine facility in Japan. It was being used for production trials and was outmoded, with mechanical relay controls instead of high-tech programmable logic controllers, as these machines would have today. And it only had the capacity to produce 375 engine blocks a day; Lincoln needed 450 at least.

The team in Lincoln updated and rewired the casting equipment and replumbed the hydraulics, a relatively inexpensive job, and put the refurbished casting machine online. "We figured once we expanded, we could buy new equipment," Ernst said. "As it turned out, we did our job too well. After optimizing the machine, we tested it and ended up running over six hundred pieces during a twenty-four-hour period, more than adequate. And our workers learned a lot more about maintaining and operating the equipment by rebuilding it than if we had simply purchased something new."

That saved $500,000. An additional $600,000 came out of the budget by importing idled machining indexes, which essentially hold raw materials like steel in place for cutting or shaping, from Honda's engine plant in the United Kingdom. And more savings were found in an unused module transfer machine, also left for dead in the UK; this machine enables a number of different engines to be manufactured on the same line.

The recycling strategy was more than just a way to minimize the overall price of the factory; it had immediate implications for the bottom line. "In total, we saved $2 million with equipment that had minimal book value—just the cost of shipping and remanufacturing. If you pay less in investment costs to move something into production, there's less depreciation and you can become profitable more quickly."

By almost any accounting, Honda's Lincoln factory surpasses other auto plants in space utilization and cost efficiency, two key manufacturing productivity metrics. Although the Lincoln plant has since been enlarged, initially it spanned 1.7 million square feet and produced 130,000 each of cars and engines annually. The total price tag for the Alabama facility was about $500 million—which includes not just equipment inside the plant but earth moving, building construction, and real estate expenses. By way of comparison, Volkswagen's factory in Chattanooga, Tennessee, which opened in 2011, covers 3.5

million square feet, makes only 150,000 cars per year (no engines), and cost $1.4 billion. It's twice the size of the Lincoln plant at three times the cost with a much lower production volume.

Toyota, too, has not been able to replicate Honda's efficiency. Its massive 7.5-million-square-foot factory in Georgetown, Kentucky, produces 500,000 cars and engines a year. A Honda factory of that size would manufacture about 200,000 more vehicles and motors. Recently, Toyota announced plans to invest $300 million on a new line in Georgetown that would make about 50,000 additional cars a year, a relatively low number by Honda's standards. Since it opened, the Lincoln plant has expanded to about 3.5 million square feet; and its annual output has steadied at 300,000 cars and engines, mostly light trucks and V6 motors.

"Honda never had the deep pockets that other automakers have had," said Ron Harbour, senior partner specializing in global automotive manufacturing at consultants Oliver Wyman. "From making motorcycles to cars they've operated on a shoestring and now that factory efficiency, adaptability, and efficient use of space is all the rage, suddenly in the past decade there is interest in how Honda does this so well."

And he added, "But the point is, Honda's ability to make efficient factories didn't just start yesterday, even if no one paid much attention before. It's a product of their history going all the way back to the way the founder hated waste and always looked for ways to save money through internal innovation."

Harbour is one of the auto sector's most knowledgeable experts on factory design and output. His annual ranking of plant performance, the *Harbour Report*, based in part on his own on-the-ground reporting, is a must-read for automakers. He said that the secret sauce setting Honda apart from other manufacturers has been what is now commonly called factory flexibility. In plainer terms: Honda can make any number of different types of cars on the same assembly line without any downtime between models.

Traditionally, entire factories in the auto industry were dedicated to a single type of vehicle, like the rows of Model Ts that grainy black-and-white pictures of an earlier industrial era show Henry Ford pointing to proudly. Problem is, when those cars fall out of favor, the factories must be shut down. Moreover, relatively low-volume autos—popular but only to a small market, such as the Ridgeline truck—are shelved because their sales revenue is insufficient to cover the exorbitant costs of making them on a single line. In contrast, Honda's assembly line flexibility allows it to make a small profit on the Ridgeline and, hence, to continue to dabble with new designs that could lead to even greater returns in future, potentially more lucrative vehicles.

Besides minimizing costs, building a factory capable of manufacturing multiple vehicles simultaneously was at the very top of Chuck Ernst's agenda in 2000. It was a target that Honda had come close to in other plants but not quite fully achieved. However, the five-zone manufacturing system provided the perfect platform for assembly line flexibility.

With Honda's new factory layout, in effect, workers in each zone became experts in specific, relatively large sections of the automobile. As long as all of the vehicles coming into the zones shared common designs, broadly speaking, such as similar locations and installation techniques for functions like brakes or transmission, a team of assemblers in the zones could without difficulty manage the small variations that would differentiate, say, an Odyssey from an Accord V6. In other words, the key to building a flexible factory, Honda found, was as much in synchronized engineering among models as in the assembly process, a relatively easy stratagem for Honda to implement.

In plants with traditional assembly-line stations, the individual tasks are diced up into small, separate pieces. That precludes workers from having a sufficiently holistic view of the assembly process to handle different models in rapid sequence.

More recently, other manufacturers have attempted to mimic Honda's flexibility techniques to varying degrees of success. Not surprisingly, Toyota has come the closest to successfully following Honda's lead, but no companies have yet fully equaled Honda's assembly line speed or fluidity.

"Honda is really good at that," said Harbour. "When they want to change the mix of cars because demand has shifted, it doesn't matter. They just have to make sure to deliver the right parts to the line."

And where this strategy pays off the most is in new car launches, which typically require shutting down a plant to retool the equipment and train assemblers, a process that can take months, during which the factory loses money daily. Instead, Honda's method allows it to introduce a car virtually without disturbing a factory's normal productivity.

The late Jerome York, a well-respected industry insider who was CFO at Chrysler and led billionaire Kirk Kerkorian's ill-fated attempt to take over General Motors a decade ago, told automakers at a meeting in 2008 that the flexible factory was "tomorrow's war" in the auto industry. And exhorting his American colleagues not to belittle the significance of Honda's achievements, he added ruefully but with grudging respect: "Honda can go from building 100 percent Accords on Friday, to 100 percent Civics on Monday. Their only limitation is the response time for ordering vehicles."

York's assessment was validated a few months later when, in the wake of the recession and roller-coaster gas prices, SUV and minivan sales collapsed worse than other segments of the market. Honda quickly moved production of the Ridgeline and Accord V6 into

Lincoln to make up for decreased demand for the Odyssey and Pilot. This single rapid changeover ensured that Honda could continue to operate Lincoln at relatively high capacity even in the worst days of the economic crash and remain profitable with no firings while GM and Chrysler were facing bankruptcy and Toyota had slipped into the red for the first time in its history.

Implementing this novel approach meant that the Lincoln assembly line would, ironically, be one of the least automated among automobile plants. To be sure, computers in the assembly zones scan barcodes to help determine the specific parts needed for the cars entering the work area. But that's about the extent of high-tech in many parts of the factory. To ameliorate the distinctions, slight as they may be, between models entering the zones, to be responsible for whole subsets of the car, and to manage quality control within the zones, more people—and fewer machines—were necessary. In fact, by default, Honda's manufacturing system, as sophisticated and advanced as it is in other ways, is fairly labor intensive. Conversely, auto companies that have spent heavily on robotics in the past decade or so are among the least nimble in altering production schedules to respond to unanticipated demand shifts for individual cars.

"The problem is that even with vision systems [machines that can see], you have to tell that piece of automation what's acceptable and not, but you can't possibly program all of the abnormalities that could occur," said Mike Oatridge, vice president of Honda Manufacturing in Alabama and part of Ernst's Lincoln development team. "I can teach a robot to pick up this bottle of water and put it down in the same spot every time, but I can't make it care whether the table is scratched or the table is some other color, at least to the degree that we need those discerning judgments in making cars."

It is important, however, not to put too fine a point on statements like these and miss the larger valuable lesson that Honda's reasoning on this issue offers. Indeed, Honda is not, by any means, averse to automation. The automaker has some of the industry's most skilled robots in sections of Lincoln and its other factories where people are not equipped to do the assignment well or where automated equipment has been shown to be clearly better at the particular task. But deciding whether to automate or not is viewed by Honda as a value judgment, one that its executives do not make lightly because in general they see automation as a deterrent to innovation. They believe that assemblers become disengaged and less prone to proactively elevate the processes in their work area when they share it with a machine. Further, output and quality standards are too often set to the levels that the technology can achieve, Honda maintains; consequently, to enhance performance you often have to buy a new piece of equipment.

"Once you automate, you're incapable of further improvement," said Sean McAlinden, chief economist at the Center for Automotive Research, paraphrasing Honda's perspective. "And when you look at the efficiency and sophistication and creativity of their factories, despite the somewhat lower amount of automation, they're making a good argument."

In taking this stance, Honda is going against the grain of almost every major industrial company in any sector. Robotics has been eagerly welcomed by manufacturers of all stripes, who see it as a convenient way to satisfy two of their most elusive desires: improved productivity and lower labor costs. Remarkably, by 2015, Apple's Chinese iPhone manufacturer, Foxconn, will have more than a million robots in its factories. And in their book *Race Against the Machine*, Massachusetts Institute of Technology economists Erik Brynjolfsson and Andrew McAfee contend that industrial automation will have the same dramatic impact on manufacturing that agricultural automation had on farming in the twentieth century, when employment on farms declined to below 5 percent of the workforce from more than 40 percent.

Punctuating this argument, Mike Dennison, president of Flextronics High Velocity Solutions, an electronics component manufacturer in San Jose, California, described how widespread robotics is in manufacturing with an allusion to an earlier place and time: "The tantalizing question is at what point does the chain saw replace Paul Bunyan?" he asked. "There's always a price point, and we're very close to that point."

It's impossible to prove a negative so it can't be said with certainty that Honda's less aggressive approach to automation is a more profitable course than filling a factory with robots. But at least a few executives at automobile parts suppliers offered anecdotes about carmakers that had so fully automated their plants that they've stopped updating certain vehicle components, usually less obvious ones, because they are not giving the whole car the same attention that they used to. Engines, headlights, and brake systems may be continually redesigned, but starters and alternators, for example, may be neglected because the robotic machines would have to be upgraded at a substantial cost to handle installing new parts with different specifications, according to these executives. As a result, one supplier said, he was selling "very obsolete equipment to a very techno-savvy customer."

Given recent trends, it's likely that Honda and the rest of the auto industry will diverge even further on the question of automation in the coming years. While this issue is continually debated inside Honda, Ernst says, there is little hunger to change the company's stance, primarily because it is woven deep into the threads of the automaker's culture. "We want the associates to really understand how a car goes together, not rely on a machine to do it for them," he said. "And there's this as well: there is very little joy in manufacturing when you know that someone else or something else deserves the real credit for building the car."

Lincoln's unparalleled manufacturing flexibility continues to evolve in large part because of the presence of Honda's in-house engineering team, which is responsible for, among other things, devising proprietary equipment to enhance assembly line speed and versatility. Honda's competitors have tried to separate as many manufacturing processes as possible from the factory in order to simplify work flow; often this means outsourcing complex production jobs to suppliers and housing their engineers in large centralized teams near or in headquarters, where they are far removed from the immediate needs of individual assembly lines. For its part, Honda prefers to concentrate as many tasks under one roof as possible; the automaker believes that this prevents quality deterioration, streamlines inventory management, encourages local innovation, facilitates communication among all aspects of production from tooling to design to assembly, and makes more economical use of factory space and manufacturing investments.

The high-water mark of the engineering team at Lincoln is an extraordinary welding system, a tool that amplifies the potential of flexible manufacturing to an extraordinary degree. Welding massive body panels and roof components to a vehicle frame is the most cumbersome and time-consuming aspect of building a car. The prevalent welding approach is known as fixed tooling, in which heavy stationary robots are set up to aim at specific welding points on a single vehicle model. To assemble a second type of car on the same line, the welding tools must be torn down and rebuilt, a process that can introduce long delays—hours in some cases.

At Lincoln (and now at other Honda plants) this unwieldy equipment has given way to a much more nimble "general welder," or

One of Honda's initial motorized bicycles with the company's first engine, the A-type, circa 1947. For fuel efficiency, air and gasoline enter the engine through a rotary disk valve attached to the side of the crankcase instead of through the intake valve on the pistons.

Soichiro Honda (left) and Takeo Fujisawa (right) agreed to colead Honda Motor in 1949; it was a tempestuous but rewarding partnership that lasted nearly twenty-five years.

Honda's first full-fledged motorcycle, the Dream Machine, built in 1949.

Honda's research and design center near Tokyo soon after the company spun off the department as an independent entity, circa 1960. Honda remains the sole major manufacturer with separate R&D subsidiaries.

Honda's first foray into the United States: a storefront in Los Angeles where a small staff introduced the company's small motorcycles, dubbed Super Cubs, to a country that adored choppers.

Soichiro Honda with racing trophies. Honda later became the first non-Western motorcycle maker to earn a top spot at the prestigious 1961 Isle of Man TT motorcycle race.

Honda's first production car, a 1963 S500, which Japanese journalists disparaged as being "just a four-wheeled motorcycle."

You meet the nicest people on a Honda. It's largely a question of personality. A Honda is easy going, dependable. Makes few demands. Prices start about $215*. And it runs around all day on a nickel's worth of gas. That's the kind of friend to have. Frugal. How about one in your family? World's biggest seller!
HONDA

One of the most successful marketing campaigns ever: Grey Advertising's "You Meet the Nicest People on a Honda" print ads. Seen here in a 1965 version, these ads showed housewives, young couples, rich matrons and their dogs, delivery boys, and even Santa Claus, to name a few, riding a Super Cub.

Soichiro Honda with a prototype of the Honda vehicle that won the Formula 1 race in 1965, a year after the company initially entered the circuit and two years after it built its first automobile.

Soichiro Honda with the CVCC engine in 1972; it was the first motor made by any automaker to meet strict 1970 U.S. Clean Air Act pollution regulations.

The 1974 Civic, the first Honda vehicle equipped with the "clean" CVCC engine.

The first car Honda manufactured in the United States, a 1983 Accord. At that time, Honda was the sole non-American automaker to produce vehicles in the country.

Soichiro Honda (left) and Takeo Fujisawa (right) nearing the end of their run as coleaders of Honda Motor. They retired on the same day in October, 1973. Soichiro commented, "Takeo Fujisawa and I, we're half good each. We're like apprentice geishas who count as one geisha together."

The 2014 Honda Ridgeline, an American-designed vehicle for the U.S. market that *Car and Driver* wrote "turned conventional thinking on its ear."

The 2014 Honda Brio, a car originally developed and conceived by Honda's Thailand subsidiary, one of many independent Honda companies around the world that exemplifies its global localization strategy.

Honda factory workers at the Lincoln, Alabama, plant, wearing the white uniforms required of all Honda employees on the job—from executives to those on the production line—with their first names in a red oval on the top right side of the shirt.

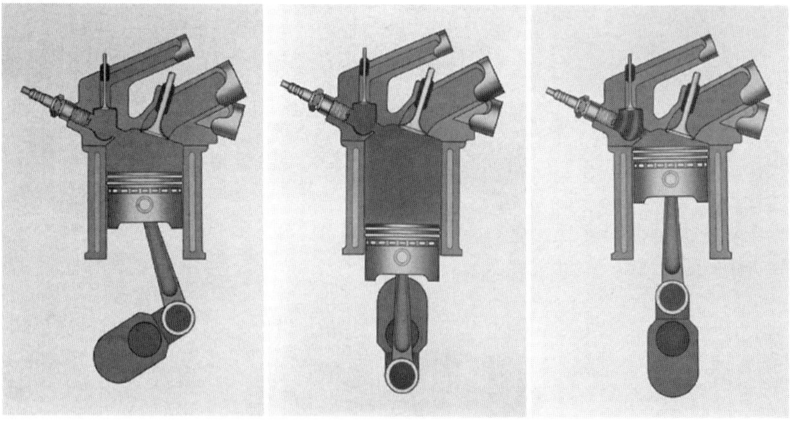

CVCC Engine Diagram.

GW, with lightweight aluminum jigs that hang on the end of robotic arms to place the body part on the chassis; the robot adroitly uses the specific position of the car on the assembly line to control its own speed and clamping force. Then, with a shower of sparks that lasts no more than a nanosecond, electric servo welding guns fasten the vehicle's body parts together.

If every second car on the line is a different model, the GW can continually change its own jig to match the vehicle arriving at the welding station. The machine's arms literally glide over to the appropriate bin and gracefully swap out one jig for another in seconds. New models can be accommodated as quickly as if the same model as the one before had just arrived at the welding zone. The entire automated maneuver is choreographed in rhythm with the pace of the assembly line, with no slowdown or interruption.

The design of the Lincoln factory and the new manufacturing process that was introduced there have generally been duplicated at all other Honda plants, although local affiliates can alter them to suit their preferences and requirements. By having a single global manufacturing platform, Honda is able to shift production of a vehicle from one plant to another with virtually no disruption in output and introduce an existing automobile into an additional region seamlessly.

The innate value of Honda's new flexible manufacturing system has been borne out by any number of statistics: in one benchmarked plant, the defect-free manufacturing rate rose by 20 percent in the first year of implementation, while rejects (cars that needed actual repairs before leaving the factory) dropped by 75 percent. Cost of manufacturing per vehicle declined by 10 percent, and investments in welding were slashed by 30 percent. In addition, electricity usage fell by 10 percent throughout the factory and 20 percent in welding.

As for the town of Lincoln, it is still in desperate search of an identity. It's too sprawling for a small hamlet and too antiquated for a community without a past to celebrate. But since Honda's arrival more than a decade ago, there are signs of life that would not have been possible before. Parks are sprouting up, one even has a jogging path, and the current mayor has promised to rebuild the old downtown and turn it into an attractive city center. Moreover, all of Lincoln's schools are newly constructed.

The people of Lincoln, however, are a different story. Or I should say, the people of Honda who live in Lincoln are. They have decent jobs, challenging but satisfying, in a clean, state-of-the-art manufacturing facility. They are earning salaries larger than any they could have expected in the region when Lincoln's fortunes had faded. Even starting assembly-line workers are making more than $50,000 a year. And many of the Honda employees I spoke to said they feel good about themselves again, respected at work, and with enough job security to be less tense at home.

Perhaps the most colorful and insightful description of Lincoln and its unlikely relationship with Honda belongs to Richard George—he of the best barbecue ribs in the world (I tried them; they are, in fact, just as he said). "Lincoln was never going to make much of itself," George told me. "But then again sometimes you have to look real ugly before someone sees how pretty you are, leastwise in their eyes."

7

HONDA'S INNOVATION MACHINE

Soichiro Honda and Charles Handy did not know each other but their minds had clearly met. Just as Honda was among the most eccentric and creative engineers in automotive history, Handy stands out as a wholly original thinker in the area of organizational behavior and management, fields that suffer from a shortage of nonconformist ideas.

And although they came from very different upbringings, the pair viewed many aspects of life through the same lens. You can hear Soichiro's disdain for formal education—how little it teaches about common sense and the ways it stifles do-it-yourself ingenuity—in Handy's words: "Instead of a national curriculum for education, what is really needed is an individual curriculum for every child."

Or you can see the contours of Honda's global localization strategy in Handy's support for the decentralized organization—or as he calls it, the Federalist model: "With people scattered around the world, you really have to let them be on their own. . . . That means you have to run the organization on the basis of professionalism and trust—subsidiarity. If you run an organization like that, you really have to base it around relatively small, long-term, continuing units where each member has a high level of commitment."

Given the intellectual kinship between the two men, it is not surprising that one of Handy's most valuable and practical concepts for continuous innovation in a company has had perhaps its most skillful application at Honda Motor. It involves paradox and thinking one or more steps ahead of everyone else, two ideas that are closely linked to Honda's success.

Handy, who was born in 1932 in an Anglican parsonage in Ireland's rural County Kildare, lived a fairly conventional first half or so of his life—a degree from the royal Oriel College Oxford and soon after, in 1956, a marketing executive job at Royal Dutch Shell. But Handy left Shell in the mid-1960s after being threatened with a posting to Liberia. He pursued a career in academia, including a stint as a professor at the London Business School. And by the early 1980s, Handy was on his own, leaving the "shelter of organizations . . . (to) fend for myself," as he wrote in his totally enjoyable autobiographical tome, *The Elephant and the Flea.*

In that book and in many lectures, Handy describes a world made up of, among other things, elephants, which are the large corporations and multinational conglomerates, and the fleas—individuals who either on their own or through downsizing have found themselves feeding off a number of elephants as independent contractors with a portfolio of jobs.

Handy loves being a flea; it was the path he chose. But he believes that proper education utterly fails to prepare people for the less structured and more autonomous work that occurs outside an organization's walls. Schools offer neither the emotional nor the intellectual tools to handle that type of life, Handy contends. And yet, he posits, an increasing number of people now either are compelled to face a career as a flea or would prefer it to working in an identityless corporation. Soichiro and his company, of course, have been immersed in a sixty-plus-year journey to build an organization whose culture encourages people to be fleas—independent, self-motivated, and unafraid to think differently—while faithful to the goals and rules of a publicly traded elephant with shareholders to satisfy.

Though he sometimes sounds like an embittered leftist, Handy is not anticapitalist, any more than Honda was. But both men believed (a bit radically) that corporations exist in large part to improve the lives of their customers and workers as well as to be profitable—equal, inseparable ambitions that are ultimately dependent on each other. Honda advanced this sentiment when he asserted the Three Joys as fundamental principles of his company. Handy's version, written more than two decades later, has clear echoes of Soichiro's startlingly modern (for the 1950s) interpretation of what makes a great and sustainable corporation. "The companies that survive longest," Handy said in an interview, "are the ones that work out what they uniquely can give to the world—not just growth or money but their excellence, their respect for others, or their ability to make people happy. Some call those things a soul."

Handy's idealism is noteworthy. Too few organizational experts place such significant emphasis on a company's values and beliefs—and hold them responsible for living up to these tenets. But Handy is not so romantic as to ignore that even the best-intentioned and most enlightened companies can be undone by a serious shortcoming that organizations commonly suffer from: namely, the inability to understand cycles of innovation.

For most manufacturing companies, knowing when to add new features to popular products or replace them entirely—and having the will to do so—is a paralyzing dilemma. As a result, it's not unusual for even the most well-run organizations to sacrifice substantial market share and sales opportunities by innovating too slowly. Indeed, Soichiro chronically feared that his company was falling into this trap, and Honda's three primary principles evolved implicitly from these concerns. *Waigaya*, *sangen shugi*, and respect for the individual encourage reevaluating and reimagining products and processes frequently—and not just a new feature here or there, but serial, continual, groundbreaking advances.

Handy has a unique notion about continuous innovation, an intriguing analysis depicting the precise conditions that make many companies risk averse and frightened of change. Instinctively and driven by Soichiro's many warnings about the perils of standing pat, Honda Motor has avoided these scenarios by adopting a series of organizational schemes involving intradepartmental product development and R&D's central role in the company that ensure a constant flow of new ideas. Because Honda's approach essentially parallels Handy's, the automaker is a perfect proving ground for his premise.

Handy's innovation theory, which he first wrote about in *The Age of Paradox*, is based on an old and complicated mathematical function called the sigmoid curve, or more frequently S-curve. Very simplified—and taken out of the realm of calculus—the sigmoid curve is a stretched-out *S* laid on its back that represents the natural cycle of virtually every biological and physical system and human behavior common in politics, art, business, and even intimate relationships.

Following the *S* from left to right, life starts out slowly; we dip and falter until we get our bearings. Then it's all on the upswing as we gain in strength and confidence, as we learn what was there before we arrived and create things that weren't, as we fall in love and give birth to new lives. And finally, we wane, softly and smoothly,

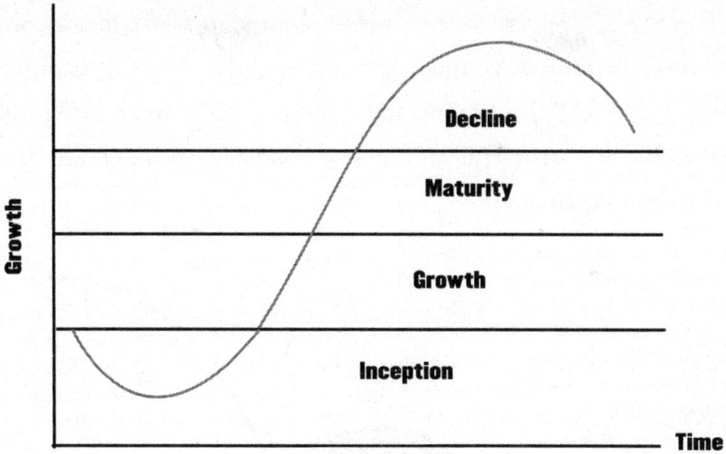

Sigmoid Curve

and end up somewhat above where we started. Even giving the S-curve's progression an anodyne cast, as I tried to do in describing it, it is hard to camouflage its depressing message that, well, all good things come to an end.

Applying this theory to the business world and specifically to companies that make things, Handy argued that popular products ride the S-curve, often in telescoped time. At first, during a short window, potential customers learn about the product through advertising, marketing, and public relations. If they like what they hear, sales for the item balloon, as happened with the iPad, for example, after the initial flurry of publicity that began even before Apple launched the tablet. And then, eventually, customers turn away, often toward some new product in the same niche but with novel and captivating features.

Handy proposed that companies need not be victims of the S-curve's unyielding march toward irrelevancy. Instead, he wrote, businesses should start a fresh sigmoid curve before the first one abates to build on the popularity of the original product by introducing an improved version before competitors do. Ideally, this new product initiative would begin when there are still resources and energy within the organization to take on a fresh ambitious project—that is, before the first curve is past its peak (Point A in Handy's sigmoid curve).

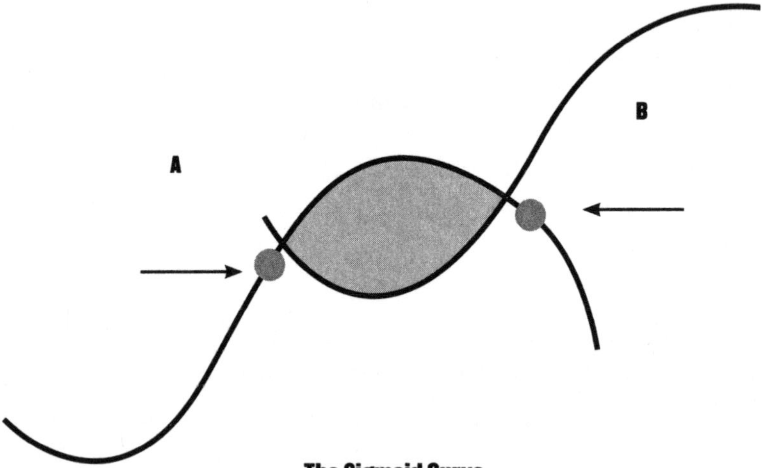

The Sigmoid Curve

But that's where the paradox comes in. When sales are skyrocketing and the original product is still in demand, the last thing companies want to do is replace it with something better. To most businesses it would seem foolhardy and damaging to supersede a bestselling item with an upgrade that puts it on a path to obsolescence. Companies are loath to leave millions of untapped customers, dollars behind while also spending an equal amount of money to develop and launch a new version of a product. Indeed, the real motivation to change course tends to take hold only when the downhill slide has begun (Point B in Handy's sigmoid curve).

However, by that juncture it's often too late. As sales slip, organizations may pour significant financial and labor resources into keeping the product alive by, for instance, discounting or conducting a marketing blitz. And when that costly effort fails because the product has fallen inexorably behind its rivals and is perceived by customers as old-fashioned, morale flags. Moreover, excess cash for a new development campaign is at a premium. There is little that anyone can do to recreate the enthusiasm and the internal support that were in full bloom at the beginning of the initial sigmoid curve.

With these dire prospects for companies that dawdle, the shaded area in Handy's sigmoid curve between Point A and Point B can be characterized as a time of confusion and simultaneously a period of greatest opportunity for a company and its products to maintain their market position and, if possible, augment it. (The same sigmoid curve trajectory and renewal sequence would apply to an organization's culture, strategy, or operating model, according to Handy.)

Apple, which has avoided the pitfalls in the S-curve, is clearly an outlier. With the iPad as well as much of the rest of its "i" line, the computer maker has done a remarkably good job of refreshing its products before its competitors supplant them (although competition in the smartphone sector is so feverish now that the S-curve seems to be cycling through at an unparalleled pace and even Apple is struggling to keep up).

More typical are the many companies that have fallen victim to the sigmoid curve. A classic example is the U.S. television manufacturing industry, dominated since the advent of TV networks in the 1940s by RCA, Magnavox, Zenith, GE, and others. As televisions grew from small screens to large color boxes, the vacuum tubes that powered them increased in size, complexity, and development costs. Profit margins from replacement sales of tubes were enormous, and these companies became addicted to the earnings stream. So much so that even when their research divisions developed transistor-based, solid-state semiconductors for next-generation TVs—as occurred at RCA, one of the giants in electronics R&D at that time—the business side of the organization refused to design consumer items based on this technology, fearful that it would cannibalize sales of existing products.

By the 1980s, Japanese electronics companies like Sony, Sharp, and Panasonic flooded the American market with solid-state televisions, radios, microwaves, and any number of other feature-laden products, effectively riding the wave of a new sigmoid curve while the American TV makers still held tight to one that was forty years old. The last U.S.-made television was built by Zenith in 1995. By then, all of Zenith's former American rivals were either out of business or out of the sector. The same sigmoid curve lapses plagued other once dominant U.S. business lines—IBM PCs, Blockbuster video stores, and, certainly, Detroit autos made by GM, Ford, and Chrysler, caught flat-footed by the arrival of Honda and its Japanese competitors.

Handy has a favorite anecdote to describe the paradox that makes the sigmoid curve so difficult to navigate for most companies. He talks about trying to find his way to the Wicklow Mountains outside Dublin, an area of unmarked roads and native beauty. Handy asked a passerby for directions.

"Sure, it's easy," the local replied, "just keep going the way you are, straight ahead, and after a while you will cross a small bridge with Davy's Bar on the far side. You can't miss it!"

Handy said that he understood—just head straight to Davy's Bar.

"That's right. Well, half a mile before you get there, turn to your right up the hill."

In Handy's words: "His directions seemed so logical that I thanked him and drove off. By the time I realized that the logic made no sense he had disappeared. As I made my way down to Davy's Bar, wondering which of the roads to the right to take, I reflected that he had just given me a vivid example of paradox, perhaps even the paradox of our times: by the time you know where you ought to go, it's too late to go there, or, more dramatically, if you keep on going the way you are, you will miss the road to the future."

As detailed in chapter 3, Honda understands well the prevalence of paradox in the business environment. The automaker's culture is designed around the concept of continually weighing opposing ideas to determine which one to embrace and to reject long-held beliefs when they are no longer valid. *Waigaya* sessions are meant to drive people away from their comfort zones and to challenge the value of conventional ways of doing things. They are aimed at viewing the many facets of Honda—cars, manufacturing processes, mobility, the nature of assembly work, and anything else that affects the company's performance—from alternative perspectives, to at least temporarily take the side of the unorthodox against the status quo.

But beyond the questions raised by Honda employees about the usefulness of existing systems and the virtue of new proposals, the automaker has adopted an unusual organizational model to outmaneuver the paradox of the sigmoid curve and to anticipate the imminence of the downward slope. In a restructuring rare among companies of any size, in 1960 Honda spun off its research and design team into a separate entity, Honda R&D, with its own distinct agenda, budget, and leadership. As mentioned in chapter 2, this gutsy move, conceived by Soichiro's business partner, Takeo Fujisawa, was intended to separate research from short-term financial goals; or expressed differently, to remove the fear of risk that paralyzes companies on the sigmoid curve between Point A and Point B.

As Fujisawa designed it, Honda R&D could choose everything germane to the company to explore and advance. In Honda's current lexicon that translates into experimenting with concepts and features that further mobility, a term that encompasses a broad spectrum of products including robots, planes, cars, motorcycles, lawn mowers, snowblowers, and tillers. Some of the research is essentially applied R&D; for example, the group's engineers play a primary role in new car and motorcycle designs. But other R&D efforts are much more basic, with fewer obvious immediate applications—such as the study of the kinesics of cockroaches and bees to better understand the nature of movement.

Honda's emphasis on R&D is a distinctive characteristic of the company, a competitive edge in Soichiro's view that firmly alters the dynamics of how Honda interacts with potential customers. "We do not make something because the demand, the market, is there," he said. "With our technology we can create demand. We can create the market."

There are upward of two dozen Honda R&D labs in five regions around the globe—North America, South America, Europe, Asia, and China. And beyond those, there are separate Honda Research Institutes in Japan, the United States, and Europe, which provide venture capital, equipment, scientists, and facilities for local research endeavors involving long-term projects, such as nanomaterials and artificial intelligence.

Each Honda R&D site operates independently within the formal R&D structure, enjoying levels of local autonomy and decision-making authority that large corporations never confer on their R&D functions. In fact, in most companies, R&D is strictly tied to corporate objectives. If the company is investing heavily in gaining blue widget market share, R&D's focus must be to advance the blue widget line.

Honda believes that approach wastes the imagination of research engineers, who given the latitude to think independently will produce more useful and creative ideas than if their work is dictated from a centralized bureaucracy at the top. Moreover, Honda's global localization strategy is based upon allowing regional preferences, biases, and customs to influence the agenda of Honda's teams—whether manufacturing, design, sales, or R&D. In Honda's view, management from afar would be at a loss to supervise these activities.

"Honda operates as a series of businesses around the world, not as one business with many little dependents," said Michael Robinet, managing director of auto industry consultants IHS Automotive. "Giving R&D substantial independence within that structure is a gamble that most companies wouldn't take. What if you don't get the product features or designs that you need when you need them since R&D is essentially free floating? So far it's paid off for Honda, though."

Scanning R&D's track record, it's hard to argue with that. The unit has consistently proven itself capable of generating practical innovation that has kept Honda a step or more ahead of its rivals. The 1973 CVCC engine, which set the pace in the auto industry for clean air standards, the 1991 VTEC motor with its automated cylinder intake adjustments, and more recently the world's first hybrid and fuel-cell cars have crystallized Honda's reputation for generating fresh and timely automotive concepts that in most cases were believed to still be years away. Perhaps not as well known, in 1990 Honda R&D introduced the first front-passenger airbag that deploys upward rather than at the passenger, reducing the potential for injury, and later in the decade the unit released a Collision Mitigation Brake System (CMBS) that alerts drivers to the risk of an accident. Moreover, Honda would have been unable to speedily manufacture its first car in 1963, responding to the Japanese Ministry of International Trade and Industry's threat to bar the company from making automobiles, had R&D not already prepared vehicle prototypes unprompted.

And beyond cars, a wealth of other equally inspired ideas is in progress; among them, the ASIMO robot, the HondaJet, and a technique to make cellulosic ethanol from rice straw. Globally, a Honda R&D team in Europe recently introduced the first commercially available robotic lawn mower that lets you stay indoors watching football on the telly while a machine the size of a canister vacuum cleaner cuts your grass. Meanwhile, China's R&D crew is readying twelve new vehicles by 2015, almost half of them tailored specifically for the Chinese market. Included in this group is the oddly styled but eye-catching dragon-faced Crider, a midsize sedan at a relatively low price built for the post-Mao generation—or, in Honda's self-referential, culture-bending nod to the preoccupation with Western ideals and fads among younger Chinese, for "those who were born in the 1980s, known for the energetic pursuit of their dreams."

Each year, Honda's autonomous R&D unit hatches literally thousands of inventions. In a 2012 report by the Patent Board, Honda was third in the number of patents granted for automobile and power-train engineering among 183 automotive and transportation companies. That year, Honda received 1,049 patents, while GM earned the top spot with 1,123 patents and Toyota came in second with 1,111 patents. Considering that Honda's revenue is about one third of Toyota's and half of GM's, the company's patent production compared with its much larger rivals' is extraordinarily high. Further, those numbers comprise automobile patents only. Taking R& D's portfolio as a whole, Honda outpaces its auto industry competitors by as much as ten to one, according to patent experts.

Still, Honda R&D's value is hardly demonstrated solely by a patent horse race. Far more important and distinctive is Honda's nimble blending of R&D into the automobile development process, a degree of company-wide cross-pollination that Honda alone among car companies has been able to master. Typically, during a model update or new launch in the auto sector, engineers—researchers and designers—are relatively isolated from manufacturing and sales. Each manages their tasks separately and then hands off project responsibilities to the next department as they conclude their work. Although it is obvious that these silos impede communication, efficiency, and innovation, anxious attempts by automakers to dismantle them have been met with resistance from teams who fear that a shared effort will dilute their importance to the company.

Honda's approach is sharply different: A multidisciplined team, comprising representatives from R&D, engineering, manufacturing, and sales, oversees each vehicle development project. Usually, an R&D executive is in charge of the group, primarily to ensure that the most novel ideas in the organization, sometimes years old and hidden deep in R&D's vaults, are considered for the new automobile. Moreover, this intradepartmental team remains intact during the entire launch program, often four years or so, working as a single entity on every phase of the project. This grants R&D a wall-to-wall role in the venture, including the opportunity to amend blueprints and introduce new features as late as the first test manufacturing runs—sometimes, even when the initial vehicles are being built. In Charles Handy's terms, R&D's participation throughout guarantees that new sigmoid curves are routinely layered over the development process well before the old ones have descended.

Quite at odds with the pass-the-baton scenario other automakers employ, this strategy creates a virtuous circle in which the expertise of Honda's research engineers enriches the manufacturing process, while the accumulated knowledge of factory leadership, assembly workers, and sales and marketing staffs has an impact on design. For every bauble that R&D proposes to add to a vehicle, manufacturing can offer its two cents about whether the supplier network is capable of producing the new component and at what cost, or about a factory improvement that would make the new feature easy to install, if it were altered a tiny bit; meanwhile, sales can speak to how customers will likely respond to the added function.

Aspects of Honda's three principles are skillfully combined in this approach: decision making based on disparate recommendations and data points; the team's continuous presence at the spot (in this case, the spot is each phase of the development process, from research to finished vehicle); and respect for individual contributions involving all aspects of the car's development from each member of the vehicle team.

Honda's unusual vehicle development model is a valuable asset, a manifestation of a dynamic *monozukuri*, in the words of a respected Japanese industrial expert. An unfamiliar term to most Westerners, *monozukuri* is an essential ingredient in the success of Japanese firms. It refers to the intangible organizational elements that, although not readily perceived by customers, ultimately enhance a product's market value. These hidden but nonetheless discernible factors include plant productivity, production costs, defect rates, product development lead times, design and manufacturing efficiency, and an understanding of consumer tastes. Japanese businesses believe that the quality of a company's *monozukuri* (which literally means the process for making things) ultimately determines the competitiveness of its products.

Honda's version of *monozukuri* sprang out of the automaker's indigent roots, said Hiroshi Ito, the specially appointed researcher at the University of Tokyo's Manufacturing Management Research Center. In his view, because Honda was a small, start-up enterprise at its origin with little money to support rapid growth, the company did not have the wherewithal or the sales volume to hire large numbers of employees and establish boundaries separating R&D engineers, product developers, and manufacturing specialists. "It was natural for (Honda) to adopt concurrent interdepartmental engineering or simultaneous engineering," Ito noted. "This helped keep all individuals concerned fully informed of the design data and created an uninterrupted flow from process to process."

Additionally, Ito pointed out that as a result of its more collaborative engineering and manufacturing environment, Honda has avoided the temptation to segregate and streamline factory processes by deconstructing them into smaller and smaller segments, as Toyota and Nissan have generally done. Instead, said Ito, "Honda keeps its (assembly) lines lean by concentrating as many tasks on one process as possible. This prevents quality from deteriorating."

By placing R&D in the forefront of its multifunctional development teams, Honda enjoys a continuous stream of innovation. A fitting example occurred in 2007, during the planning of the second-generation Acura MDX, when a now standard Honda feature, which other companies are still trying to emulate, bubbled up unexpectedly.

Updating a luxury brand vehicle like the MDX, a bestselling crossover SUV, involves a delicate series of financial and feature trade-offs. Customers who are willing to pay upward of $50,000 for a car expect to be seduced by technology and gadgets that they can, in turn, boast about; they want to be the first to say that they have keyless start-up or backup cameras. They may prize a responsive engine and a chassis that takes curves like it's riding on air, but they also want physical evidence of the car's value—something fresh and unforeseen that they can easily show off.

The MDX design team had already souped up the SUV with an intimidating motor that could go from 0 to 60 in six seconds and such new features as a remote-controlled lift gate, a power moon roof, and xenon headlights. The all-wheel-drive transmission and the sound system had also been completely overhauled. And the suspension contained a Honda original concept: a computer-controlled damper system that anticipated actual road conditions and body movements in the car to automatically adjust vehicle stability and comfort. Still, while fully loaded from a driving standpoint, the MDX lacked new features that were eye-popping or sexy; functionally, it was greatly improved but it was a bit short of sizzle.

Frank Paluch, a Honda R&D president and an MDX project leader, asked his research colleagues to pitch some as yet untried technologies that they had been working on to spruce up the vehicle. Among the ideas that were presented, an automatic humidity control system was particularly intriguing, although at first it appeared to be a bit low-tech.

The concept was intended to solve a common predicament for drivers, which Paluch described vividly for an audience of engineers in upper Michigan: "Imagine yourself here in Traverse City in the winter months. The snow you kick off your shoes inside your vehicle melts overnight in your heated garage, soaking the mats. The next morning you get in your car and drive out into the cold. As soon as the outside air hits the windshield, humidity fogs the inside of the glass. You hit the defrost button. Your eyes dry out, the noise is loud, and the heat is pointed to the windshield instead of keeping your feet warm."

In addressing this annoying problem, Honda R&D had two goals: improved driving satisfaction and also greater fuel efficiency by minimizing the drag on the power train imposed by always-on auto AC systems—the primitive solution provided in most cars to reduce humidity levels and fogging. Combining hardware and algorithms, the R&D team had devised a system that could detect temperature and humidity levels outside and inside of the car and automatically start to bleed warm or cold air to the windshield before condensation occurs. Or, to extend Paluch's example, the vehicle's mats would still be soaked, but the car would be warm and the glass clear. Moreover, this system turns off the compressor when the AC is not needed, potentially decreasing fuel consumption by as much as 4 percent.

"It spoke to a critical customer issue in a novel way," Paluch said. "However, upon first hearing about it, it seemed to all of us on the team to be an innovation too limited for the added expense of putting it in the car. So we rejected it."

Not satisfied with that answer, Honda's researchers installed the humidity control system into a previous-generation MDX to demonstrate the concept. The researchers poured water over the floor of the vehicle, placed it in a humidity chamber overnight, and made plans to meet the MDX development team at five A.M. the next morning. Seven MDX members showed up, piled into the vehicle, and drove off.

The SUV's windshield fogged up instantly; then the researchers turned on the climate system. Within seconds, the glass had cleared, while the temperature and humidity in the inside of the car remained at comfortable levels. This exercise was repeated the next day in an MDX without the humidity control equipment. That car was undrivable, no matter how long the defroster remained on.

"We were sold," said Paluch. "We knew that it could cost a little bit more to put in and perhaps we knew we would take a little hit on profit margin, but this was a winning idea. It gave the customer a better experience and better gas mileage; that ultimately drives satisfaction and loyalty. Manufacturing and sales liked it as much as R&D; it addressed all of our interests. It wasn't a new gadget, but it solved a bothersome issue for drivers with the best possible solution. That's just as good."

Beyond innovation, Honda's cross-functional design and development system provides cost savings and efficiency in what is known as the new product life cycle, the central aspect of industrial production that has resisted attempts in most companies to simplify and gain control over. Typically, the new product life cycle—comprising conceptual and preliminary design, preproduction tests, full-scale manufacturing, and eventually customer sales—is a wasteful, skewed undertaking. Normally, about 80 percent of total product life cycle costs are baked in by design decisions made in the first 20 percent of the effort—that is, during the preliminary design phase with no participation from applied engineering, manufacturing, sales, or marketing.

After that stage, the price of altering the design or the manufacturing plan or fixing flaws in the finished product increases enormously. Whether it involves swapping out technology and features, retraining assembly line workers, expediting shipments of materials and parts changed in the last minute, or covering warranty repairs and recalls, the amount of money that potentially can be lost on the back 80 percent of a development project (when R&D is nowhere to be seen) could sink any hopes for product profitability. And that's without considering the so-called soft consequences: specifically, sluggish sales for unreliable products with poor word of mouth, which in turn results in damage to the manufacturer's reputation. By breaking down the barriers in the product life cycle—that is, by giving a single, multidepartmental team the all-inclusive task of designing, building, and selling every new and upgraded vehicle—Honda escapes the expense, inefficiency, and missteps that plague other manufacturers.

I recently observed the tangible benefits of Honda's development model in the Lincoln plant. After a four-year effort, the latest iteration of the Acura MDX was finally moving down the assembly line in its last trial run when a team in one of the zones held up the operation to point out a serious problem. To install the center console, which controls heating, air-conditioning, radio, GPS, and other equipment, the blueprint called for a robotic lift to lower it through the windshield and onto the dashboard. Then, assemblers were supposed to smoothly slide the console into place before attaching it with screws.

But the holes in the console and dashboard only lined up after Honda workers got on their knees in the chassis and shoved the parts together. "There's a lot of variance in a manufactured part, more than people know," said Bob Schwyn, the Lincoln plant manager supervising the MDX line. "The design spec has to guess at the right manufacturing variance or you will have problems. That's a crapshoot. Sometimes it works, other times—like in this case—it doesn't."

And typically when there is a small discrepancy in a factory during an initial run, one of two things happens: One, the part is installed with a slight gap because either assembly line workers or supervisors deem the issue to be too minimal to delay production plans; repairs can come later when customers complain. Or two, the line is halted and the car is sent back to the engineers to address the problem either with suppliers or internally before the project resumes.

At Lincoln, though, there was a third option. The MDX development team, including R&D, was on the ground, overseeing the building of the first vehicles. As soon as the line stopped, the entire crew funneled into the assembly zone to diagnose and fix the problem. Within an hour a repair was agreed upon: widen the holes in the console manually for the existing batch of parts and give the supplier these new specifications for future deliveries. It was a simple setback with a relatively simple solution, but the time and cost saved in resolving it instantly as opposed to either not addressing it at all or sending the vehicle on a detour back into the development process enabled Honda to take immediate advantage of the growing anticipation and demand for the new MDX.

"The design and development process is difficult to decipher for many auto companies, so there are only limited cases where it can be viewed as a competitive edge," said John Casesa, the auto industry expert and senior managing director at Guggenheim Partners. "Honda has a smart approach that mostly differs from others in the industry. And its success is evidenced in part by its warranty record."

Which is by far the best in the industry. In 2012, Honda's annual warranty cost per vehicle hit a multidecade low of $182, and stacked against sales, Honda's warranty outlays were a minuscule 1.3 percent. By comparison, Toyota's warranty-to-sales figure was about 2 percent, Volkswagen's was 3.5 percent, and Ford came closest to Honda with 1.7 percent, according to *Warranty Week*.

Other factors besides Honda's comprehensive development team strategy also account for the automaker's minimal warranty costs. For one thing, Honda has steadily produced dependable vehicles that are relatively free of flaws by placing quality experts in factory manufacturing zones and putting its products through a grueling test drive before they are released for distribution. But Honda's warranty claims would not be nearly as low if the back end of the automaker's new product development cycle were disconnected from the initial stages.

And in one of the more ambitious and imaginative steps to further diminish the potentially costly boundary between design and manufacturing in the new product life cycle, Honda R&D has created a breakthrough computerized tool that eliminates the need to build expensive and often useless vehicle prototypes before actual production.

Normally, when a car design is close to completion, an order is placed to manufacture about a dozen physical beta versions of the vehicle to at least get a basic sense of what it is going to look like in real life and whether the body parts adequately fit together. These first factory runs are assembled with what is known as soft tooling, which are essentially limited copies of the dies, stamping equipment, and other precise machining tools called for in the automobile blueprints. Invariably, vehicle chassis specifications will change based on irregularities found in these beta versions, so it is too risky and pricey to purchase or make final manufacturing gear—so-called hard tools—until the definitive final drawings are completed.

"Making ten or twenty prototypes of a car is hyperexpensive," said Erik Berkman, president of Honda R&D Americas. "And these cars have many characteristics that are not real, because they are made with manufacturing processes that are basically pretend. For example, the dies may be plastic, instead of metal. They'll cut well but not last very long. You may need more than one die or you may have to repair the one you have. That's not cheap, and even after spending money on the prototypes, the car's performance on the assembly line could be different because we were not working with real-world conditions."

Vehicle safety guidelines complicate this problem. For example, U.S. National Highway Traffic Safety Administration rules require that automobile bumpers must protect the car from damage to headlamps, the fuel system, and other functional components in a crash that occurs when the vehicle is going 2.5 miles an hour or less. Bumpers made during the prototype phase are similar to a single piece of fiberglass as opposed to a double-sided mold held together by thick pressurized polypropylene used during actual production. As a result, the test bumper may be too thin to damage the headlight during a collision, while the thicker bumper that will be on the car might crack right through it.

"So we would often lead ourselves down a rosy path of yeah, that two-and-a-half-mile-an-hour bumper test was fine, no problem," said Berkman. "And then we get to hard tooling and T minus six months from production, and we've got real good bumpers now, and we do a safety test and we go, 'Crap, we're breaking the headlight.'"

The excess costs of making prototypes or redesigning problematic vehicle specs that slipped through in the prototype stage and the potential production delays inherent in this two-step process were disconcerting, but accepted by automakers as the norm. However, a few years ago, some engineers at Honda proposed creating computer-aided design tools to analyze automobile material properties, structural geometry, stress points, and the way the chassis responds to a variety of conditions to produce a near-perfect final blueprint that would let the automaker skip directly from design to hard tooling in the factory, without having to create a physical beta version of the vehicle. At first, the idea was rejected. Trusting a computer to unearth every possible specification deficiency and automobile design flaw without physical tests on prototypes to verify the machine's output seemed like a gamble too perilous to shoulder, despite the enormous savings and efficiency gains if it worked.

"It just wasn't the way things were done; we didn't like soft tooling, but going straight to manufacturing without a life raft, now that's revolutionary," Berkman noted. "But the new-school people, the young engineers, they said, 'You old guys are idiots. Virtual is the way forward. If we don't do it some other company will take advantage of our hesitance. Trust us; we know what we are doing.' And they actually do know what they're doing."

Indeed, it took a couple of years and plenty of software coding to prove their point, but the computer-aided design supporters at Honda finally convinced enough of their colleagues that it is worth testing out. The company's no-prototype development system, a radical tool for vehicle development that Berkman and the other leaders at Honda R&D have now enthusiastically endorsed, is in the midst of its maiden voyage on the redesigned 2015 Acura TLX luxury sedan. It blurs the distinction between research and manufacturing more than ever before.

"So far, so good," Berkman said. "We have real confidence in the technology and I think we'll be doing away with prototypes on all cars as we proceed down the road, at least here in the U.S."

That would be a change in automobile development that no one could have imagined just a few years ago. And it goes a long way toward proving Charles Handy's point that the fittest companies have the foresight to make sure that the path to Davy's Bar is clearly marked.

8

AN UNCOMMON SUPPLY CHAIN

The first time the American auto supplier's VP saw this trick, he was taken aback. Now, in his dealings with Honda, he had seen it often enough that it lost its shock value. But it still was amusingly odd.

The session was an annual cost-down negotiation, one of many that Mark VanDeVelde, Honda purchasing division manager in Lincoln, would attend. In these meetings with each of the largest vendors in his division, VanDeVelde and his team revisited the supplier's previous-year agreement to see if it had to be amended, hoping to get better terms for Honda for the coming twelve months. The supplier in this incident (we'll call the company AAA because Honda executives were concerned that the anecdote revealed sensitive information about its relations with the vendor) had signed an agreement that was strikingly favorable to the automaker in the prior year. But AAA did it to gain a more secure foothold with Honda and to be in line for more orders involving additional cars in the future. And although the profit margins were skimpy, AAA nonetheless earned some money on the deal.

The atmosphere was different this year. AAA's VP had taken heat from his boss for being too lenient with Honda; so he was clearly less indulgent this time around. The primary sticking point was the volatility of raw materials prices; in particular, petrochemical costs were unpredictable from one week to the next, making contracts linked to fixed feedstock prices extremely dangerous for suppliers like AAA.

"We went through weeks of negotiations and it was much more testy than ever before," said VanDeVelde. "They were determined to get some relief from raw materials fluctuation."

But automakers, like most industrial companies, are hesitant to take on the risk of unstable materials prices. Some supplier agreements are adjustable monthly or quarterly based on a commodities price index. However, in most cases, car companies prefer to be insulated from the problem and ask their vendors to protect themselves by hedging against rising materials costs.

"That option wasn't going to work in this case," said VanDeVelde. "Asking this supplier to continue to absorb raw material prices could severely harm them over the long term since raw material cost can represent a significant portion of the finished product. Although it may be painful for us to take on some of that cost, we decided we had to walk through that door at some point. We want to secure the best possible terms, but our aim is also to make sure our suppliers are healthy and productive—not to harm them."

So VanDeVelde offered AAA's VP a way to resolve the impasse. Honda, he said, was willing to share some of the possible losses if the cost of materials rose. But in exchange, Honda expected AAA to improve its factory efficiency by a slightly higher degree in the first year of the agreement and to pass that on in annual cost savings to Honda. The VP nodded his head, actually trying to be friendly yet noncommittal, but he was too late. VanDeVelde had quickly written the terms on the whiteboard in the room—and so the deal was done.

In Honda's rather eccentric practices, once terms are written on the whiteboard, no more discussion was needed.

"I took some heat for it because I had to give away more on raw material than the prior year," VanDeVelde said, recalling the way his colleagues responded. "However, we also received a commitment to improve efficiency and productivity from the supplier. The result was a stronger supplier partner for Honda. It was the right way to end these negotiations. It showed mutual trust."

That phrase isn't heard often in negotiations between automakers and suppliers. Indeed, Honda's whiteboard agreements and virtually every other out-of-the-ordinary aspect of its interaction with suppliers have become legendary in the auto industry. While U.S. auto companies have spent the past many decades forging contentious and cynical relationships with their vendors, pitting their interests against their suppliers', Honda (and to some degree the other Japanese car manufacturers) has fashioned transparent partnerships with these companies. Although sometimes these arrangements are a bit too cozy for the parts makers themselves, Honda is motivated by a single unorthodox goal—that its suppliers become carbon copies of Honda, with the same ideals, methods, and objectives.

Honda's parts community is an essential hub in its localization strategy. In order to build self-contained, autonomous operations in lucrative markets around the world, Honda requires a durable group of reliable, disciplined, and creative suppliers to support its factories. This manufacturing cluster, replicated globally in every Honda region, is both symbiotic and independent. The companies in it feed off Honda's success—indeed, many of them would not exist without it—while drawing upon the automaker's distinctive operating principles to shape their own identity, separate from Honda's. Just as Honda wants its employees to be simultaneously dedicated to the Honda Way and actively subverting tradition, so it does with its suppliers.

By contrast, U.S. automakers have viewed parts companies as adversaries. Until very recently, virtually all contracts out of Detroit were primarily awarded to the lowest bidder, relegating quality and manufacturing skills to secondary considerations. Whether the supplier was lean or bloated, cared about quality or cut corners shamelessly didn't matter, as long as the company delivered the parts at the bargain basement price agreed upon. In fact, after a contract was signed, it wasn't unusual to never see the automaker's purchasing agent again, until the agreement was up for renewal. And there was no reward for above-par performance, but rather only for promises of bargain basement prices; each new parts order was bid out again, without preferential treatment for companies already in the existing supplier community.

Since their collapse in 2008, the revived Detroit 3 have put better supplier relations on the top of their to-do list. But it's extremely hard to wipe away the mistrust that separates U.S. automakers and parts companies, particularly when GM, Ford, and Chrysler showed no interest in throwing their suppliers a lifeline during the automakers' fiscal crises. They were clearly focused solely on their own survival.

As a result, suppliers I spoke to said they are pleased that the American carmakers are trying to improve their relationships with parts companies, but until the auto manufacturers make the quality demands and forge the open partnerships that Honda does, it is hard to take this change seriously.

An Ohio-based brake manufacturer described his company's interactions with Honda and General Motors as "the difference between dealing with your perfectionist friend or your son who has gone away to college. If you send Honda one defective rotor or a shipment missing a single brake pad, they will call you immediately and tell you that they view the entire delivery as unacceptable. 'Tell me how you are going to do better in the future.'

"GM won't even call you; it's too much work for them to care that much."

Comical, perhaps, but for a manufacturer this distinction has grave consequences. As globalization took hold in the past few decades, multinationals expanded their factory operations into parts of the world that were traditionally their export markets. Japanese companies moved into North America, Europe, and throughout Asia; American and European firms into Eastern Europe, China, and Vietnam. And many other similar ventures.

To profitably do business in such far-flung and complex factory footprints, constellations of dependable and loyal local suppliers are needed to meet sensitive just-in-time and global logistics schedules. Companies for which supplier antagonism has been a comfort zone or that simply have never thought it necessary to learn how to develop a superior supplier base are at a distinct disadvantage in this manufacturing environment.

"For a long time, the big automakers could make the rules for how to manage suppliers and the suppliers had no choice but to go along with them," said John Henke, president of supplier-relations consultants Planning Perspectives Inc. "It may not have been the most desirable situation, but it was profitable enough. Now the field has shifted: success in global business is shared, not hoarded."

If the supplier relationship is the most important that a manufacturer will have, then Honda's approach to this partnership would best be called tough love. Honda is unyielding in the demands that it places on its suppliers because these companies are not ancillary actors but rather central figures in Honda's business model. Although Honda makes a greater array of its own parts—from transmissions, dashboards, and engines to dies and robotic jigs—than any automaker, it also relies more than other companies on its supplier network to mirror the flagship in delivering cost control, quality, and innovation.

Honda's uniquely structured bond with its parts manufacturers is, by all accounts, a crucial element in its success. It should serve as a model for other multinationals, although few have followed Honda's lead. For most companies, Honda's supplier strategy is too arduous and expensive, both in resources and time, to execute.

But the returns, as Honda has learned, can be enormous. Considering that parts purchases account for nearly 75 percent of the cost of a vehicle, the skills, imagination, and efficiency of Honda's suppliers clearly play an outsized role in the company's industry-leading profit margins. Indeed, manufacturing costs for some of Honda's bestselling vehicles, including Accord and Civic, routinely dip as much as 25 percent during the four-year model cycle, a direct outcome of supplier innovation. In the past, when public verbal attacks on suppliers were not considered gauche in the auto industry, other carmakers routinely complained that their trend lines went in the opposite direction. Moreover, by working as a team, Honda and its suppliers have trimmed the new car launch time from finished design to production to between twelve and eighteen months, compared with the industry standard of two to three years.

"Having a strong relationship with your suppliers actually has good, hard, solid business results," said Thomas Choi, professor of supply chain management at the W. P. Carey School of Business at Arizona State University.

Honda's supplier strategy began somewhat by accident, a by-product of the way Honda's history differs from that of its older rivals. The Detroit 3 were early-twentieth-century companies, the pioneers of the auto industry to whom suppliers were merely other businesses that sprouted up around the primary activity of making cars. And the large Japanese automakers, founded in the 1930s, tended to buy the loyalty of their suppliers by placing them in *keiretsu*, interlocking business grids that were chiefly owned by the car companies. Although Japanese *keiretsu* are out of favor now, dismissed as crony capitalism and blamed in part for Japan's decades of economic stagnation, Toyota maintains its hold on its supplier lattice. The Japanese company still owns stakes in more than two hundred of its primary parts suppliers and seventy of its equipment manufacturers. Much of Nissan's *keiretsu* was dismantled in the late 1990s when French carmaker Renault took a big stake in Nissan, and Renault CEO Carlos Ghosn became the Japanese company's top executive.

Debuting its first car in the 1960s, Honda never had the innate attention from auto parts companies that the Detroit 3 enjoyed or the financial leverage over suppliers that Toyota wielded. As a result, Honda had to build its supplier base from scratch, in Japan and then in the United States, Europe, China, and wherever else it pitched its factories. But that was a difficult task because in Honda's earliest meager years the suppliers themselves—especially those that had substantial orders from the established automakers—were wary about committing to a company whose survival was uncertain.

Faced with this reluctance, Honda could choose suppliers from two groups: makers of motorcycle parts that were already working with Honda but would have to be taught how to make automobile components; and the smallest automobile parts companies, which would need to be persuaded to invest in new production capabilities in exchange for a promise of more business in the future. As Honda executives saw it, in reality this was only one option; either way, suppliers would require significant training and technological support to reach the standards of quality and customer satisfaction that Soichiro Honda and his successors demanded.

Consequently, Honda decided to create a supplier network made up of companies that were willing to be molded in Honda's image, regardless of their technical expertise. "Simply, they had to have the right attitude," said Rick Mayo, a Honda executive who worked on the supplier development effort in the United States.

Which meant, among other things, wrote Susan Helper, former economics professor at Case Western Reserve University, and John Paul MacDuffie, associate professor of management at the Wharton School, in a seminal 1997 paper about Honda's supplier base called "Creating Lean Suppliers," a willingness to 1) take risks, consistent with the "racing spirit" that Soichiro Honda worked hard to maintain in Honda's culture; 2) invest in new technologies in advance of competitors; and 3) invest in organizational and human resource capabilities—that is, advanced engineering and production control staff, sophisticated management systems, and worker training.

In return, Honda offered a lifetime relationship, unless the supplier failed to meet certain operational and performance criteria that Honda would, in fact, help the supplier achieve. And Honda promised that existing suppliers would be given the first claims on new business before any other companies are brought inside the circle.

"As we saw it, it was a mission, not a job," said Mayo.

That initial supplier network foray resulted in many improbable partnerships. Parts makers whose tactical missteps had led them to the brink of bankruptcy suddenly had the prospect of working for an automaker, albeit a fledgling one—a chance that seemed out of reach as long as the Detroit clique dominated the industry. But first they had to satisfy a rather amorphous set of conditions that Honda appeared to be making up as it went along. They had to prove that their corporate personality fit the somewhat odd definition of a supplier in a new era of automobile manufacturing that Honda claimed to represent. To be sure, Honda managers were, in fact, relying on their intuition and their firsthand observations; yet this period of trial and error proved valuable, because it set the tone and drew a road map for the way Honda still chooses suppliers to this day.

One unlikely company that made the grade when Honda was building its supply chain in the United States was Progressive Industries in Toledo, Ohio. Honda learned about Progressive—and vice versa—strangely enough through an ad that the automaker took out in a trade journal in 1986, looking for stamping companies to cut body parts for its just opened Marysville plant. More than one hundred companies replied to Honda. Progressive was the smallest, a $1 million, barely profitable family business with a 1,600-square-foot factory located in the middle of a bean field.

At one time, Progressive had contracts with the auto industry, but by this point the company was doing run-of-the-mill stamping jobs for local industries, specializing in keeping costs and wages down and squeezing the most it could out of old machines. Honda sent Progressive and the other applicants a questionnaire asking about the company's background, equipment, goals, and principles. Not long after, a team of Honda purchasing specialists showed up at Progressive's factory.

Progressive's history and size were unimpressive; its client list was mediocre—and, indeed, the Detroit 3 had consistently rebuffed Progressive's sales calls because of the insignificance of its résumé. But Honda was attracted by something unusual in Progressive's application: although consigned to routine jobs, Progressive unexpectedly had an acute interest in alternative types of equipment and cutting-edge techniques. For one thing, Progressive used Japanese dies, which were engineered from softer metals than U.S. stamping tools; as a result, they were less expensive but required frequent maintenance. Honda was impressed that Progressive had the deep knowledge of dies in the organization to keep this equipment operating; most stampers lacked those skills.

In addition, Progressive had created its own die-sensoring gauges to monitor whether the stamping equipment was operating within certain benchmarks. Typically, stampers do this by ear and sight—and the calibrations are more often than not less than perfect. Seeing this, Honda's purchasing team was pleased that although Progressive was mired in a relatively mundane commodity business, the company's leadership sustained a creative, curious, and motivated workforce and could boast about actual technical advances. And Honda's enthusiasm grew even more upon hearing from Progressive's young CEO, Ruston Simon, who had just taken over the business from his father, that the company had laid off only one worker in its forty-year-history and that employees received quarterly profit sharing based on performance targets and a bonus at year's end.

Progressive got the contract, one of seven to win orders from Honda out of the original one hundred applicants. "They liked our quality, management, and modern equipment, but, most of all, I think they were impressed with our flexibility and our desire to be a first-class supplier," said Simon.

Three years later, Honda offered to train Progressive in welding and assembly of stamped parts, something that Progressive had never attempted. "They started us off on small, simple tasks and we were able to show good results early," Simon explained. "We needed to earn our spurs with them and we were given more leeway at first than the bigger guys."

On the wings of its relationship with Honda, Progressive signed deals with other major automakers as well. Honda encourages suppliers to have a diverse customer portfolio because overdependence on a single contract could put a company's long-term stability in jeopardy and make managers risk averse, tempering their appetite for investing in equipment, workers, and improvements. "Customer makeup is one of many things we look at now," said Tom Lake, division manager of Honda's North American Purchasing unit.

By 1990, Progressive's annual sales had grown about 700 percent in seven years, to more than $7 million. Employment had more than tripled to seventy, and the original factory was expanded to forty-three thousand square feet. Toward the end of the decade, Midway Products, a large automobile industry supplier in Monroe, Michigan, acquired Progressive from Simon for nearly $20 million—and expanded the company's operations in Ohio substantially.

Honda doesn't have to run trade journal ads anymore to find parts makers and the company doesn't have to convince suppliers these days of its viability. But the traits that most attracted Honda to Progressive—a family business with an entrepreneurial streak—and the other aspects of Honda's culture that the automaker looked for in a supplier back then continue to influence Honda's choice of suppliers today. Consequently, visiting Honda suppliers is a monotonous experience; at one after another you hear the same guiding principles. They all claim to value employee ideas, work-life balance, continuous improvement, and Japanese-inspired cooperation inside the company and with its external partners.

With this set of criteria, since the 1980s Honda has assiduously pieced together a network of suppliers in the United States, now comprising some six hundred companies in thirty-four states, and $20 billion in sales—one fifth of Honda's global revenue. In Alabama alone, since the Lincoln plant opened a little more than a decade ago, more than one hundred new Honda suppliers or new supplier relationships have sprung up. And Honda has established similarly large groups of suppliers in all of its key regions around the world, each reporting to local Honda management.

After Honda purchasing executives choose a new parts company—often very early in the initial discussions about an upcoming model or vehicle upgrade, perhaps as long as three years before the actual launch—the automaker sends in a multispecialist team to refashion the supplier's operations to fit Honda's requirements. At this juncture, Honda knows little about the supplier's day-to-day operations and quite a bit about its personality and ideals. In Honda's view, if its culture is right, any company can become a first-class manufacturer.

The same Honda departments participate in this rigorous and frequently (for the supplier) unmooring campaign as those in the new vehicle model development team—that is, R&D, engineering, manufacturing, and, sometime, sales. In essence, these Honda staffers unroll their sleeping bags at the supplier's factory and begin a three-month, six-month, nine-month, even a yearlong boot camp. During this time—and, in fact, throughout the period that the supplier works with Honda—the automaker demands total access to information about the vendor's technology and free rein to move around the factory.

Each supplier differs in its shortcomings, but typically during the reeducation process Honda asks the supplier's manufacturing workers—from supervisors to graveyard shift clock punchers—to reexamine their assembly line routines and come up with fresh, untried methods and techniques. In turn, these alternatives could be hashed over during *waigaya* and assessed in real-time experiments on the plant floor to ultimately be implemented or rejected.

Waste is also tackled at this stage. Few supplier plants have eliminated *muda* (literally idleness, uselessness, and superfluity in Japanese) and achieved the smooth production flow of Honda and Toyota. *Muda* comes in many forms. It could be three different parts placed in the same bin on the factory floor, making it difficult for workers to immediately find the component they need. Or it may be excessive inventory or inordinate distances between one assembly zone and another. Or even leftover sandwiches and sodas in the work area, obscuring important paperwork. (In Honda factories, no food is permitted on the assembly line.)

Any of these issues can, in fact, indicate larger problems with the parts maker's own suppliers or its logistics and purchasing systems as well as possible flaws in other parts of the assembly line. Until these concerns are resolved—and the supplier's systems and processes resemble the simple fluidity of those in a Honda plant—the go-ahead to produce Honda components will not be given. Once the supplier does get the green light, a manufacturing plan is drawn up for the production test run, including defined benchmarks for materials, tolerances, and defects.

After the initial intensive stages of the supplier improvement program, Honda teams will make themselves scarcer; the number of visits will drop off to at least two times a week as opposed to every day. But that schedule, including spontaneous drop-ins, will be in force throughout the agreement between the two companies.

On the business side, Honda's supplier contract contains specific cost targets, which will decrease each year of the pact, and quality goals, which will increase. Some agreements call for reevaluating these objectives annually, although Honda is resistant to making many substantive changes in them, in large part because the automaker believes that it has a built-in mechanism to ensure that the initial targets are appropriate: namely, the supplier arrangement gives Honda the right to examine the vendor's financial records at any time. This requirement, a bitter pill for some suppliers who are used to the hands-off attitude of other auto manufacturers, provides full transparency of the supplier's books and an excellent tool—at least in Honda's view—for establishing attainable cost goals.

"Honda purchasing knows what suppliers pay for raw materials, how much they pay their workers, what their profits are," said Dave Nelson, a former senior vice president of purchasing at American Honda Motor Co. and coauthor of *Powered by Honda*. "The Honda buyers often know more accurately what the supplier's parts costs are than the suppliers do."

Generally, if a supplier complains that the component price was set too low, Honda will send engineers to the factory to look for flaws in the manufacturing process that may be affecting costs. If the engineers fail to find or fix the problem, Honda will be more willing to change the terms.

"Honda's constant presence kind of feels like Big Brother looking over your shoulder sometimes," said the plant manager at a Honda parts supplier in northern Alabama. "And it can be annoying the way they are always right until they're wrong. But I have to admit even when I am most critical of Honda that we are improving as a manufacturer because of the attention and the demands. That helps sell other business."

Higher costs are not always the result of plant deficiencies. And rather than place blame on suppliers for factors that may be out of their control—an attitude that the Detroit 3 maintained for so long, to their detriment—Honda has conducted an analysis of potential supplier expenses that are divorced from the factory and has identified hundreds of prospective ways to minimize them. Where possible, Honda helps the supplier implement these savings. A good example is worker compensation. According to recent industry studies, reducing labor expenses by even 5 percent could be the difference between profit and loss for a low-margin automobile component.

However, if Honda and its suppliers competed for the same relatively small group of workers, wage levels would escalate, adding additional expenses to a vehicle part—and making profitability that much more challenging. Consequently, Honda assists parts companies in finding factory locations sufficiently far from the automaker's plant, though still in the regional neighborhood, to tap a distinct labor pool with suitably low wages to produce Honda parts economically. (It's worth noting, though, that while keeping labor costs in check is important to Honda and its suppliers, their average employee compensation—benefits and wages—is above $50 an hour, about the same as other manufacturing workers anywhere in the United States. Many Honda North American workers earn $60,000 or more per year, a high salary in relatively low-cost regions.)

Honda's approach is a far cry, for example, from that of Mercedes-Benz in Vance, Alabama. By and large the German company's suppliers are clustered within a few miles of the Mercedes factory, many of them in industrial parks built to serve the plant. Wages and benefits costs in that region are about 10 percent higher for semiskilled workers, according to Alabama economists.

"It's a really interesting and unusual model: when Honda came to Alabama they not only looked out for themselves but also for their potential suppliers," said John Shrout, plant manager at TS Tech in Boaz, Alabama, which makes seats for the Lincoln factory. "So we're close enough—within that one- to two-hour range where Honda is comfortable—but far enough that we can pay a bit less and make money."

TS Tech is a Japanese company (TS stands for Tokyo Seat) with four factories in the United States. It's a paradigmatic Honda supplier, a virtual replica of the automaker. Its managing philosophy is strewn with Honda-inspired terms: "pursuing our dreams through creating products and challenging infinite possibilities; bright working atmosphere; harmony and communication among people; push past the present boundaries to a higher level of comfort; company welcomed with joy"—and it goes on.

Like Honda, TS Tech has a flexible factory and can make Ridgeline or Odyssey seats on the same line using a sophisticated interchangeable platform. If a third car is added to the order, as occurred not long ago when the supplier was directed to make seats for the Accord, only a short retooling is needed. Based on Honda's daily work order, TS Tech stays about ten hours ahead of Honda's schedule, leaving plenty of time to truck the seats south to Lincoln before their intended vehicle hits the assembly line. What's more, the open office structure so evident at Honda is also a fixture at TS Tech; the company president and clerks have desks in the same bullpen.

And recently, when Honda appealed to its supplier base for a costly favor no other automaker would have the temerity or the affinity to ask of its parts companies, TS Tech was one of the few suppliers that acquiesced to Honda's request. It occurred during the dark period from 2008 to 2011, when the global recession decimated worldwide auto sales and subsequently the Japanese tsunami shuttered a critical Honda and Toyota supply chain pipeline, forcing both companies to lower their factory output. Although its plants were operating at less than three-quarters capacity, Honda hoped to adhere to its no-layoff policy, in place since Honda's founding except when a factory is closed completely. And Honda wanted its suppliers to do the same, explaining that the slowdown could be used for factory and manufacturing process improvements. More important, Honda argued, a full team of employees will be needed at a moment's notice to quickly ramp up production when customers begin to buy cars again. Preserve their jobs now and you'll have an energized workforce eager to return the company's unanticipated commitment with their own loyalty later, Honda said.

Most of Honda's suppliers could not afford to make this sacrifice. And while TS Tech saw the long-term wisdom in Honda's tactics, it might have lacked the fortitude to do as the automaker did had Honda's entreaties been less persistent. "We had a lot of conversations with Honda managers and they kept saying, 'Find a way to use this time to prepare for the upswing when we come out; strengthen your environment; strengthen your manufacturing; strengthen your workers,' " said Shrout. "It was a cold pool of water to jump into but we agreed.

"And soon after, we spent a few minutes with Boaz's mayor and told him, 'Look, I'm sure that you're worried about what's going to happen here. We're going to do everything we can to keep everybody at work. We're going to give them their forty hours, whether it's training, cleaning, painting, fixing up.' And he said, 'Man, you don't know what that means to a small community that relies on sales tax to keep the schools going.' Our workers live in this community and they respected us for this. My guess is that it helped us with Honda as well. It was worth it, but I can't say that we were profitable during that period."

After the supplier is online and the vehicle is in steady production, Honda's in-person appearances may be a bit less frequent, but the automaker is no less vigilant, or exacting, about detecting potential trouble. Each day Honda collects data about every supplier's performance: output, timing of shipments, defects, plant safety, and worker productivity, among many items. In addition, after supplier visits Honda employees are expected to report potential problems that they observed—generally, obvious infractions like idle equipment or workers not wearing goggles.

All of this information is translated into a monthly supplier report card. If a supplier fails in certain aspects of its operation and is unable to fix it within a short period of time, Honda will send a team to eliminate the deficiency. (In the supplier community, the white-uniformed Honda workers who unannounced suddenly speckle the assembly line when something is amiss are known as "snowflakes, bringing with them relief and anxiety," as one parts company executive put it.)

More often than not, though, a serious supplier problem will get the attention of Honda's early warning system, well before the monthly reports are issued. This computer-based monitor is sensitive to even slight changes in a vendor's performance that may foreshadow systemic issues and ultimately threaten Honda's supply chain. Subtle metrics raise red flags: a lot of additional overtime for workers, a single defect in a component that had a perfect quality record for the previous six months, a couple of late shipments on the same route explained away by two different implausible excuses. These and other possible symptoms of an imminent breakdown, small as the lapses may be, would warrant at least a phone call from Honda to determine whether there was a real problem or just a data aberration.

However, a more dire disruption in operations will bring a SWAT-like response, as NTN, a Columbus, Indiana–based maker of driveshafts for twelve North American automakers, found out. Unlike TS Tech, NTN had rejected Honda's request to maintain full employment during the sales slump that began in 2008. Thus, when global auto purchases skyrocketed in 2012, NTN could not keep pace with the increased demand for parts. The supplier's managers then had to take the extraordinary step of asking the automakers to reduce their orders for the foreseeable future, a request that not surprisingly infuriated the car companies, which were finally feeling their way out of a very dark tunnel.

To address this crisis, NTN's customers each sent a couple of people to investigate the plant's performance gap and offer possible fixes. But Honda took a different tack. Initially, Honda dispatched two teams of four people each not as advisers but to actually work at NTN, helping to oversee the two shifts. Their primary responsibility was to speed up production by improving work-flow schedules and quality control procedures for all of NTN's parts, even those destined for Honda's rivals.

Instantly, though, it became clear that NTN's shortcomings, which had been masked before the sales revival, were deeper than merely ineffective management. Instead, NTN had consistently underestimated its labor needs, maintaining an inadequate workforce regardless of the demand. To fill orders, even before the increased activity, NTN workers often had been glued to the assembly line for twelve hours a day with no days off for weeks at a time.

"They were having turnover issues and they weren't hiring quickly enough; they lacked worker loyalty," said Lincoln's purchasing manager, Mark VanDeVelde. "We could see that they weren't going to find their way out of this by themselves."

So Honda threw more resources at the problem, putting two crews of eight people each with a supervisor and a back-end inspector directly on the assembly line, this time as production workers. This gave NTN's manufacturing staff a huge lift, allowing them to work more normal hours in a more relaxed environment—and their output rose commensurately. After the arrival of Honda's emergency production team and a subsequent spate of new hiring, NTN's factory performance improved quickly. Within four weeks, Honda and the other automakers could go home.

Intriguing dynamics unfolded behind the scenes in this incident that amplify the benefits of Honda's supplier strategy. Although Honda was only one of a dozen NTN customers, it earned a privileged vantage point by dint of its frequent supplier interactions during noncrisis periods. By phone, computer, or in person, Honda makes its presence known to suppliers; indeed, VanDeVelde estimated that, although a manager, he visits as many as ten individual parts companies each month. Almost immediately upon Honda's entrance, NTN either asked the other automakers' advisers to leave or parked them across the driveway, away from the factory. Moreover, Honda's willingness to work on the assembly line itself, rather than to merely recommend from a distance, was a welcome respite for NTN's management, which was wilting under the pressure of too many meddlers and too few solutions.

"Secretly, we were very proud of this," said VanDeVelde. "NTN trusted us because we had earned it then and before. And that was a big win for us: we got the parts we needed, we even learned something about how their driveshafts are made—knowledge we can use in the future—and we improved our relationship with the supplier."

Although it's an aggressive goal, Honda aims to shrink the overall cost of every automobile part by 25 percent or more during the model's life cycle, about four years. In so doing, Honda hopes to pump these savings back into the updated version of the car in the form of supplementary features, which ideally can be added to the new vehicle with only a minimal sticker price increase over the prior model. Cost cutting is merely one part of the equation. Factory improvements and quality gains can be equally beneficial in reducing the price of a part. And while the supplier is responsible for reaching the overall cost targets, the Honda workers who are routinely dispatched to parts companies each day help identify and execute new plant ideas that could help them achieve their numbers.

Many of these initiatives are small, even unusual, but they add up. For example, there was the episode involving the alarming number of bulb failures in Honda headlights produced by Stanley Electric in London, Ohio. With returns multiplying, Stanley was slipping well behind its price improvement objectives for the part. But despite the company's attempts over many months to manufacture the headlamps more precisely, even using better components, the problem persisted.

Finally, a team of Honda and Stanley workers examined Stanley's quality monitoring procedures themselves, which are often assessed last because it is akin to blaming the deficiency on a diagnostic tool rather than identifying the cause of the flaw. And after many months of trial and error, the teams discovered that by testing the headlights for longer periods on the assembly line the number of rejects dropped. For one thing, the extended inspections enabled Stanley to catch the deficient parts before they were shipped to Honda. But in addition, although it is not completely clear why, the shorter tests had apparently corrupted some of the headlights. With the new monitoring techniques more lamps were free from flaws at the end of the assembly line and there were fewer returns.

"Fortunately, Honda worked with us on that for a long time, and didn't just throw us to the wolves and say 'That's your problem,'" said Mark Cowan, Stanley's executive vice president. "In fact, the idea of improving our testing procedures is now something that we're implementing throughout all of our product lines. For example, we've made changes to the layout of the conveyor belts to increase the amount of time workers can monitor parts for quality before they are passed along to the next station. That's delivered a huge return, a very nice cost savings."

Honda suppliers I interviewed appear to be extremely motivated to meet price and quality objectives. For one thing, they stand to be rewarded with a contract for the next model of the vehicle they are providing parts for. Plus, a high-scoring supplier may be in line for additional orders in new car launches. Notionally, there are more immediate gains as well. So the theory goes, by keeping costs in check Honda sales will rise through the life of the model, which in turn can increase the supplier's monthly production volume. Also, Honda vehicles are exceptionally durable and rank at or near the top on virtually all reliability surveys—indeed, recently a 1990 Accord surpassed one million miles—a performance that Honda ties directly to the quality of the equipment in its vehicles. As a result the aftermarket for Honda components can be remarkably lucrative for many years. On my visits to Honda supplier factories, I routinely saw sections of the plants devoted to making parts for ancient Hondas that haven't yet given up the ghost, some going back to the 1970s.

If Honda seems to be overly obsessed with the performance of its suppliers, almost to the point of micromanaging, consider the alternative. Seduced by promises of discount parts, usually from regions with low wages, many manufacturers have been stung by signing up suppliers they know little about and are too removed from to oversee. A textbook example is Boeing, whose latest jet, the Dreamliner or 787, is an engineering marvel in many ways: the plane is made chiefly from composite materials so it's lightweight and strong, uses 20 percent less fuel but reaches the same top speed as other large transcontinental jets, and its passengers enjoy the industry's roomiest seats, largest windows, and plasma televisions.

Problem is, the plane struggled to get off the ground. Originally slated for a maiden voyage in 2007, the Dreamliner suffered delay after delay and finally flew commercially for the first time in 2011. Almost all of these postponements can be blamed on the jet's troubled supply chain. In order to save money, Boeing risked all by farming out the design, engineering, and manufacturing of whole sections of the jet to suppliers from around the world who were then supposed to deliver these huge subassemblies to Boeing's factory in Everett, Washington, where they would be pieced together like a jigsaw puzzle into the final product. No manufacturer had ever given its supplier base so much control over a high-profile project before.

Not surprisingly, because the subassemblies were designed and produced independently, they didn't match when they arrived at Boeing's plant. Many of these separate pieces failed to fit tightly against each other during assembly, leaving minute but unacceptable gaps in the fuselage. As a result, huge portions of the Dreamliner had to be torn down and rebuilt. Additionally, some suppliers were late with shipments, complaining about a shortage of fasteners to assemble their portions of the plane. And in many cases, the suppliers had neglected to produce documentation and instruction manuals.

Perhaps worst of all, Boeing paid little attention to its suppliers, a far-flung group with plants in Asia, Europe, and North America, believing that supervision would slow down this streamlined production model. That decision proved foolhardy when some of Boeing's suppliers revealed that they were in serious financial difficulty and unable to operate at full capacity; Boeing executives were caught completely unawares. As Mike Denton, a Boeing vice president, told me when the company was still struggling to build the first copies of the Dreamliner, the plan was "not to encumber the partners with the Boeing way of doing everything. So we erred on the side of giving them more free rein than in retrospect we should have."

Although Boeing has recently tried to make up for its flawed supply chain strategy by taking more control over manufacturing the plane, the Dreamliner continued to suffer glitches well into its initial commercial flights. The plane has been grounded numerous times for defective batteries, fuel leaks, and faulty wiring. And in January 2013, the Federal Aviation Administration began an in-depth review of the 787, including its design, manufacture, and assembly, to determine why the Dreamliner is known more for its defects than for its time in the air. Analysts estimate that Boeing lost tens of billions of dollars from Dreamliner delays and order cancellations due to its cavalier supply chain management attitude.

The Dreamliner debacle may be a worst-case scenario, but to some degree most multinational manufacturers are making the same mistakes as Boeing by being too indifferent to their supply chains. On the face of it, Honda's distinctive supplier strategy should allow it to avoid their fate.

Still, even Honda's approach is not foolproof, as the company learned in 2011 when a devastating Japanese tsunami in March and Thailand floods in late October forced the automaker to shut down as much as 50 percent of its North American production for almost a full year. As a result of these twin natural disasters, Honda faced a shortage of a single set of critical semiconductor components, a specialty of Asian companies since the 1970s, that was produced outside the United States or Canada for American cars. Many of the firms making these parts were so-called Tier 2 or Tier 3 suppliers; that is, they provided electronic circuitry to Honda's main parts providers, which were in many cases outside the disaster areas. This was an embarrassing blow for Honda. It exposed a vulnerability in the automaker's supposedly disciplined supplier management program and in its localization strategy, which was centered on self-reliant market regions.

Since then, I have asked at least two dozen Honda executives how they could have overlooked such a looming threat to the company's business model. They were at a loss to explain it, except to say that their attention was so fixed on improving the manufacturing skills of their primary suppliers that they neglected to make sure that these companies had multiple channels for the components in the parts they made.

But to eliminate the possibility of a similarly costly parts deficit in the future, Honda undertook a massive initiative to map its entire supply chain, down as far as third- and fourth-tier suppliers. Scanning this chart, Honda managers can uncover weaknesses at a glance, primarily overreliance on lower-tier suppliers that are either unstable or in danger zones. Honda officials concede that although ambitious and time-consuming, this undertaking opened their eyes to areas of exposure about which they were completely in the dark.

"There's no risk-free scenario, but we believe we've mitigated the risk throughout the supply chain," said Honda North American Purchasing executive Tom Lake. "Every time we fail, we learn something. And what happened in North America proved that we were right all along: you can't be too obsessive or overinvolved with your suppliers. Anything less than total, you'll pay."

9

THE LOCAL MULTINATIONAL

Five anonymous, uninhabited islands in the East China Sea between Okinawa and China, a two-thousand-acre chain known as Senkaku in Japan and Diaoyu in China, have been objects of enmity between the two countries for some time. But in 2012, this little-known dispute with ancient roots suddenly had a very modern impact on the world's biggest businesses. Unexpectedly bursting into the open, the Asian quarrel roiled the auto industry and in so doing exposed the illusions behind the unrealistic promises of globalization. Although some multinationals still do not fully grasp the connection, the Senkaku affair provided the most salient explanation yet for why an operating model based on the hope of minimal trade boundaries, cheap labor, risk-free global manufacturing, and, in essence, corporations without borders has proven to be utterly disappointing and mostly unprofitable.

Japan had long eyed the Senkakus, but Tokyo didn't annex the islands until 1895, the same year that the First Sino-Japanese War concluded with a Japanese victory, effectively signaling the end of the Great Qing, the last imperial Chinese dynasty. Japan justified its takeover of the islands by citing the relative proximity of the Senkakus to Japanese-controlled Okinawa as well as the lack of apparent claims on the property. At the time, China did not formally oppose Japan's decision to oversee the Senkakus.

In fact, the islands were mostly an afterthought, neglected and rarely mentioned, until 1969 when a United Nations commission identified potential oil and gas reserves in the waters offshore. At once, interest in these tiny, barren outposts perked up in the region. China soon protested Japanese oversight of the islands, asserting that it is "fully proven by history" that the Diaoyu have been Taiwanese-owned fishing grounds since ancient times. But Japan refused to acknowledge China's assertion. However, to tamp down a possible diplomatic row, Tokyo prohibited development of the Senkakus.

Until recently, stasis held. Every so often the Senkakus disagreement would flare up after a Chinese trawler or fishing boat veered too close to the islands or a Japanese business hinted at starting an operation on the Senkakus. But these incidents passed with little, if any, damage.

However, in 2012 an unanticipated Japanese move abruptly escalated the Senkakus dispute into a full-blown international crisis, perilously heightening the age-old mistrust between the two nations. In September, Japan purchased the three Senkaku Islands that it had ceded to influential Japanese families before World War II. Officially, Japan said that it had taken this step to keep the islands out of the hands of Tokyo's anti-Chinese, right-wing governor Shintaro Ishihara, who had announced plans to use public money to acquire the Senkakus.

That explanation, which Tokyo thought would earn goodwill from the Chinese, couldn't have been more tone deaf. Beijing leadership viewed the Japanese acquisition of the islands as a transparent provocation, not as a favor. They saw it as a signal that the Japanese intended to assert control over the islands and box the Chinese out once and for all. Beijing threatened military retaliation.

Although in the past China had seemed uninterested in vigorously affirming its claim to the islands, this was no longer the case, for two reasons. First, China is desperate for oil (as is Japan) to power its economic expansion, and the waters around the Senkakus may contain a fossil fuel bonanza. So far, neither country has attempted offshore drilling in the region, in large part because the technology for ultradeepwater exploration was perfected only in the last five years or so; as a result the precise amount of the reserves in the East China Sea is not known. But now that it may be feasible to extract oil from the region, the petro-political value of the islands has appreciated significantly.

Moreover, the economies of China and Japan are vying anew on the world stage and particularly in the Asian region. And for the first time since as long ago as the Middle Ages, China believes that it has the upper hand on its old enemy; its roaring GDP growth stands in stark contrast to Japan's faltering attempts to escape more than two decades of on-again, off-again recession and deflation. Losing the Senkakus permanently to Japan would be an embarrassment for China, an unvarnished gesture of disrespect from a country that China considers to be its inferior in size and global economic muscle and significance. It would make China appear feckless.

A flurry of confrontational incidents ensued, mostly involving standoffs between warships and destroyers but ending just short of actual military engagement. In the most fraught episode, the Japanese Coast Guard arrested a group of Hong Kong activists after they attempted to swim ashore from boats just off the Senkakus' coast. China was not shy about wrapping the two-day detention of its citizens in nationalism. Beijing leadership proclaimed the islands a "core interest" of the country—Chinese code words for places or property that may be protected by force—and said that the dispute was "about sovereignty and territorial integrity." The *China Youth Daily*, an official Communist Party newspaper, called for a boycott of Japanese products to "express the inviolable dignity of the Chinese people."

That triggered violent protests in Shenzhen, just north of Hong Kong, as well as in a half-dozen other large Chinese cities. Japanese flags were torn and burned; shops selling Japanese goods were vandalized. But the protesters' anger was felt most sharply in the auto industry. Japanese cars were perfect targets for Chinese resentment. Big and shiny and not Chinese—and seemingly ubiquitous in the streets—Nissans, Toyotas, and Hondas were randomly turned over, sometimes to be set on fire, other times trashed. In the most disturbing confrontation, a middle-aged man, Li Jianli, was driving a Toyota Corolla in the populous city of Xi'an when a crowd surrounded his vehicle, pulled him out, severely beat him and left him lying in the street. More than a year after this incident, the right side of Li's body was still paralyzed.

To many Chinese, including those not participating in the riots, the activists' message was unmistakable: drive a Japanese car in China at your own peril. And within weeks, the Chinese auto market, the biggest in the world by volume, was turned upside down, essentially by a small, bitter mob.

Between April 2012 and October 2012, Japanese automakers' share of new car sales in China declined from 21 percent to a mere 9 percent. In October alone, Honda and Toyota both lost as much as 40 percent of their Chinese sales compared with the same month the year before, when Japanese automakers as a group had the highest market share of any cluster of foreign companies by country in China.

Meanwhile, General Motors and Volkswagen took advantage of the weakness in Japanese car sales to solidify their number-one and number-two sales rankings in China, each with upward of 20 percent market share. Because China, like the United States, accounts for about 25 percent of worldwide vehicle sales, rapid, radical changes in the performance of companies in either of these countries have an instant impact on global auto industry sales rankings.

The Chinese auto sector is still relatively nascent and, hence, extremely mutable. So sudden sales dips are not necessarily something to be alarmed about. In fact, by mid-2013, the Japanese automakers had already recovered about half of their lost sales. Still, the fight over the Senkakus remains a very real deterrent to their return to top spots in China.

Honda's response to its dwindling results and the troubling Chinese backlash was telling. The company blamed itself, not the churning geopolitical winds in the East China Sea. Taking a cue from founder Soichiro Honda, who warned that success is 99 percent failure, Honda's leadership perceived the turn of events as indicating that their company had fallen short in implementing the most critical aspects of its localization strategy in China.

In Honda management's assessment, as opposed to the company's U.S. business or, for example, its operations in Thailand, India, Brazil, and the United Kingdom—where Honda cars, motorcycles, lawn mowers, and other iconic items are not only often locally designed and manufactured but strike such an emotional chord with customers that they are virtually perceived as domestic products—the Chinese subsidiary had stumbled in its efforts to become a local firm. It had not achieved the status of a company that Chinese society wants to exist. Otherwise, Honda executives concluded, it wouldn't be under attack.

Precisely why Honda had been unable to blend into the Chinese economic landscape was confounding. After all, the automaker had followed its own localization recipe as well as could be imagined, starting with taking the unorthodox and dicey step in 1998 of becoming the first Japanese vehicle manufacturer to produce cars in China. At that time, Honda acquired a plant in southern Guangdong Province and a joint venture with the Chinese GAC Group, both of which Peugeot had abandoned after giving up hopes of turning a profit. The French automaker's management and the Chinese workers had clashed frequently over which language would be spoken in the plant and working conditions.

But with Honda's arrival, the factory's fortunes changed almost immediately. Honda layered a local accent over the plant by installing a management team led by two Chinese and two Japanese executives and establishing a supply chain in which nearly half of the parts makers were Chinese companies. Moreover, within a few years Honda's independent engineering and research and development companies had set up shop on the Guangdong campus to stimulate local innovation and customize Honda factory technology from other plants in other regions for Chinese needs. In doing all of this, Honda had moved purposefully to fully integrate with the Chinese economic culture, to prove that it was willing to share its global knowledge and experiences with its Chinese partners, even to give them local control of the business—measures that other multinationals would have considered too risky in the early 2000s. Some still feel that way now.

The returns validated Honda's approach. The company's Chinese factories have proven to be among the most productive auto plants in the country, capable of assembling a car in as few as twenty-one hours. And until the recent troubles, Honda had among the highest profit margins of multinationals in China.

Yet notwithstanding this performance and this strategy, Honda still found itself in an unfamiliar and untenable position in China: it was, essentially, an outsider in a country where it had painstakingly attempted to assimilate. The antipathy toward Japan—and by proxy, Honda—unleashed by the East China Sea row was evidence enough. But equally revealing, a couple of years ago Honda factories in China were hit by a series of wildcat strikes over low wages and the company's decision to increase plant output without hiring additional employees. To quell the walkouts, Honda raised factory salaries by about 25 percent and promised improved training to enhance productivity and minimize the hardship of higher production goals.

However, some of the assemblers continued the job action for more than another week, hoping to call attention to more generic and long-standing labor grievances—such as the Communist Party's undue coziness with manufacturers—that were unrelated to the Honda negotiations. This added millions of dollars to Honda's losses from the strikes. But the Chinese government was in no rush to send the workers back to the factories. In fact, the Honda job action was one of the few labor protests of many that had broken out around the same time that the country's leadership permitted to be publicized. China was apparently eager to embarrass Honda for its Japanese pedigree and to slow Honda's localization ambitions, which were a threat to domestic Chinese automakers. In addition, Honda represented a convenient scapegoat for Chinese authorities to divert attention from labor's simmering resentment toward the government.

Viewed through the serpentine optics of Chinese politics and motivations, Honda's inability to mutate into a domestic automaker in China was easier to understand but of little help to the company. Although geopolitical jockeying may explain Honda's dilemma in China, the automaker's executives say that it would be a mistake to use that as an excuse for the shortcomings of its localization strategy there; it would be foolhardy, they say, to let fluid international rivalries and suspicion dissuade the company from adopting the same global market tactics it uses everywhere in the world.

A Honda manager reminded me that in the 1980s when the automaker became the first Japanese company to manufacture cars in the United States, the backlash and prejudice were at first unrelenting and, looking back, embarrassingly public. For example, in Wapakoneta, Ohio, twelve miles north of Honda's Anna plant, William Leitz made headlines across the United States for angrily resigning as mayor soon after Honda began to build its factory in the area. Leitz testily said that he could not work side by side with the Japanese: "I was on a destroyer (in the South Pacific) that was sunk . . . and I was in the hospital. . . . I'm an American, and I love my country."

And on a larger stage, Honda's competitors and American manufacturing trade and labor groups ran national xenophobic TV ads showing, in one case, a herd of angry-looking Japanese cars, their slanted eyes ablaze, running roughshod over U.S. bridges, highways, and even the Statue of Liberty, drowning it in the Atlantic. The voiceover, a hoarse baritone with a threatening staccato cadence, says ruefully as atonal brass clangs perilously in the background: "When it started, America was unprepared. From across the ocean they came. Little cars determined to change the buying habits of a nation. And for a while there was no stopping them."

A Lincoln-Mercury newspaper ad for a Yonkers, New York, automobile retailer typified the anti-Japanese spots that regional dealers were routinely running. The full-page copy targeted both Danny, a nerdy fictional salesman in Honda's commercials, and a Japanese politician who had baited U.S. trade representatives by saying that America's economic troubles were caused by lazy U.S. workers, about a third of whom "cannot even read." In bold letters, the ad reads: "Sorry Danny, not all Americans are stupid!" And among the selling points for the Mercury Sable was the responsibility to save American jobs.

Yet this deep if not wide rage against Honda was relatively short-lived. It was sufficiently dispelled in less than two decades to permit Honda's pioneering U.S. localization strategy—which began with the company's "start small, grow big" motorcycle distribution program in Los Angeles and culminated with automobile plants in the Midwest and South run by autonomous American management, engineers, researchers, and designers—to become the model for the company's stepwise market entry approach everyplace else in the world. Consequently, with this history to fall back on as a guide, Honda hopes to improve but not profoundly change its localization agenda in China, despite the unfriendly conditions.

"We are disappointed in ourselves, not in our business model," said Masa Nagai, who ran Honda's Chinese operations from 2004 through 2010 and is now an assistant to CEO Takanobu Ito in Tokyo. "If your business model is right—and if it has proven to be right many times before—then you will find that failure and success coexist on the same road. You need to learn from the first to achieve the second. That means we must keep doing what we have already been doing in China but we have to do it better with deeper engagement in the local community to overcome the obstacles."

As a result, in the midst of the furor over the Senkakus, when fearful Chinese consumers were posting on Weibo, the country's social media platform, variants of "I can't purchase a Japanese car now; it is too dangerous," Honda daringly made its own headlines. The automaker doubled down on localization by announcing an aggressive effort to plant more meaningful stakes in China.

For starters, the company broke ground on a third production line in Guangdong, a new leg of its joint venture with the Chinese

GAC Group (all nondomestic automakers must partner with a Chinese firm to manufacture cars in the country). This will be a combined factory and engine plant incorporating two of Honda's most novel manufacturing breakthroughs: the Intelligent Painting Technology invented in Marysville, Ohio, which markedly reduced the company's annual carbon footprint in the United States, and a state-of-the-art laser for welding aluminum and steel in the stamping department. Prior to Honda's development of this laser equipment, consistently reliable welds between the two disparate metals were considered impossible to achieve. Also, Honda plans to hire additional designers and engineers specifically to conceive additional local products that are expected to eventually outpace sales of the so-called global models Honda makes in each of its regions—the Civic, Accord, and CR-V.

And in perhaps the biggest surprise, Honda introduced three new Chinese-designed vehicles, two of which were ready to go on sale immediately: the dragon-faced midsize sedan Crider, which *Car and Driver* snidely described as "an unhappy mishmash of styling cues from a plethora of Hondas and Acuras," but which sold an impressive 12,500 units in its third month of production; and the Jade, which the magazine called a "sultry little wagon." The third Chinese car is an Odyssey-like minivan, and the company said that two more Chinese originals would be released by 2015, when Honda hopes to double its sales in the country. After these cars are on the streets, Honda will boast the most domestically developed models in China of any non-Chinese auto company. In all, Honda expects to add twelve new vehicles, including the global models, to its Chinese manufacturing portfolio by 2015.

At about the same time as the Guangdong expansion was unveiled, Honda opened a second automobile and engine factory in Wuhan, a city some six hundred miles north of Guangdong in the nation's interior. This facility, part of a ten-year-old joint venture with Dongfeng Motor Corporation, is distinguished by a pair of extraordinary assembly line achievements developed by Chinese Honda employees at Honda's existing Wuhan plant.

The first is a height-adjustable assembly line. Rather than conveying vehicles from zone to zone via rigid overhead hangers, the new Wuhan line uses adaptable platforms that support the car's undercarriage and can be raised or lowered to place the automobile frame at the most efficient and comfortable height for the workers. For example, with this system Wuhan assemblers can avoid the awkwardness and inconvenience of lifting an engine aloft to mount it in the chassis by bringing the vehicle down to eye level, which positions them better to securely and accurately install the huge piece of equipment in its precise fixed position in the car. This height-adjustable assembly line dovetails well with Honda's flexible factory concept, because it provides a single vehicle conveyance system that can be altered moment to moment to the specifications of any automobile size or type.

The second Wuhan innovation is a delivery scheme that carries small and medium-size parts down the production line in concert with the vehicle or engine that they are intended for. This channel eliminates the need for frequent, noisy parts deliveries to assembly line zones and the plethora of workstation dollies in the factory's aisles where the inventory is typically stored until needed. It also reduces the danger of accidents involving forklifts scurrying to and fro and minimizes delays due to late-arriving parts. As a result of this single lean advance, Honda was able to shorten the assembly line in the second Dongfeng factory by about 30 percent from the original design, sharply curtailing energy use and factory clutter.

Speaking of the Dongfeng factory as a whole, Masa Nagai said, "It reflects well the Chinese culture where it was born, particularly in the lovely way it combines simplicity with choreographed efficiency. Many of the new local ideas in the factory will be useful at other Honda plants around the world. Sometimes they have to be altered to fit another region's way of doing things but their inherent value remains the same."

Honda arrived at its global localization strategy organically, a natural outgrowth of the company's three operating principles, manifested in this context by going to the spot for firsthand knowledge, having respect for unorthodox ideas and cultural differences, and encouraging indigenous innovation. Rather than entering a country with the brute force of a foreign military—shipping over from home the plans, programs, concepts, people, designs, and platforms, the way multinational manufacturers do to a large degree—Honda expands into new markets from the ground up and nurtures these enterprises to gradually blossom into autonomous operations.

To accomplish this, Honda initially may train workers on advanced technology borrowed from other production facilities, but only to spur their creativity. Shortly, however, the new factory is expected to take on a domestic flavor with homegrown manufacturing improvements surfacing from the local teams. Simultaneously, nearby parts makers are recruited; those that survive initiation into the Honda Way will join a local supply chain that is intended to provide at least 90 percent of the components that Honda doesn't make itself.

Before long, Honda R&D and engineering companies establish operations in the country, populated by local technologists who work alongside experienced Honda engineers and designers helicoptered in to spend as much as a year at the new site. Local management is installed as well to eventually run the Honda subsidiary independent of headquarters. At first, global models are produced at the factory. But within a few years, these facilities are expected to launch their own domestic vehicles, or at least customized versions of products made in neighboring countries.

Soichiro Honda grasped the value of multinational operations very early in his business's history. In the mid-1950s, when Honda Motor had been in existence for only about five years and Japan was still emerging from the fog of World War II, Soichiro exhorted his company to look outward from the insular Japanese islands and view the rest of the world as its potential customer base and factory footprint. Well before any Japanese manufacturers of complex items considered themselves capable of competing with deep-pocketed and entrenched global industrial outfits, Soichiro bemoaned the limited growth opportunities in "little Japan," as he put it, and declared that Honda Motor must "maintain an international viewpoint . . . dedicated to supplying products of the highest efficiency."

Soichiro stoked his global ambitions by overseeing the development of the powerful yet nimble motorcycles that would score stunning victories in the 1961 Isle of Man TT races in England. Within two years of that event, which sealed Honda's international reputation as a maker of preeminent engines, the company took its initial step toward localization by constructing its first non-Japanese factory in Aalst, Belgium, a small town about twenty miles northwest of Brussels. No other Japanese manufacturer—and, in fact, virtually no Western companies—had yet built a plant outside their home borders.

Although the Aalst facility bore just a passing resemblance to what Honda's global localization plan would eventually evolve into—for example, in this venture research and design remained firmly rooted in Tokyo—the factory nonetheless had a decidedly Belgian flavor because all parts were obtained from nearby suppliers. Debuting without glitches, the plant immediately met capacity goals of ten thousand motorcycles and mopeds monthly. And inside Honda, the Aalst facility offered a clear glimpse into the global strategic thrust that would in a few decades be second nature to the company.

"You might think that [the monthly production] was unreasonably small for a market that had yearly demand of more than two million motorcycles," said Kenjiro Okayasu, the plant's manager. "But it was the first time [that Honda or any Japanese corporation had engaged in overseas production]. So we thought along the lines of rearing a small child and raising it to adulthood."

By the early 1990s, with successful motorcycle and automobile factories in Belgium, New Zealand, the United Kingdom, and the United States under Honda's belt, the basic principles of global localization had, in fact, matured sufficiently that the company could articulate them more concretely. That is apparent in *The Machine That Changed the World*, the landmark book about automobile lean manufacturing published in 1990. Presciently, the authors included a section on the importance of global enterprise but it is sketchy at best because, save Honda, car companies were not willing to fully invest, financially and culturally, in overseas operations. However, Honda was singled out for "its conviction about doing it all in one place"—meaning combining engineering, design, and manufacturing functions in each of its large local facilities. And the authors praised Honda for its "plans during the 1990s to develop a set of products unique to each region," which would be sold to local customers and, if necessary, exported to other regions to fill market demand.

"Honda seems to have been the first to see the advantage of this approach," the authors wrote.

In the realm of operating models, localization is the antithesis of globalization, the concept that has transfixed and bewildered multinationals for two decades. Under the guise of globalization, multinationals hastily opened factories in developing countries such as China, Vietnam, Thailand, and nations in Latin America and Eastern Europe, eager to take advantage of cheap labor for products that could be exported around the world. In most cases, these facilities were solely for production. The skilled tasks, like engineering and design, remained at corporate headquarters, or were at least micromanaged from there.

In theory, globalization was to act like a rising tide, lifting all boats in poor and rich countries alike. Buoyed by hundreds of thousands of new assembly line jobs in emerging nations, the middle class would swell, which in turn would propel higher local consumption. More factories would be needed to meet the demand, further raising local standards of living and handing the multinationals a vast and enthusiastic new customer base to sell products to.

Meanwhile, back home in the United States and in Europe, consumers would have their pick of inexpensive items made by people thousands of miles away whose salaries were much lower than theirs. And as this virtuous circle of global manufacturing grew, trade barriers would fall because, to put it colloquially, we're all in it together. Policies that reduce exports and imports would be out of fashion because they harm factory workers, consumers, and multinationals equally.

Unlike localization, in which companies like Honda attempted to harmonize with a region's social, political, and economic dynamics—no matter how distressed or in turmoil these dynamics were—globalization ostensibly offered multinationals a less precarious proposition: to be outsiders with insider privileges, safe from quotidian crosscurrents and risks by dint of their special business relationship with the country.

In short, multinationals would enjoy a benign, prosperous, and flat world, the latter term famously coined by *New York Times* columnist Thomas Friedman to describe the gifts of globalization. With win-wins scattered throughout the global commercial landscape, corporate borders would be eliminated and teamwork would be virtual, thanks to continuing breakthroughs in computer and communications technology. A designer in Detroit could change the shape of a headlight fitting and instantly share the CAD file with an engineer in Mumbai who would adjust the dimensions of the part in three different ways to fit into three different automobile models. Next, a factory manager in China would be pinged to look at the file on his tablet on the plant floor and send it to the supplier who would produce three hundred new parts within twenty-four hours. Presto. Done. The fitting is placed on the vehicles within a day of its design.

Not quite. The more likely scenario is that each step of the process introduces a small deviation. It could be in the design, which may be based on old headlight dimensions that were changed months earlier on the fly in the factory but never actually altered in the car's master blueprints. Or perhaps the supplier's metal-cutting machines inserted a sizing variation that is invisible to the naked eye. As Boeing learned from the losses and delays resulting from aggressively outsourcing virtually all the components for the struggling Dreamliner, aberration is the norm in these situations. And when the part doesn't fit, a typical plant supervisor's reaction would be to set it aside to tackle at another time; after all, he has vehicles to produce.

Instead of flat and seamless, globalization is full of hurdles and obstacles. Though presented as a panacea for a world with haves and have-nots—a way to eliminate economic disparities and magically expand multinational revenue streams—globalization is still a barely profitable and perplexing strategy for most companies and a dubious asset for many emerging economies. Indeed, the fault with globalization lies in its fundamental premise, which for a hard-charging business concept is oddly Rousseauian: it hinges on the belief that an innate altruism stirs in people and their institutions and that the desire to cooperate in an equitable worldwide economic order is just under the surface, waiting to be tapped.

That idea, of course, has no basis in reality. It disregards the weight of nationalism, cultural sensitivities, and historical antagonism in framing global relationships, while neglecting the way self-interest motivates people, companies, and governments to seek gain at the expense of others. Incomprehensibly, proponents of globalization assumed, or at least proffered the notion, that the mere prospect of significant economic growth would persuade individuals and nations to bury their differences to take part in the system.

The Senkaku Islands dispute belied the myths of globalization by shattering the most seductive of them—that it would usher in a post-nationalist era of conflict-free economic growth. The Chinese response to Japan's acquisition of the East China Sea properties demonstrated in a very public venue that even the most business-obsessed countries would not hesitate to upset lucrative arrangements with multinationals to defend their geopolitical interests. Certainly, there have been other flare-ups around the world that endangered corporate well-being; for example, the frequent Iranian threats to block oil shipments through the Strait of Hormuz until U.S. sanctions were lifted have put multinational energy companies in an uncomfortable spot. But these incidents, like many others, tend to deescalate well before global business is seriously affected. By contrast, the Senkakus confrontation was alarming precisely because the Chinese refused to back down, even though their second-largest trading partner's biggest companies would suffer dramatically.

"That was what most surprised me—the extent to which China was keen to harm companies like Toyota and Honda; they are major companies with lots of business in China," said a General Motors executive in the power train division. "We all shuddered a bit at that. The U.S. and China are not exactly on best-friend terms, so is GM's position in China in danger as well?"

In fact, GM has good reason to worry—but not purely because of Chinese capriciousness or patriotism. As much as any multinational,

GM has placed a huge bet on globalization and, like most multinationals, GM has been frustrated by the minimal returns. Including a recently announced investment, by 2015 the automaker will have spent more than $20 billion on a series of joint ventures in China. GM has even expanded R&D facilities in China, although its R&D teams are still ultimately beholden to management in Detroit. And General Motors has designed a few Chevy models—for example, the Sail and the Spark—specifically for China and other low-income markets.

This blitz of activity has earned GM bragging rights to being number one in auto sales in China, with Volkswagen close behind. However, GM's Chinese profits are disappointing at best. In 2012, GM made $2.2 billion in the Asian region, less than a third of its earnings in North America, where it sold 250,000 fewer vehicles. The problem is, about half of the vehicles that GM sells in China are Wulings, inexpensive, low-margin little minivans designed by one of General Motors' Chinese partners, targeted mostly at commercial buyers. To GM's dismay, Chinese customers purchased 1.3 million Wulings and only 35,000 Cadillacs in 2012. In the United States, GM's sales mix is much more profitable, with high-margin trucks, vans, and SUVs dominating the list.

As much as China is a domestic market for GM's partners, such as Wuling, their factories are little more than low-cost production facilities for General Motors. Some of the cars made in these plants—for example, the same vehicles that may be sold as Wulings in China—are slapped with the Chevy nameplate and exported to low-income markets as far away as Latin America. Consequently, GM's connection with China, forged only through the prism of globalization, is tenuous and remote. In fact, GM is consistently overshadowed by its largest Chinese ally, Shanghai Automotive Industry Corporation (SAIC), a state-owned enterprise that is the country's biggest domestic automaker.

"Make no mistake, even though GM is bringing the brands and the designs and the technology and the marketing know-how, SAIC is the leading partner, at least in Chinese eyes," noted John Rosevear, a GM expert who is The Motley Fool's senior auto analyst. "There's a reason that their main joint venture is called Shanghai GM and not GM Shanghai."

Or more explicitly, twenty years after GM's arrival in China, meager earnings and low-rent factories are about all that the automaker has to show for its trouble. A lucrative presence in the country with a growing customer base for profitable cars is almost as far away now as it was when GM first got there. Not quite the bounty that globalization was supposed to deliver.

As the Senkakus quarrel took center stage in Asia and the sales losses piled up for Japanese companies, globalization itself came under increasing scrutiny from corporate experts and executives around the world. Where business leaders had expected more global stability and growth, they were seeing disintegration. In the view of Kazuko Mori, an international affairs expert and a professor at Tokyo's Waseda University, "The huge contradiction at the center of Japanese-Chinese relations is the fact that politics and economics are moving in completely opposite directions."

The same could be said for other would-be global commercial partnerships, including the United States and China, the United States and South America, Europe and the Middle East, and on and on. In point of fact, the primary threads of globalization have been unraveling for many years. However, only recently have dispassionate analyses into the lack of rewards from globalization dampened the optimism that it is simply a young concept yet to be fully realized.

Paltry earnings are the most troubling issue. Virtually every multinational is struggling to maintain stable profits in emerging nations. GM's China numbers are emblematic of most of the biggest multinationals, which often boast of getting more than half their sales from outside their home country but usually don't report earnings by region—a sure sign that they have nothing to brag about. With little solid data available about multinational profits and margins in China, recent surveys have had to suffice—and they paint a dour picture.

A study of multinationals by the American Chamber of Commerce in Shanghai found that in 2012 the percentage of companies whose Chinese profit margins increased over the prior year tumbled to 48 percent, from 65 percent in 2010. The percentage reporting profitable operations slipped to 73 percent from 79 percent, while year-over-year revenue growth was down as well—to 71 percent of multinationals from 87 percent two years earlier. Not surprising, then, that the number of multinationals viewing China as "critical to global strategy" declined to only 37 percent in 2011 from 53 percent less than a decade earlier, according to *The Economist*. These grim figures came even as China was pumping money into its economy to bolster consumer and industrial spending in the post–global recession period.

If multinationals are disappointed with globalization, as these survey results would indicate, they have good reason to feel this way. Instead of a level playing field and chummy business relationships with local governments, multinationals face policies that favor domestic companies and make it difficult for an outsider to gain traction. The most pernicious of these is captured in the rise of state-owned enterprises (SOEs): central-government-backed businesses that enjoy special treatment, such as low-cost loans and no-bid contracts. Ninety-five percent of Chinese companies are SOEs; Russia (81 percent), Indonesia (69 percent), and Malaysia (68 percent), among other countries, have high SOE penetration as well, according to research published by the global economic Web site

VoxEU.org. In Vietnam, state-owned enterprises are so prevalent that they tie up 50 percent of government investment and 60 percent of bank lending because finance companies are often SOEs as well; SOEs also account for more than half of the nation's bad debt.

While state-owned enterprises were intended to be conduits for capital reinvestment inside a country, thus spurring local expansion and improving domestic standards of living, their impact on economic growth has generally been lamentable. Studies of SOE performance show that without the imperative to be lean, productive, and competitive hanging over their heads, SOEs are often guilty of "overcapacity, inefficient cost control and slow industrial upgrading," said analyst Li Jin of the China Enterprise Research Institute. In other words, they soak up available capital without providing sufficiently meaningful returns to the economy. Moreover, they squeeze out or discourage domestic and multinational rivals that could boost innovation. As a result, SOE profits tend to increase more slowly than private companies and the GDPs of their countries, dampening consumer spending and making the region less enticing to multinationals.

Worse yet, multinationals are required to financially support SOEs. In most developing economies, companies must form joint ventures with state-owned enterprises if they hope to manufacture products in the country. This is the case in the Chinese auto industry in which the SOEs are allocated at least half, sometimes more, of the partnership's profits. These deals limit the ability of multinationals to improve factory productivity and manufacturing processes, even for companies like Honda that reject typical globalization practices. In fact, the leadership of Honda's principal Chinese partner, GAC Group, which is owned by the city of Shanghai, has been an impediment that the automaker has worked around only by demanding a high level of quality and performance as the price of continuing the joint venture. Still, without Honda's persistent presence and unyielding pressure, success is not guaranteed as the executive suite of GAC, like that of most Chinese SOEs, is entered through a revolving door that carries one former government apparatchik after another whose industrial experience is gained solely at state-owned enterprises.

Trade barriers have also whittled away at multinational profits, despite the hope that globalization would minimize punitive tariffs. China and the United States have skirmished repeatedly in recent years over a wide range of claims involving dumping and new trade duties. The United States has alleged that China is subsidizing exports of its rare earths, auto parts, and solar panel industries, while raising tariffs on American-made cars and sport-utility vehicles. For its part, China argues that the United States has made it increasingly expensive for Chinese companies to sell a growing number of products in the United States, including kitchen appliances, paper, steel, tires, magnets, chemicals, and wood flooring.

And protectionism is not limited to those two countries; indeed, it is endemic and covers virtually every aspect of global trade. Some recent tariffs may seem trivial—for example, Argentina imposed import restrictions on bottle caps and water balloons—but they only illustrate the sheer scope of trade sensitivity. For every tiny Argentine maneuver, a larger, more costly curb is enacted, such as India's ban on cotton exports or South Africa's increased tariffs on artificial turf. In all, the G-20 countries (the biggest economies and trading partners in the world) added more than one hundred restrictive measures from October 2011 to April 2012, according to the last available World Trade Organization data, despite a so-called standstill agreement to limit trading walls protecting their businesses.

Perhaps the most visible evidence of dissatisfaction with globalization is the Bedouin-like migration of multinationals. Unable to establish a foothold in China free of political and economic uncertainties that threaten their businesses, the world's largest companies—at one time, globalization's most ardent supporters—have begun to pull back from the country and seek more attractive places to manufacture products. Rather than finding stability in China and expanding outward into other regions in Asia and even Africa, large companies appear to have decided to simply move to where they can reap the greatest rewards. More than 50 percent of manufacturers and importers surveyed in late 2012 by the factoring company Capital Business Credit said that they are considering leaving China, while 26 percent said that they had already left. Many of these companies had operations in China for less than a decade.

Absent the hoped-for benefits of globalization, such as vast domestic markets in hospitable business environments to plumb and profitable factories to export from, costs have become a paramount concern. And in China the price of doing business is rapidly rising. In 2000, Chinese factory wages averaged 52 cents an hour; in 2015, manufacturing compensation will reach $6 an hour in many industries, according to the Boston Consulting Group (BCG). At that time, factoring in anticipated gains in the Chinese yuan against other, more stable currencies and increases in shipping rates, some analysts forecast cost parity between manufacturing big-ticket items in China to be shipped to American markets and simply making the products in the United States. For lower-margin businesses—such as textiles and inexpensive furniture—countries where wages are still low, like Vietnam, Bangladesh, the Philippines, and Cambodia, are already becoming more desirable than China.

For many multinationals that have closed Chinese factories in favor of new plants in the United States—including big and small makers of appliances (General Electric among them), Frisbees, water filters, padlocks, home improvement hardware, auto parts, and software—the productivity of American manufacturing is a significant plus. U.S.

factory workers produce about $75 an hour in output, twice the rate of Chinese workers, says the Bureau of Labor Statistics.

Globalization has foundered because it is predicated upon countries' acting in ways that are, well, foreign to them. Countries are protectionist, insular, suspicious, nationalist, colonialist, or competitive precisely because global financial power depends upon some combination of these behaviors—none of which are conducive to globalization. But it is naïve to think that countries would break these ancient habits for a concept based on a cooperative new world order that elevates multinationals while lessening the influence of the nation-state.

By contrast, localization, as Honda practices it, is designed to camouflage the multinational in the colors of the country's culture itself. In the United States, Honda is American; southern sometimes, midwestern other times. And in Thailand, where Honda is the number-one automaker by sales, the company is Thai. Honda's current factory in Thailand, located in Ayutthaya, about an hour north of Bangkok, opened in 2000; since then, it has been the scene of a series of intriguing new car designs aimed at a country with the biggest auto market in southeast Asia yet not known for much besides plain vanilla vehicles. For example, the $13,000 and up Honda Brio, conceived in large part by the Ayutthaya R&D and engineering team in 2011, began life as an ultrasporty, hatchback subcompact that tightly hugs curves in the road like more expensive vehicles and is light and efficient enough to get 40 miles to the gallon. The target audience: the many first-time car buyers with a limited amount of money to spend but who are willing to pay a bit more for style and quality. Since then Honda's Thailand subsidiary has released slightly pricier two-door and sedan models of the Brio, which is by far the most popular native automobile line in the country and a top seller among all vehicles, including imports.

To build on this success, Honda's Thai subsidiary is investing about $500 million in a new factory in Prachinburi Province, about two hours east of Bangkok. Scheduled to open in 2015, this plant will be designed by local engineers to incorporate many of the production process shortening techniques and new painting and welding advances that Honda is implementing in China and elsewhere but also to produce even greater levels of CO_2 reduction and more marked improvements in materials and water recycling than in other Honda factories. No other industrial facility in Thailand yet approaches this ambitious level of environmental protection and manufacturing sophistication and efficiency.

Honda has replicated this experience to one degree or another in Brazil, Malaysia, Indonesia, and numerous other places, depending on the maturity of the domestic auto market and the skills of the local workers. Next step for Honda is its African push. Although it's an admittedly inchoate effort, Honda recently took the somewhat bold step of establishing an independent subsidiary in Nigeria, Honda Automobile Western Africa Ltd., to first sell cars in the region while the seeds are planted to build auto and motorcycle factories in the country (the same strategy that Honda originally employed in the United States).

Through local manufacturing ecosystems, Honda can take advantage of currency fluctuations and raw material price movements while gaining the loyalty of domestic governments, consumers, and workers, making it much more difficult for punitive and protectionist policies as well as bad publicity to unexpectedly affect the business. Indeed, if the withdrawal of manufacturers from China to developed areas like the United States and Western Europe has a macro message it is this: making products where customers live is a more efficient, less risky, potentially less costly, and more consumer-targeted strategy than globalization's idea of manufacturing products where the labor is cheap and shipping the items around the world. Certainly, Honda's localization tactics plant the company deeper into a region than other manufacturers' strategies, but if nothing else the multinationals' Chinese disengagement validates the local thrust of Honda's plans.

Localization ultimately succeeds because it is, simply, homegrown workers, ideas, and innovation combining to produce the best products for domestic markets, where the real profits lie in emerging economies like China, India, Thailand, Brazil, and Vietnam. As such, it is essentially a people-driven concept, not a production strategy. Which is ultimately how Honda differs from other multinationals—in the autonomy and individual creativity it demands of its global offshoots. "Honda is a local company wherever it goes, because it doesn't impose a system from the top; it lets a system emerge out of the culture," noted John Casesa, senior managing director at Guggenheim Partners.

Or, put more poetically, Honda CEO Takanobu Ito said: localization "nurtures the invisible part of the tree—the roots in the ground—without which the beautiful part of the tree would not exist to look at."

10

A MANUFACTURING MANIFESTO

Soichiro Honda viewed manufacturing as a cleansing process, which crafted simplicity out of complexity and purity out of raw parts. He saw it as a beautiful—even ennobling—human activity, summed up in this way: "After materials are carried into the factory, nothing but perfect products should be carried out."

Honda believed that by creating attractive and durable objects—in his case, anything with an engine in it—an individual could make people happy and their lives more fulfilling. Mobility and freedom presented in exquisite packages can be a complete gift, one that satisfies the material and spiritual soul, Soichiro would say.

And he measured a person's value by his output—in Honda's words, "by the quality and quantity of work accomplished within the limited span of life. I must determine that a person who makes inferior products, which may break down after a short while, has an inferior personality."

Honda's elevation of manufacturing to a nearly mystical plateau was old-fashioned, a vestige of the era that he grew up in when factories, particularly in Japan, were known to house talented craftsmen. Yet, taken alone, his sentiments don't come across as musty or archaic or irrelevant, in large part because we still revere the handiwork and skills of people who build things with their own hands. We recognize the splendor and inspiration in the artisan's achievements. We just don't equate his or her work with manufacturing anymore. By today's calculus, a Tiffany lamp or a Lamborghini Aventador sports car are art; a pressed board desk that can be purchased at Walmart is what factories produce.

In its perfectionism, devotion to detail, homemade tools, respect for individual improvement, and preference for human labor over robotics, Honda Motor is one of the few companies that can claim to apply the principles of craftsman manufacturing to mass production. The influence of Soichiro's unorthodox appreciation for a factory's elegance is felt everywhere at his company.

But to much of the rest of the world, manufacturing does not merit such lofty consideration. Instead of dignity, the face of global manufacturing has a dark, sooty character, not much different from what we saw during the Industrial Revolution some 150 years ago. It is emblemized by sweatshops in Bangladesh, China, and Vietnam; or by people who are so indigent and desperate that the chance to receive a few dollars more than they would from begging in the streets is a godsend. And in developed countries, manufacturing is perceived as a second-class profession, a punch-the-clock job that the less intelligent and least privileged are forced to endure.

The disturbing state of manufacturing in emerging markets is both a symptom and by-product of the failure of globalization. Instead of widespread prosperity, income equality, and consistently rising standards of living, globalization has brought poor nations a string of low-cost factories and spotty economic growth. Making matters worse, multinationals have generally turned a blind eye to the bare-bones wages, long days, and precariously crowded and combustible working conditions in the overseas plants where many of their goods are produced; in so doing, they have unwittingly dispelled the canard that globalization is an altruistic, inclusive manufacturing strategy.

In developed nations, the antipathy toward manufacturing has been equally costly. These countries, primarily the United States but also the United Kingdom, France, Spain, and other Euro-zone nations, have exposed their economies to perilous shortfalls in trade, cash flow, innovation, and personal income by dismissing the importance of manufacturing and ceding industrial output to others. In lieu of factory work, growth was predicated upon income from an abundance of service jobs—doctors, lawyers, janitors, bellhops, bankers, actors, rock stars, chimney sweeps, and consultants, among dozens and dozens of other positions. Which, as one economist told me, is akin to modeling an economic future on Greece.

Because manufacturing brings in a steady flow of hard currency from global customers and stimulates discernible gains in domestic employment and consumption, it is the most important economic activity that a country can engage in; it is the primary means of attracting cash from other countries at virtually no additional cost while simultaneously improving currency circulation at home. Indeed, when a nation stops making things, its economy becomes unmoored; it has nothing tangible to barter or trade and, dangerously, its ability to borrow becomes its sole survival skill.

To calculate the true value of manufacturing, consider the multiple stages in which each Honda Odyssey minivan produced in Lincoln, Alabama, primarily for sale in the United States boosts GDP: first, when Honda acquired supplies and materials to build the Lincoln factory; second, when an American purchases the new car (and, equally important, doesn't buy an import); and third, when

Honda sells an Alabama-produced Odyssey in the Philippines or the United Arab Emirates, where the automaker doesn't yet have manufacturing facilities because the market is too small.

Factory exports, as opposed to services sold abroad, are especially lucrative for the home country. While the auto dealership and its logistics providers in the Philippines retain a small portion of the purchase price for an Odyssey bought there, the lion's share of the money is sent back to American Honda Motor Co. for reinvestment or to be spent by Honda workers. By contrast, a George Clooney movie or an Alicia Keys album might have originated under the aegis of an American media company, but by the time the worldwide money it earns is divvied up among global investors, international distributors, and the artists, it's anyone's guess where that cash is spent and which country's GDP is the better for it. Similarly, although a small portion of the fee charged by an American consultant in Abu Dhabi may return to her employer in the United States, she will probably recirculate most of the money in the Arab city.

The importance of manufacturing—and the consequences of downplaying manufacturing as little more than underemployment—is slowly dawning on some American business leaders. For example, General Electric CEO Jeffrey Immelt, who has been a lightning rod of criticism for his company's all-in embrace of globalization that sent thousands and thousands of U.S. jobs overseas, has recently begun to reevaluate his position on global manufacturing. He has shuttered plants in China and renewed factory operations in North America, although his company still has a disjointed, "partially pregnant" global manufacturing policy, halfway dependent on low-cost labor but wishing it weren't.

Perhaps, then, as one of globalization's earliest cheerleaders and now an apostate of sorts, Immelt's assessment of the developed world's rejection of manufacturing carries additional weight. It seemed so to industrial leaders who were unnerved by his unexpected stinging attack on current U.S. manufacturing policies offered not long ago in a speech at West Point. He said: "Many bought into the idea that America could go from a technology-based, export-oriented powerhouse to a services-led, consumption-based economy—and somehow still expect to prosper. Our economy tilted towards the quicker profits of financial services. We need a new strategy. We should clear away any arrogance, false assumptions that things will be okay if we stick to the status quo. We need to make products here and have the self-confidence to sell them around the world."

Any number of economic variables can be chosen to illustrate the stiff price a country pays for surrendering its manufacturing sector. For example, base wages and total hourly compensation, which includes the value of medical insurance and pensions, are as much as 13 percent higher in manufacturing than in other sectors—a testament to the tangible role that industry plays in unleashing a country's middle class and awakening consumer spending. Moreover, these better-than-average salaries are spread across a group of less-educated employees whose opportunities to climb the economic ladder are otherwise limited: nearly half of all manufacturing workers have never gone to college, compared with 37 percent in non-manufacturing jobs.

But as palliative as higher salaries are to economic growth, most industrial experts cite trade balance, or the difference between the value of exports and imports, as the area in which manufacturing has its greatest influence on a nation's well-being. This benchmark gauges a country's ability to generate cash flow or, conversely, its need to borrow money by whether it supplies more goods and services to the rest of the world than it purchases.

The United States has run a trade deficit since 1976 but more recently the imbalance has risen to extreme levels—about 3 percent of GDP after sinking to that nadir only once before, during the mid-1980s recession. Manufacturing is by far the largest component of the trade deficit and between 2000 and 2012, the United States accumulated an aggregate negative trade balance in goods of about $8 trillion. In six of those years, the deficit topped $700 billion, which means that each U.S. household purchased about $5,000 in foreign-produced items for every $1 in American exports.

Not surprisingly, these figures coincided with a huge drop in manufacturing jobs in the United States. In January 2000, manufacturing's share of total employment was 13.2 percent; by 2013, it had fallen to about 9 percent—and that includes the slight uptick in manufacturing jobs since the end of the 2008–09 recession.

At 12 percent of U.S. GDP, manufacturing has an outsized impact on the overall U.S. economy, magnified by the fact that for every dollar spent on manufacturing another $1.40 is added to the economy. That is the highest so-called multiplier effect of any sector. By contrast, services add only about 60 cents to the economy for every dollar spent. Including the multiplier effect, the endemic trade deficits and concomitant factory job contraction are responsible for over 1 percent a year in lost economic growth.

And while GDP slows, the trade deficit adds to the nation's indebtedness to other countries. These loans must be repaid out of future U.S. income, which itself is at risk unless the weaknesses in the manufacturing sector are alleviated. As Harvard economists Kenneth Rogoff and Carmen Reinhart wrote in *This Time Is Different*, an examination of economic downturns since the medieval era, large trade imbalances may not be the direct cause of deep recessions, but they are an unequivocal sign of an unhealthy economy and are in fact harbingers of serious financial crises.

Innovation is another victim of manufacturing's lowly status in the United States and other developed nations. Manufacturers rely on conceiving new factory processes and products to lift sales and earnings far more than any other companies. According to a 2008 National Science Foundation survey, 22 percent of U.S. manufacturing companies bred a new or significantly improved product, service, or process between 2006 and 2008, compared with only 8 percent of nonmanufacturing companies. Moreover, manufacturers account for 68 percent of U.S. private sector R&D spending. And they allocate, on average, 3.6 percent of sales for R&D versus only 2.4 percent in nonindustrial sectors. As noted earlier, Honda is consistently the leader in R&D expenditures in the auto industry, earmarking over 5 percent of sales per year for its autonomous research and design company.

The speed and frequency of innovation in its midst are indispensable components in a country's economic growth. Innovation sparks improvements in worker output, materials usage, energy conservation, product design, lifestyle, and other vital facets of a society's productivity. In turn, jobs are created and standards of living rise.

Indeed, the Commerce Department estimates that about 75 percent of U.S. GDP growth since World War II can be directly linked to new products and processes. And taking a broader view, Ohio State University economist Richard Steckel pointed out that between 1820 and 1998 the overall GDP per capita of the world increased by a factor of 8.6. But in the industrialized countries, which have benefited from wave after wave of technological advances, this figure rose at a much more rapid clip. Western Europe saw a tenfold increase while the United States enjoyed a twentyfold gain. Meanwhile, GDP per capita went up by only a factor of 3.3 in Africa and India and 5.5 in China.

One of the more dubious ideas promulgated by globalization is that factories and R&D can be separated by thousands of miles and myriad cultural differences without affecting the ability to innovate—an example of the flat-world syndrome at its most naïve. And most multinationals have, in fact, embraced this notion, in large part because they prefer maintaining design units close to corporate headquarters where new ideas can be centrally managed and adapted into global company product strategies. Honda has taken the opposite approach, establishing independent research companies that are linked directly to local factories, ultimately to foster grassroots innovation throughout the organization.

Many leading economists favor Honda's strategy, viewing it as a competitive advantage for the company and an economic benefit for the countries where Honda's manufacturing and R&D facilities are located. They argue (as Honda has) that exposing engineers to the challenges addressed by production and design teams fuels debates and experimentation about the potential for accelerating improvements in existing technologies, enriching them for new markets and transforming them into new products. According to Susan Helper, chief economist at the Commerce Department and former senior economist on the White House Council of Economic Advisers, "We've learned from numerous studies that the proximity of production and innovation will determine which countries lead in current and future technology, design, and process advances."

In a 2012 white paper for the Brookings Institution entitled "Why Does Manufacturing Matter? Which Manufacturing Matters?," Helper and two colleagues provide convincing anecdotal evidence of vexing R&D shortcomings in the United States that occurred after companies sent production overseas. They point to the decision to transfer battery and electronics manufacturing to East Asia a decade ago, which has given this region a substantial knowledge advantage in the contest to perfect rechargeable batteries for electric cars. The same thing happened in the area of solar panels assembly techniques, a process known as thin-film deposition. After shipping much of the related semiconductor manufacturing to Asia some time ago, the United States is ill equipped now to develop new technologies for this complicated operation.

And perhaps the most costly American innovation deficit that the paper's authors describe involves rare earths, the highly prized elements used in an expanding array of modern devices including wind turbines, hybrid-car batteries, smartphones, flat panels, fluorescent light bulbs, and hard drives. The United States has abundant rare earths reserves, but American companies began offshoring the harvesting of these elements to China and other countries more than three decades ago. Since then, patent applications in the United States for rare earths technology have dried up. And now U.S. companies no longer have the infrastructure or the intellectual property to refine rare earths into pure metals and alloys required for manufacturing.

"The ability to make things is fundamental to the ability to innovate things over the long term," said Harvard Business School professor Willy Shih, coauthor of *Producing Prosperity: Why America Needs a Manufacturing Renaissance.* "When you give up making products you relinquish a large part of your economy in the short run—that's obvious. But although less immediately visible, in the long run the damage is even worse."

With so much to lose when a country abandons its manufacturing base, the ease with which the United States and other developed nations were seduced by the specious promises of globalization is perplexing. The ramifications of this policy have begun to come to light only recently, and many economists and pundits continue to argue that globalization will yet pay off. But Western countries cannot afford to wait much longer before addressing the deficiencies in their manufacturing sectors.

In the course of my research for this book I asked multinational executives, academics, consultants, and policy makers for their ideas about how manufacturing in the West can be revived. Some favored extensive participation by governments in backing essential industries and funding industrial ventures (to a degree, Germany and China have chosen this approach). That's probably not possible in the United States and other countries averse to any whiff of socialism.

Others said that the best thing political leaders can do is give multinationals a low-tax, low-regulation environment in which to operate and the companies themselves would address the manufacturing decline for their own benefit and ultimately the country's. That disengaged approach sounds curiously like current U.S. manufacturing policy, except in a much more lenient setting for multinationals. No research or historical precedent exists to indicate that a laissez-faire posture would trigger a manufacturing renaissance in the West of the size and scope necessary to overcome the economic instability plaguing developed nations.

But despite the sharp divisions in this debate, there were areas of agreement—some strong, some less so—that pointed to a few simple, relatively easily executed strategies that could in fact draw large pockets of manufacturing back to the United States and its ilk. These recommendations reflect a commonsense and viable approach for which Honda, among very few other companies, can largely serve as a model.

All of the specific policy prescriptions fit under a single umbrella: active support for high road manufacturing, a rather new term to describe companies that harness the knowledge, experience, and creativity of their workers for continuous factory and product innovation. Obviously, Honda is in this camp (and was well before economists coined its latest name). And potentially, so could be many of the companies that are closing plants in China to shift production back to the United States, a slow but steadily swelling stream. These firms are primarily motivated by the performance gains inherent in siting factories close to a majority of their customers and by cost inflation in China, especially rising prices for labor and logistics. But much of this global realignment involves high-margin, durable items—autos, appliances, turbines, engines, expensive home hardware, and the like—which depend for their success on repeated improvements in processes, productivity, and design; in short, the facets of industrial life that high road manufacturing is perfectly suited for. Other, commodity-like, limited-profit goods—basic textiles, electronics, office supplies, and inexpensive kitchen ware, for example—will still primarily be made in the lowest-cost countries.

High road manufacturing has its own virtuous rhythm. It pays above-average wages to workers capable of consistently generating product and process enhancements, which in turn reduce defect rates, increase market share, drive factory efficiency, deliver cost savings, and embellish the company's reputation. This boosts revenue and customer loyalty; as a result, wages scale up further and turnover is kept to a minimum. Because of how logical this concept sounds, many companies claim to favor it. But as with lean techniques, few businesses are sufficiently persistent and attentive to detail to fully espouse it; certainly not to the granular extent that Honda has. Still, even imperfect high road manufacturing can provide a demonstrable lift in sales and profits and quicken economic growth.

A recent study by Case Western Reserve University of automotive stamping companies found that only about one third adopted two of the most basic worker-directed factory improvement programs—and those firms far outperformed the rest. One was preventive equipment maintenance, which draws on and ultimately broadens employee knowledge about the causes and rates of machine failures, greatly minimizing downtime. The other was quality circles, or cross-company employee teams that meet frequently to explore ideas for process and product improvement. Between 2007 and 2011, stampers with preventive maintenance routines and quality circles enjoyed sales gains of 5.1 percent and 3.5 percent, respectively. Stampers eschewing these programs suffered corresponding sales declines of 31 percent and 9.9 percent.

Generally, the stampers that engaged in high road manufacturing were among the best-paying firms, offering salaries as much as 70 percent higher than their more tentative rivals. Since direct labor makes up less than 20 percent of a stamper's costs, additional revenue and cost savings from process innovation more than made up for the generous wages. In addition, about 10 percent of the stampers took it upon themselves to improve designs provided by their automaker customers—a level of autonomy that Honda expects of companies accepted into its supplier community—and these presumably higher-margin parts accounted for a very profitable 70 percent of the stampers' sales.

This is a small window into a small industry, but in other similar studies of high road manufacturing the same narrative unfolds of real and durable increases in wages, product innovation, sales, consumer spending, factory construction, and productivity—all of which are vital elements of overall GDP growth.

"The most progressive manufacturers are not focused on a quick fix or a quick exit; instead, they represent long-term value creation that echoes throughout the economy year after year," says Hamdi Ulukaya, the founder of Chobani yogurt, who converted an abandoned Kraft Foods facility in South Edmeston, New York, into an impressively efficient dairy plant that employs two thousand people and has spurred new business for local farmers, restaurants, gas stations, and hotels while helping revive the local real estate market.

"These manufacturers can be a foundation for consistent economic expansion that builds upon itself, product by product and process by process."

Economists believe that the most sensible industrial policies would influence companies to choose high road manufacturing, but not subsidize it. There is virtually no desire in the United States for Washington to pick industrial "winners" to bankroll directly; the bailout of the auto companies in 2008, although necessary, still veers disturbingly close to government industrial favoritism for most Americans. Instead, U.S. economists tend to back broad incentives to make applying high road manufacturing more desirable without forcing companies to adopt the concept.

Promoting R&D investments is an obvious place to start. Most companies are hesitant about earmarking a large portion of sales for research because the payoff is too uncertain and, usually, not immediate. Tax credits or deductions for R&D spending are the simplest and most prevalent way to address this reluctance. In effect, they reduce the impact of R&D budgets on quarterly earnings, making research more palatable to many companies. However, the U.S. R&D tax credit is among the least generous in the world, amounting to about 20 percent of research expenses, and thus is considered too meager to significantly buoy R&D activities. Other countries, notably the United Kingdom, Brazil, Australia, Israel, and Germany, grant much more attractive inducements to innovators, in some cases returning more than 100 percent of R&D expenditures to the companies.

The miserly U.S. research credit is worsened by tax policies that hinder manufacturers from claiming deductions. As the Internal Revenue Service has interpreted the R&D rules, most prototypes that eventually become commercial products and virtually all improvements in production processes are ineligible for the credit.

Under the agency's definition, R&D is a pure and inchoate activity; that is, basic experimentation not directly linked to a profit-seeking part of the operation. The government is reconsidering this stance, which prevents manufacturers from sharing in the tax credit for the very types of innovation that are most critical to their businesses.

But even at its most unfettered, R&D tax forgiveness is a rather passive way for governments to foster innovation. A more direct approach for Washington would be to support a network of industrial research centers, in which neighboring universities and companies match public-sector funding to jointly develop new materials, technologies, and processes. Ideally, these centers would undertake both basic and applied research, giving companies access to immediately useful new technologies and systems while other ideas are incubating.

Although the U.S. business landscape is dotted with dozens of government-backed research facilities, most of them are defense related or focused on extremely speculative areas of investigation, such as space travel to distant planets and cures for untreatable diseases. Less exotic industrial research tends to be by necessity self-funded and tethered to a single company or perhaps to a joint venture comprising two or more firms. For example, Honda and General Motors recently agreed to work together on developing fuel cell and hydrogen storage technologies for electric cars by 2020. Similarly, Intel and GE have had a long-standing partnership targeted at advances in health care equipment, and the pharmaceutical industry is well known for its many group drug development efforts.

Because these private-sector R&D initiatives receive little if any government money, many of them are short-lived, starved for cash when the sponsor companies lose interest or hit a financial wall. Usually, they are idled well before they achieve their goals. U.S. economic policy makers told me that there is a growing sense in Washington that the government's lack of support for industrial R&D has been a mistake. And they boast about efforts to make up for this; among them, a new program called the National Network for Manufacturing Innovation (NNMI), slated to eventually house fifteen separate institutes.

The pilot site is a facility in Youngstown, Ohio, where researchers will explore new avenues in additive manufacturing—essentially 3D printing—for the industrial sector. This public/private partnership—participating universities and firms have anted up $40 million to match the government's $30 million—has attracted a cast of big names like Alcoa, Northrop Grumman, Lockheed Martin, GE, Carnegie Mellon University, and Johnson Controls. Like most other research centers funded by the government, NNMI is collaborative and the intellectual property will be shared. The hope is to stoke rivalries among members to develop proprietary technology from NNMI's basic research; in turn, it is assumed that the most innovative applications—at least those that appear to be improving profitability and, if commercial, attracting customers—will act as pace cars for other companies to try to surpass.

But research efforts like these are relatively small and will still leave the United States at a distinct disadvantage to other industrialized countries that count on their manufacturing sectors to drive a substantial portion of the economy. The United States ranks twenty-second out of thirty countries in government-funded research as a share of GDP. Germany spends about twenty times more on manufacturing R&D than the United States, with much of its money targeted at factory floor activities, such as industrial design and robotics. In addition, the vast network of sixty-seven research centers known as the Fraunhofer Institutes concentrate primarily on practical industrial technologies, such as advances in solar cells and lightweight construction, and spin off private-sector firms that partner with more established manufacturers, helping to seed and promulgate additional innovation. Given this emphasis, it's not a coincidence that manufacturing in Germany accounts for a stunning 30 percent of GDP. And unlike most Western countries, Germany's trade balance in goods is reliably positive.

Honda has enjoyed the same degree of success with its R&D strategy. In effect, the automaker has an internal research network that is as extensive and fixed on industrial innovation as Germany's. The company's two dozen R&D labs and three regional Honda Research Institutes are unmatched by other industrial firms, which don't put the same premium on research and innovation. But U.S. policy makers would be wise to emulate Honda's model, particularly its flexible combination of applied and basic research that has produced more automotive, engine, factory process, and individual mobility patents and designed-in features than any other manufacturing operation.

Industrial clusters offer governments another possible channel for promoting manufacturing innovation. A cluster is a local web of integrated, cooperating companies, suppliers, service providers, trade associations, and associated institutions, such as university research labs. Well-known clusters exist across the United States: Silicon Valley; the life sciences companies in eastern Massachusetts; and the aerospace outfits around Huntsville, Alabama, and Wichita, Kansas. Clusters tend to form naturally—Silicon Valley grew out of the local influence of Stanford University—but some companies purposely build their own. For example, Honda's localization strategy is in part designed around a constellation of suppliers located within a short hop of the manufacturing facility, which itself is an amalgamation of R&D, engineering, and assembly.

Clusters routinely bring together, face-to-face, people who share the same manufacturing goals, creating an echo chamber in which new ideas, business plans, production processes, and product concept experimentation can emerge. In fact, according to Commerce Department chief economist Susan Helper, innovation is primarily a local activity, the fruits of which can be intensified substantially in a geographically concentrated operating model, like Honda's, or in a manufacturing cluster. As evidence, Helper said that an examination of patents found that inventors disproportionately used the output of nearby scientists as the stimulus for their work. Other studies concurred, showing that the benefits of R&D appear to be confined to the borders of the region or country where the research originates. These results can be explained in part by the motivational quality of clusters acting as self-supporting communities that inspire workers to innovate and embellish their palette of skills through daily interaction.

The federal government can provide limited support for clusters, mostly by backing research centers geared toward the particular products and manufacturing systems that are unique to the cluster. However, state and local officials can assist in the development of a cluster that appears to be evolving organically by investing in roads, rail lines, communication links, harbors, and airports as well as proposing tax incentives and other enticements to attract companies to the group.

Innovation is just one side of the equation. High road manufacturing also depends on skilled, intelligent workers who are excited by discovery and change and enthusiastic about influencing new product designs and factory improvements in their companies. That's a bit of a tall order these days. The steady decline of manufacturing in the West and the very public implications that factory work is a second-class, dying, low-income occupation, which anyone can do with the same aplomb anywhere, has soured many of the brightest young people on industrial careers. A recent survey of engineering, science, and math students by consultants Booz & Company found that while 80 percent of the engineering students had some exposure to manufacturing—mostly through college courses or field trips to factories—only 50 percent regarded it as an attractive career. Of science and math students, only 20 percent did.

Local and federal education programs should help prepare young people for manufacturing jobs far better than they do today. It can start with the industrial arts curriculum—in other words, the once common shop classes, which have been phased out in most high schools because they are increasingly preoccupied solely with college preparation. But for the large number of students who are not college bound (as well as many that are), manufacturing represents a chance to participate in a field that is inventive, rapidly changing, and quickly modernizing. Many of the most noteworthy environmental, mechanical, robotic, and electrical breakthroughs of the past fifty years have been the handiwork of manufacturers, as Honda's history clearly shows. By reviving shop classes, schools can provide teenage students with attractive alternative career paths.

In addition, federal and state funding should be made available for programs that teach manufacturing workers the additional skills that their companies feel they need. Some states tie educational opportunities of this sort to the local community colleges and tend to provide guidance in, for example, operating new machines that are being installed in the plant. But these programs can be expanded to cover more high-level and complex skills like process improvement and product development. They can also be used to retrain assembly line workers who have lost their jobs.

Meanwhile, with the shortage of American engineering students robbing the labor pool of high-quality manufacturing workers, immigration reform advocates and manufacturers are pressuring Washington to relax visa restrictions. They've asked the government to allow foreign national students in U.S. science, technology, engineering, and math programs to remain in the country for industrial jobs after they graduate, rather than return home and use the skills they've learned to benefit manufacturers there.

Drawn together, these many recommendations could represent the beginning of a cohesive industrial policy with limited government involvement and a strong course for manufacturing's future set at the national level. It should be noted, however, that this approach completely ignores intractable issues that are too politically delicate to seriously tackle now. For example, every economist believes that the U.S. corporate tax code is stacked against American manufacturers. At 40 percent, the U.S. statutory corporate tax rate is higher than that of any other manufacturing country. Germany's is about 39 percent; Brazil, 24 percent; Mexico, 30 percent; and China, 20 percent. Reducing taxation levels would make other leading economies less attractive and encourage manufacturers to open new factories in the United States. The tax base would thus expand, potentially resulting in higher government income. It's logical, but precisely how much to lower the rate and which tax loopholes to eliminate has Washington tied up in knots. Equally thorny are efforts to reduce unfair global trade barriers and currency manipulation, both of which are endemic throughout the world and favor local manufacturers.

Still, even with woefully deficient tax rules and global hazards, the U.S. manufacturing sector is in remarkably healthy shape. With companies moving back to the United States from low-cost countries, American factories have added more jobs since the end of the 2008–09 recession than all of the G-7 countries combined. Moreover, U.S. manufacturers produce about 75 percent of the products that the nation consumes, a high rate for a developed nation. Economists believe that with the right mix of initiatives to buoy factory innovation and worker engagement, the hallmarks of high road manufacturing, that figure could increase to 90 percent. At that level, GDP growth, salary gains, and trade imbalances are no longer intractable concerns.

■

When Soichiro Honda was in his last years, he slowed down quite a bit. His speech, formerly lively and lilting, had become halting; his gait was doddering. Yet he visited Honda's research labs in Japan frequently, unable to keep away from the grease pits and gleaming metal.

He admitted to friends that he felt out of his depth there, however. He didn't understand the new machine designs or even the variations in the way mechanical parts moved, shifting from one cadence to another at the whim of computers and semiconductors. And he casually mentioned this to one of the young Honda engineers on the factory floor.

The young man, perhaps earnestly or maybe hoping to avoid insulting Soichiro, responded: "Oh, no, Honda-san, it's all very derivative. Everything we make is connected in some way to everything you made. Things change, but the basic theory is the same. You could build these engines."

"But that's not so," Honda answered. "I don't see any connection between this engine and the single-cylinder motors I first worked on. The pistons don't work the same anymore; they are not linked to the rhythm of the cylinder rings in the same way they used to be. And the transmissions are constantly in motion. Even when I made cars, our transmissions were primitive. I don't see any of me in this equipment."

The young man tried once more: "I do completely. In fact, I revere the past. The concept of how the engine works has not changed, just the equipment surrounding the engine. Those are two different things."

"That's not true," Honda said. "If I had a wrench and was asked to fix this engine, I couldn't do it."

Now the engineer had tired of the conversation. It was going nowhere and he had work to do. Obviously, Soichiro didn't. His patience gone, the young man snapped back, "You're too old. You just don't understand."

"Exactly. Why didn't you just agree with me in the first place?"

And Soichiro hobbled away smiling. Clearly, age hadn't dulled Honda's love for paradox and his taste for verbal swordplay.

Indeed, that knotty conversation captures the enigma of Honda Motor perfectly: through argument and joy, and the joy of argument, by going to the spot and then fighting over what you saw with someone who came away with a completely different impression, somehow Soichiro's company has invariably arrived at the right answer.

AFTERWORD TO THE PAPERBACK EDITION

Since the publication of *Driving Honda* in hardcover last year, Honda has racked up numerous achievements, many of which are anticipated or detailed in the book. Each of them reflects well Honda's restless impulse to be innovative and unorthodox, two of the most essential legacy characteristics that the company inherited from its founder, Soichiro Honda. In the name of helping people pursue the "joy of mobility," a term that Honda employs often to describe the purpose of its products, the company has debuted a futuristic lightweight, fuel-efficient corporate jet, as Honda became the first new company approved to build aircraft engines in twenty-three years; launched a new personality-rich Roadster designed by a twenty-six-year-old; further perfected the Asimo robot, which can walk, run, and climb like a human and perform basic tasks like holding a platter and serving food; introduced a walking-assist device for the handicapped as well as a Segway-like device called the Uni-Cub; manufactured its 300 millionth motorcycle; and continued to produce upwards of a dozen new or updated cars drawn specifically to the cultural and physical peccadillos of individual regions.

But despite this flurry of activity, Honda is probably best known at this moment for a very public mistake. During the past year, more than 35 million vehicles worldwide made by virtually all of the Japanese and U.S. automakers, as well as BMW, have been recalled to replace air bags manufactured by Takata Corp. Most of these cars and trucks were built between 2000 and 2008; however, there have also been some complaints of airbag failures in subsequent years as well. Despite the large number of vehicles involved, only a few hundred actual airbag problems have been reported, in large part because these components are used so infrequently—that is, only during an accident. When they have malfunctioned, the Takata airbags exploded upon deploying, sending shards throughout the vehicles, injuring or in very rare cases killing occupants. Although many automakers, such as Toyota and Nissan, are recalling millions of vehicles each, about a third of the cars on the list are Honda's.

While this massive recall brought Takata airbag defects out into the open, this is not a new problem. In the United States, Honda received the first complaint about "airbag inflator ruptures" as early as 2008 and in the next five years learned of more than 1,000 other Takata-related incidents during the next five years. During this time, Honda alerted the National Highway Traffic Safety Administration about these airbag failures, but not with appropriate urgency and primarily through unofficial channels that circumvented the usual computerized reporting system. As a result, Honda was recently fined $70 million by NHTSA for not sufficiently addressing an evolving but obvious pattern of airbag injuries.

This episode has been an embarrassment and somewhat of a surprise for Honda, particularly since the automaker is widely celebrated for the quality, reliability, and longevity of its vehicles as well as its trustworthiness. Indeed, I puzzled over the recall and the events surrounding it for some time, wondering whether they were perhaps a red flag, as it were—a sign that Honda was not, after all, the archetype of multinational success that I portrayed in *Driving Honda.*

But the more I explored this question—helped out by auto industry specialists and Honda experts, most of whom I had initially interviewed for the book—I realized that despite the seriousness of the Takata debacle, Honda's noteworthy response to it reflected yet again the value and dynamism of the company's unique culture and principles. Moreover, since Honda is emerging from this experience with its business, reputation, and enthusiasm for experimenting with new products and fresh ideas largely intact—its belief in its social role as a catalyst for human mobility unbroken—the company's approach to the crisis is worthy of emulation by other large global corporations.

The most striking aspect of how Honda has dealt with the incident involves the way the company turned to its most prized tenets for solutions. It's not unusual for an organization in trouble to jettison avowed beliefs and principles—often those involving transparency and accountability—while its executives cover up the problem, dive into the bunker, and point blame elsewhere. For example, the recent reaction of General Motors to fatal defects in its small-car ignition switches, which resulted in as many as seventy-five deaths, is more typical. The automaker knew about the problem since around 2004, but as emails and company documents that came to light in lawsuits and investigations show, GM executives deliberately concealed their knowledge of the serious flaws in the switch and initially took virtually no steps to address it. By contrast, neither federal agencies nor investigators or attorneys have found any evidence or indication that Honda attempted to hide the airbag ruptures; instead, Honda is under a cloud for the inadequacy of its accident reporting processes, not for purposefully downplaying or burying consumer complaints and accident patterns.

As discussed in chapter 5, Honda is among the few organizations to whom corporate culture is not merely a series of untethered ideas that can be expediently—and usually disastrously—ignored when they are inconvenient or a less palatable option. In the wake of the recalls, Honda was fundamentally guided by Soichiro's oft-emphasized fatalistic attitude about the value—even more, the necessity—of errors. He wrote: "Success is only 1 percent of your work, and the rest—bold overcoming of obstacles. If you are not afraid of obstacles, success will come to you itself." By viewing the systemic lapses that resulted in the airbag failures as an inevitable learning moment, Honda did not take a kneejerk or duplicitous defensive posture. Instead, the company stressed that this must be an opportunity for continuous improvement.

At public hearings before Congress and at press conferences, Honda executives readily admitted—surprisingly, with little or no blame placed on Takata—that the automaker had not lived up to its responsibilities both in the lack of quality of the parts in its cars and in inadequate NHTSA and customer notification that airbag problems were percolating. CEO Takanobu Ito said that there were "multiple mishandlings" and promised that the company would fix the problems that allowed this embarrassing incident to happen.

To live up to this pledge, Honda applied or examined the three operating principles that comprise its unique culture. For starters, Honda *embraced paradox* through a series of *waigaya*, contentious meetings across the organization at which all levels of employees (from executive to sales to assembly line, engineering, and maintenance) offered their opinions and ideas about Honda's missteps and how they should be addressed.

These candid sessions led to an interesting observation about corporate culture and the universal adoption (or lack of it) of a company's principles by its employees: As a small organization grows into a large one, there is an imperceptible erosion of many of the tenets that drove the business during its start-up and entrepreneurial phases, although they are still given lip service. Ultimately, creeping bureaucracy is anathema to the operational agility and employee creativity that are emblematic of the most successful emerging companies. Honda prided itself on being inured from this outcome by the strength of Soichiro's imprint on the organization, characterized by an obsession with decentralized operations held together by the unwavering responsibility of every worker to the company's success. In other words, an individual mistake is viewed as a systemic failure and everyone in the company is answerable for letting it happen.

During the Takata *waigaya*, it became clear that the expectation that a combined bottom-up and top-down accountability could fully survive as an organization aged was overly optimistic. Or at least Honda learned that this part of its culture could not exist organically without an ongoing and diligent effort to maintain it. In the context of the airbag ruptures, the shortcomings of the reporting system were obvious to those working on it—but these weaknesses did not appear to be serious enough to warrant immediate action. Similarly, the individual complaints about airbag failures seemed too small and isolated to be given a great deal of consideration. These indolent attitudes are precisely what Soichiro had hoped to quash at his company when he, often angrily and sometimes punitively, deemed that no detail, in any Honda product, could be considered insignificant. Without the *waigaya*, at which every worker is an equal and every argument is worthy of a response, the need to reroot and readdress the weight of this aspect of Honda's culture (and how it had catalyzed Honda's growth as a successful multinational) would have been lost in the fog of the Takata scandal.

Along with *waigaya*, Honda unraveled the Takata question by examining whether it adequately practiced *sangen shugi* in its relationship with the airbag maker—that is, whether it had appropriately gone to the three actualities (the real spot, the real part, and the real facts) to ensure that Takata's products and processes met the highest quality standards.

As chapter 8 explores in some detail, Honda has a rigid program of monitoring supplier activities closely and demanding annual improvements in quality and output. This policy has been in place for decades and results in a somewhat unorthodox relationship between Honda and its suppliers, one in which Honda essentially molds the companies that it buys parts and components from in its image, fusing its culture and operational practices with the suppliers' to produce real collaboration.

This approach was undone in Takata's case for two reasons: Takata had an excellent perceived safety record throughout the auto industry, and Takata's products were viewed as too proprietary and complex—unlike other parts, like electrical components, headlamps, engine components, and so on—for the automaker to diagnose potential problems. In taking this stance, Honda essentially gave Takata a free pass that few of its other suppliers enjoyed. This was a serious mistake by Honda—a disavowal of *sangen shugi*—that was not only based on a wrong premise (Takata was, in fact, not the paragon of perfect products) but displayed a fundamental ignorance of the meaning of *sangen shugi* itself. The foundation of *sangen shugi* is the notion that no product, idea, design, engineering riddle, or system is so complicated or difficult to comprehend that it can withstand the knowledge gained by going to the spot. Or put another way, *sangen shugi*, by definition, simplifies and dissects complexity; it unwinds ignorance.

Finally, Honda *reasserted the importance of individualism and the Three Joys*. Simply put, it is the responsibility of individuals in the company to practice The Joy of Creating and Selling by making the right choices, leading innovation and improvement to sell products that exceed customer expectations, which in turn inspire the Joy of Buying by improving mobility and changing society for the better.

As a result of these internal activities, each linked to its primary operating principles, Honda has made a succession of moves related to the airbag recall. Upper-level and supplier-management executives have been fired, including CEO Ito. Honda has torn down and then rebuilt its information technology system to better expose quality problems from evidence contained in isolated incidents and pieces of data and communicate these concerns more quickly with customers and authorities. Moreover, Honda is in the midst of a very challenging period of soul searching that is meant to decipher how its most treasured principles can be maintained in a large global, multinational corporate setting.

Importantly—at least as a model for the way companies should deal with crises—Honda did not allow these efforts to mitigate its internal problems to paralyze or overwhelm the company's normal and even extraordinary operations, as the steady parade of innovation and new products attests to. This is primarily because the solutions that Honda chose to implement were outgrowths of the company's culture itself and were, in fact, a testament to it strength. An organization's culture should not be a limiting or finite resource; rather, if viable and properly rooted, a culture should be encompassing and elastic, the structural foundation with which to manage and navigate unanticipated calamities and day-to-day procedures, innovation and routine processes, an unexpected shift in the business landscape and the rollout of a well-thought-out five-year strategic plan.

The Honda airbag recalls remind us again that a company is, after all, composed of people—and, hence, will certainly make mistakes, even perilous ones. The best companies are the ones that make the fewest errors that affect their customers, and even in the worst of times are focused on improving the lives and lifestyles of people who buy their products. But like individuals, companies should not be measured by single incidents (or quarterly results). They should, however, be judged by how they react to dilemmas—or, better yet, how well their culture equips them to do so.

ACKNOWLEDGMENTS

Writing a book can feel like a solo, lonely effort for authors who are compelled to follow a topic for two years or often more, to become obsessed with every little nuance that their subject offers. And yet this perception is ultimately a sort of narcissism, or perhaps masochism, that many writers—I among them—enjoy and are to a degree motivated by. Because, the truth is, it's an inaccurate impression. Rather than being a solitary affair, books are actually the product of a large team of people, all of them invaluable and indispensable.

Driving Honda's team, if I may, was a particularly stellar and competent group—and one that earns my enduring gratitude. At the head of this cast of dozens are my editors at the Portfolio imprint. Niki Papadopoulos was the main editor on the book, and her guidance and suggestions were always smart, thoughtful, insightful—and usually right.

Niki's boss, Adrian Zackheim, the president and publisher of Portfolio, also was a wonderful collaborator. He understood why this book matters—what Honda represents as a global business presence and the rich story that Honda offers—from the moment he read the book proposal. His continuing support was essential and deeply appreciated.

When I originally wrote the book proposal for *Driving Honda*, my agent was Kate Lee at ICM Partners. Although I was in a bit of a hiatus at the time, she encouraged me to get moving on another book and was instrumental in helping focus *Driving Honda* on the theme that had the greatest significance and that, in fact, Honda's story emblemized best. Kate left ICM and is now director of content at a literary blogging site called Medium, where she is, not surprisingly, exceeding expectations. My current ICM agent, Kristine Dahl, has steadily stood for my interests and is extremely competent. I couldn't ask for more.

During the course of reporting and writing *Driving Honda*, I spoke to dozens of Honda employees and visited numerous Honda facilities. The company has been extremely cooperative and has generously given me access to materials and individuals to facilitate my research. There isn't room to thank everyone at Honda, but I want to express my appreciation to all of Honda's workers who gave of their time to participate in this book. And I want to offer my deepest gratitude specifically to Ed Miller, Mark Morrison, Ted Pratt, Ron Lietzke, Marcos Frommer, and Andy Woods.

There are plenty of very bright people who follow the auto industry and helped me navigate some of the more confusing issues about Honda and its competitors. Three stand out as particularly insightful, candid, intelligent, and helpful: the extraordinary John Casesa, senior managing director at Guggenheim Partners; Sean McAlinden, one of the smartest people you'll meet and chief economist at the Center for Automotive Research; and Ron Harbour, whose remarkable yearly analysis of auto factories is an industry compulsion.

I am also indebted to two friends—two of the most accomplished publishing insiders I know—for their help in guiding *Driving Honda* at its earliest stages, when it was a nascent idea and not a particularly intelligible one. Will Balliett, the president and publisher at Thames & Hudson, listened to my initial Honda enthusiasm and astutely saw that viewing Honda through the lens of making globalization work was an apt thematic approach. At the time, I had no idea what the right direction was; Will's help was critical.

The other friend I wish to thank is Leah Nathans Spiro, who was my colleague at *BusinessWeek* many years ago and an editor on one of my prior books, *McIlhenny's Gold*. Leah now runs her own literary agency and book consultancy, Riverside Creative Management. Leah is an astute editor and wordsmith and she worked closely with me on the book proposal for *Driving Honda*, honing the theme and structure and tightening up the language. I revisited her contribution throughout the project whenever I lost the book's thread.

SELECTED SOURCES

I interviewed dozens of Honda insiders, auto industry experts, car enthusiasts, economists, globalization gurus, and corporate analysts for this book. When I could I identified them here. I also pored through voluminous research material about Honda, its history, its industry, its competitors, its strategies, its principles, and the economic landscape it is navigating. These are among the most valuable documents:

"25 Most Intriguing People of the Year." *People*, Dec. 29, 1980.

Applebome, Peter. "South Raises Stakes in Fight for Jobs." *The New York Times*, Aug. 4, 1993.

"A Renaissance at Risk: Threats and Opportunities for Swiss Manufacturing." Booz & Co. and Swiss-American Chamber of Commerce. 2010.

"A Road Forward: The Report of the Toyota North American Quality Advisory Panel." Toyota, May 2011.

"Auto Industry Sets Sights on Alternative Power." *IP Market Report*. Thomson Reuters, Jan. 2013.

"Automation: Making the Future." *The Economist*, Apr. 21, 2012.

"Back to Making Stuff." *The Economist*, Apr. 21, 2012.

Baillieul, Robert. "The Automakers' Hidden Profit Source." The Motley Fool. www.fool.com, June 27, 2013.

Barboza, David. "The Imbalances in China's Economy." *The New York Times*, May 12, 2012.

Beckley, Michael. "China's Century? Why America's Edge Will Endure." *International Security* 36, no. 3 (Winter 2011–12): 41–78.

Belson, Ken, with Micheline Maynard. "Cruise Control May Be Goal of Honda's Chief." *The New York Times*, July 10, 2003.

"Benly Machines: The Age of Innovation." www.powersports.honda.com/experience/articles/090111c0811f48a3.aspx, Mar. 6, 2013.

Büge, Max, Matias Egeland, Przemyslaw Kowalski, and Monika Sztajerowska. "State Owned Enterprises in the Global Economy: Reason for Concern?" Vox. www.voxeu.org/article/state-owned-enterprises-global-economy-reason-concern, May 2, 2013.

Cable, Josh. "Honda Celebrates 30 Years of Manufacturing in America . . . the Honda Way." *Industry Week*, May 16, 2012.

Carlisle, David. "Honda's Three Joys." Spare Thoughts. ccsparethoughts.blogspot.com, Nov. 24, 2009.

Cary, Eve. "Reforming China's State Owned Enterprises." *The Diplomat*, June 19, 2013.

Cato, Jeremy. "Honda Goes Native in North America." *The Globe and Mail*, Mar. 29, 2012.

Chakravorty, Satya S. "Where Process-Improvement Projects Go Wrong." *The Wall Street Journal*, June 14, 2012.

Cornelius, Donna. "Honda's Alabama Odyssey Begins." *Partners*, Winter 2002.

"Deep Supplier Relationships Drive Automakers' Success." *Know-WPC*. W. P. Carey School of Business, July 6, 2005.

Delgado, Mercedes, Michael E. Porter, and Scott Stern. "Clusters and Entrepreneurship." *Journal of Economic Geography* 10, no. 4 (2010): 495–518.

Elliott, Stuart. "The Media Business: Advertising; Anti-Japan Auto Ads May Backfire." *The New York Times*, Jan. 30, 1992.

Ezell, Stephen J., and Robert D. Atkinson. "The Case for a National Manufacturing Strategy." The Information Technology and Innovation Foundation, April 2011.

Fackler, Martin. "Declining as a Manufacturer, Japan Weighs Reinvention." *The New York Times*, Apr. 15, 2012.

Fahey, Jonathan, and Tim Kelly. "Engineers Rule." *Forbes*, Sept. 4, 2006.

Fisher, Lawrence M. "The Paradox of Charles Handy." *Strategy + Business*, Fall 2003.

Fishman, Charles. "The Insourcing Boom." *The Atlantic*, May 7, 2013.

Foroohar, Rana, and Bill Saporito. "Is the U.S. Manufacturing Renaissance Real?" *Time*, Mar. 28, 2013.

Francis, David. "Is This the End of Globalization?" *The Fiscal Times*, Feb. 28, 2013.

Fukui, Takeo. "The Honda Knowledge DNA and Its Transmission Regarding Corporate Culture Conducive to the Creation of New Values." Keynote Address. www.kms.jpn.org/keynoteaddress2.pdf.

Gabor, Monica. "A Welcome Sticker Shock: Made in the U.S.A." *Monthly Labor Review*. U.S. Bureau of Labor Statistics, August 2013.

Gross, Daniel. "Southern Comfort." *Newsweek*, Dec. 13, 2008.

Helgesen, Sally. "The Practical Wisdom of Ikujiro Nonaka." *Strategy + Business*, Winter 2008.

Helper, Susan, Timothy Krueger, and Howard Wial. "Why Does Manufacturing Matter? Which Manufacturing Matters?" Brookings Institution, Feb. 2012.

"Here, There and Everywhere." *The Economist*, Jan. 19, 2013.

Hindo, Brian. "At 3M, a Struggle Between Efficiency and Creativity." *BusinessWeek*, June 10, 2007.

Holford, W. David, and Mehran Ebrahimi. "A Dialectical Approach to Knowledge Creation: A Trans-Disciplinary Reflection." IAMOT, 2006.

———. "The Case of Honda: A Dialectical Yet Coherent Firm." *Proceedings of the 40th Hawaii International Conference on System Sciences*, 2007.

"Honda and Toyota Warranties." *Warranty Week*. www.warranty week.com, June 28, 2012.

"Honda Leads All Automakers in Retail Sales in Key Volume Segments." www.autoblog.com, July 20, 2013.

"Honda Ridgeline: A Truck Ahead of Its Time?" *Motor Trend* blog, Mar. 31, 2013.

Immelt, Jeffrey. "On Sparking an American Manufacturing Renewal." *Harvard Business Review*, Mar. 2012.

"Is Lean to Blame for Toyota's Recall Issues?" *Supply Chain Digest*, Mar. 3, 2010.

Ito, Hiroshi. "Strength of Japanese Monozukuri." *Kenshu Magazine*, No. 182, Summer 2007.

Iwatani, Masaki, and Shin'ya Nagasawa. "Design Management of Collaboration in Honda." *Journal of the Asian Design International Conference* 1, H-04 (2003): 1–4.

Jackson, Bill, and Michael Pfitzmann. "Win-Win Sourcing." *Strategy + Business*, Summer 2007.

"Japan Automobile Manufacturers: Creating Economic Growth and Jobs in America." Japan Automobile Manufacturers Association. www.jama-english.jp, Nov. 2012.

Jaruzelski, Barry, John Loehr, and Richard Holman. "The Global Innovation 1000: Making Ideas Work." *Strategy + Business*, Winter 2012.

Jayson, Seth. "Don't Get Too Worked Up over Honda Motor's Earnings." The Motley Fool. www.fool.com, Aug. 26, 2011.

Kaushal, Arvind, Thomas Mayor, and Patricia Riedl. "Manufacturing's Wake Up Call." *Strategy + Business*, Autumn 2011.

Kisiel, Ralph. "Adaptability Helps Honda Weather Industry Changes." *Automotive News*. www.autonews.com, June 8, 2009.

Kotkin, Joel. "Mr. Iacocca, Meet Mr. Honda." *Inc.*, Nov. 1, 1986.

Kurtzman, Joel. "An Interview with Charles Handy." *Strategy + Business*, Oct. 1, 1995.

Levin, Doron P. "Honda Decentralizes Management." *The New York Times*, May 21, 1992.

Lillis, Mike. "Foreign Auto Makers Won Billions in Government Subsidies." *The Washington Independent*. www.washingtonindependent.com, Dec. 16, 2008.

Lind, Michael. "Goodbye, Davos Man." Salon.com, May 1, 2012.

Linebaugh, Kate. "Honda's Flexible Plants Provide Edge." *The Wall Street Journal*, Sept. 23, 2008.

Lobo, Rita. "Keiretsu for a New Age." *World Finance*. www.worldfinance.com, June 26, 2012.

MacDuffie, John Paul, and Susan Helper. "Creating Lean Suppliers: Diffusing Lean Production Through the Supply Chain." *California Management Review* 39, no. 4 (1997): 118–51.

Madson, Bart. "Honda's Nicest People & Mad Men." *Motorcycle USA*. www.motorcycleusa.com, Aug. 24, 2010.

Mair, Andrew. "Learning from Honda." *Journal of Management Studies* 36, no. 1 (Jan. 1999): 25–44.

Markoff, John. "Skilled Work, Without the Worker." *The New York Times*, Aug. 18, 2012.

McAfee, Andrew. "Aspen and the Future of Manufacturing." *Harvard Business Review* Blog Network. www.blogs.hbr.org, July 7, 2011.

McArdle, Megan. "Why Companies Fail." *The Atlantic*, June 30, 2013.

McKendrick, Joe. "Toyota's Pedal Troubles: Result of Too Much or Not Enough Lean Manufacturing?" *Smart Planet*. www.smartplanet.com, Feb. 1, 2010.

Meyer, Marc H. "How Honda Innovates." *The Journal of Product Innovation* 25 (2008): 261–71.

Miller, Chad, and Mack Josep Sirgy. "Impact of Globalization of the Automotive Industry on the Quality of Life of the US Southeast." In *The Economic Geography of Globalization*, edited by Piotr Pachura. InTech, 2011.

Mintzberg, Henry, Richard T. Pascale, Michael Goold, and Richard P. Rumelt. "The 'Honda Effect' Revisited." *California Management Review* 38, no. 4 (Summer 1996): 78–91.

Moody, Patricia E. "Supplier Relationships Key to Honda's Healthy Profit Margins." *Industry Week*, Jan. 20, 2013.

Mu, Cong. "Honda's China Dream." *Global Times*. www.globaltimes.cn, June 21, 2013.

"Multinational Companies and China: What Future?" Economist Intelligence Unit. hcexchange.conference-board.org/attachment/EIU_Multinationals_and_China1.pdf. 2011.

Murphy, Colum. "Territorial Dispute Continues to Affect Japanese Car Sales in China." *The Wall Street Journal*, Sept. 11, 2013.

Myers, Randy. "Gearing Up." *CFO Magazine*. www.cfo.com, Dec. 1, 2011.

Myerson, Allen R. "O Governor, Won't You Buy Me a Mercedes Plant?" *The New York Times*, Sept. 1, 1996.

Nagasawa, Shin'ya, Shin'ya Iwakura, and Masaki Iwatani. "Design Strategy in Honda: Case Study of Civic, 2nd Prelude and Odyssey." *Bulletin of Japanese Society for the Science of Design* 49, no. 2 (2002): 45–54.

Nagasawa, Shin'ya, and Masaki Iwatani. "Design Management of Honda in Product Development of Fit." *Journal of the Asian Design International Conference*1, H-05 (2003): 1–4.

Niedermeyer, Edward. "Welcome to General Tso's Motors." *The Wall Street Journal*, Apr. 30, 2013.

Nonaka, Ikujiro, and Ryoko Toyama. "A Firm as a Dialectical Being: Towards a Dynamic Theory of a Firm." *Industrial and Corporate Change* 11, no. 5 (2002): 995–1009.

"Ohio Communities Enjoy Boom: Honda—It's Just What the Rust Belt Ordered." Associated Press, June 28, 1988.

Orlik, Tom, and Liam Denning. "The Roadblock in GM's Route Through China." *The Wall Street Journal*, Apr. 20, 2011.

Pascale, Richard T. "Perspectives on Strategy: The Real Story Behind Honda's Success." *California Management Review* 26, no. 3 (Spring 1984): 47–72.

Pearlstein, Steven. "It's Make-or-Break Time for Manufacturing." *The Washington Post*, Feb. 12, 2011.

Porter, Eduardo. "The Promise of Today's Factory Jobs." *The New York Times*, Apr. 3, 2012.

Powell, Cash, Jr. "BP the Honda Way—A Supplier's Lifeline." *Target Magazine*. Association for Manufacturing Excellence, 1st Quarter 2002.

Priddle, Alissa. "Honda's Ohio Plant Changed Competitive Landscape in America." *Detroit Free Press*, Nov. 24, 2012.

Pringle, Patricia. "Monozukuri: Another Look at a Key Japanese Principle." *Japan Intercultural Consulting*. www.japanintercultural.com, July 23, 2010.

Rapoport, Carla. "Charles Handy Sees the Future." *Fortune*, Oct. 31, 1994.

"Remarks by Erik Berkman, President, Honda R&D Americas, Inc. Center for Automotive Research Management Briefing Seminars, Traverse City, Mich." Honda. www.honda.com, Aug. 13, 2012.

"Reshoring Manufacturing: Coming Home." *The Economist*, Jan. 19, 2013.

Richardson, Adam. "Lessons from Honda's Early Adaptive Strategy." *Harvard Business Review* Blog Network. www.blogs.hbr.org, Feb. 1, 2011.

Rosevear, John. "This Could Crush GM's China Chances." The Motley Fool. www.fool.com, Mar. 14, 2013.

———. "Is GM Investing Too Much in China?" The Motley Fool. www.fool.com, Apr. 29, 2013.

Rumelt, Richard P. "The Many Faces of Honda." *California Management Review* 38, no. 4 (Summer 1996): 103–11.

Samuelson, Robert. "Globalization in Retreat." RealClearPolitics. www.realclearpolitics.com, Dec. 31, 2012.

Sanger, David E. "Soichiro Honda, Auto Innovator, Is Dead at 84." *The New York Times*, Aug. 6, 1991.

Shirouzu, Norihiko, Yoko Kubota, and Paul Lienert. "Electric Cars Head Toward Another Dead End." Reuters, Feb. 4, 2013.

Sirkin, Harold, Michael Zinzer, and Douglas Hohner. "Made in America Again." Boston Consulting Group, August 2011.

Sutton, Robert. "Weird Rules of Creativity—Think You Manage Creativity? Here's Why You're Wrong." *Harvard Business Review*, September 2001.

Takeuchi, Hirotaka. "Knowledge Creation and Dialectics." In *Hitotsubashi on Knowledge Management*, by Hirotaka Takeuchi and Ikujiro Nonaka. John Wiley & Sons, 2004.

Taylor, Alex III. "Inside Honda's Brain." *Fortune*, Mar. 7, 2008.

"The Boomerang Effect." *The Economist*, Apr. 21, 2012.

"The Experts: Countering the Biggest Misconceptions People Have About U.S. Manufacturing." *The Wall Street Journal*, June 14, 2013.

Truett, Richard. "Crafting a Pickup: Ex-GM Engineer Designed Ridgeline the Honda Way." *Automotive News*. www.autonews.com, June 14, 2005.

"Voice of American CEOs on Manufacturing Competitiveness." The Council on Competitiveness, 2011.

"Warranty Claims & Accruals in Financial Statements: Most Improved, 2012 vs. 2011." *Warranty Week*. www.warrantyweek.com, Aug. 28, 2013.

White, Joseph B. "Electric Cars Struggle to Break Out of Niche." *The Wall Street Journal*, Sept. 25, 2012.

Wieffering, Eric. "Buckley Helped 3M Rediscover Its Mojo." Minneapolis *Star Tribune*, Feb. 11, 2012.

Zhang, Yajun. "China Begins to Lose Edge as World's Factory Floor." *The Wall Street Journal*, Jan. 16, 2013.

INDEX